THE STUDENT GUIDE TO BRITAIN

This Guide gives facts about educational and social facilities in Britain. It is designed to help students to find what they need and to prevent disappointment.

A.O., Britd.

CONDITIONS OF SALE

THE STUDENT GUIDE
TO BRITAIN

HELEN PICKTHORN

A PAN ORIGINAL

PAN BOOKS LTD : LONDON

First published 1966 by
PAN BOOKS LTD.
8 Headfort Place, London, S.W.1

Printed in Great Britain by
Cox & Wyman Ltd., London, Reading and Fakenham

CONTENTS

ACKNOWLEDGEMENTS

THE information in this book is correct as far as it has been possible to check it at the time of going to print, November 1965. Amendments, corrections or suggestions will be welcomed for a next edition. It would be impracticable to list all the kind friends in the public service, private bodies and in UNESCO who have helped in the compilation of the book. Any good in it is theirs, any errors are mine.

HELEN PICKTHORN

Preface by LORD GLADWYN

IN recent years, students from all over the world, of all ages and at all levels have been coming to Britain to study. For though the nation has shed its Empire, it remains the centre of a wide English-speaking community. Above all, it is still a centre of ideas, of inventions, of discoveries, of social experiments. Anyone who, even in a general way, is interested in the nature of the great new forces which are now sweeping the world – of which the process of industrialization is the most significant – could do well to spend one or two of his formative years in Britain, for it was, after all, in these islands that such forces originated.

If the student is to make use of the many educational facilities which this country has to offer, he should be able to find out easily to what extent and to what advantage they are in fact available. He should know too that for the overseas student at any rate there are problems which must be faced. If they are to be faced, they must first be understood – the nature of British education, for instance, which has its roots deep in the past; the possibility or lack of possibility of employment while studying; the extent of xenophobia in certain districts; where and how to live; and, above all, perhaps, the need for reasonable proficiency in colloquial English if useful results are to be obtained.

Then there is Britain itself, its people, its customs and its climate. Do not be put off by depressing stories of the climate. The famous Duke of Wellington said: 'For six months of the year England has the best climate in the world, and for the other six months I'm damned if I know a better!' The right thing to do is to take no notice of the bad weather in Britain, but to walk about in the rain with good shoes and an excellent raincoat, as the British mostly do. This is called 'rising above it', and is alleged to be useful in the formation of character. The weather is, of course, one of the main subjects of conversation in Britain, and any speech with a stranger almost invariably starts with some reference to it. Anyhow, food is cheap and good, and the cooking is rapidly improving.

As for the British character, an American once observed that the English never say 'Pleased to meet you' and seldom are! But the overseas student must not be put off by this cool, or it might be thought indifferent, initial attitude. For if he perseveres he will find out that the British have a very real capacity for devoted and lifelong friendships. They are also, as a race, undoubtedly very law-abiding and polite.

So far no one publication has covered both educational and social matters, from post-graduate courses to a game of cricket, from college entrance requirements to addressing a letter. This book is *not* an official production, though all the information it contains has been checked as far as possible. It is rather an objective guide. It attempts to give a wide range of facts and to put some misunderstandings right.

To me, personally, it seems to be essential reading for any student coming from abroad and quite useful to any home student too. Nothing so comprehensive exists at present and I am sure that it will respond to a long-felt need.

Section I

General Information

Section I

General Information

Passport Regulations

All visitors and students coming to Britain have to pass through the Passport and Customs examination.

Home Office Requirements

FOREIGN STUDENTS

Admission to the United Kingdom

Genuine full-time students are very welcome as temporary visitors, but they are expected to be able and willing to leave when their studies are ended. They ought to be able to show that a place has been definitely reserved at a University, technical college, school or similar institution for a full-time course of study. They must also prove that they have enough money for their housing and maintenance whilst in the country, *without having to take a job*. Wives of students may be admitted with their husbands, but only if they have enough money for their keep.

Stateless students, or those who have difficulty in maintaining the validity of their passports, are allowed to remain only for so long as they can show that they will be able to return home. It will be useless for them to embark on a long educational course if they have no reasonable prospect of getting their return facilities renewed as necessary.

Police Registration

A foreigner must register at once if the immigration officer has noted on his passport that he is required to do so. When he registers he should take his passport and two recent passport-size photographs to the police. In the London area he should go to the Aliens' Registration Office, 10 Lamb's Conduit Street, London, W.C.1., and elsewhere he should ask at the local police-station for the address of the office to which he should report.

Extension of Stay

The immigration officer's stamp in a foreigner's passport shows how long he may stay in the country. If he wishes to stay longer he should, about a month before his stay is due to expire, give his reasons in a letter, enclosing his passport, addressed to the Under-Secretary of State, Immigration and Nationality Department, Home Office, Princeton House, 271 High Holborn, London, W.C.1. If the extension is required for study he should enclose with his application a letter from the school or college to show that he has enrolled for a full-time course of study and evidence (e.g. in the form of a bank statement) that he has enough money to keep him during his proposed stay.

COMMONWEALTH STUDENTS

Admission

Most Commonwealth citizens from overseas are subject to immigration control under Part I of the Commonwealth Immigrants Act. Broadly speaking, a Commonwealth citizen is exempt from control if:

(a) he was born in the United Kingdom, or

(b) he holds a passport issued by one of the British Passport Offices in the United Kingdom, or

(c) he is a citizen of the United Kingdom and Colonies and his passport was issued overseas by a British High Commission or Consulate, or

(d) he or she is the wife or child of a person exempted from control under paragraphs above and is included in that person's passport.

He is *not* exempt from control if he was not born in the United Kingdom and his passport was issued by the Government of a Commonwealth country or of a colony or protectorate; or if his passport is endorsed as having been issued on behalf of such a Government.

Operation of the Immigration Control

The control is operated by immigration officers at the ports of entry. The central feature of the control is that a Commonwealth citizen coming for full-time employment must be in possession of a voucher issued by the Ministry of Labour; if he is coming for employment without a voucher he is likely to be refused admission. Voucher-holders have an assurance of admission provided there is no objection on grounds of criminal record, health or security. Wives and children under 16 accompanying or coming to join the head of the household in the United Kingdom may not be refused admission.

The Control as it Applies to Students

The British Government welcomes Commonwealth students genuinely wishing to undertake a course of study in the United Kingdom. Any Commonwealth citizen who satisfies the immigration officer that he will be spending the whole or a substantial part of his time studying at a university, college, school or other institution (whether run by a central or local authority or privately) is entitled to admission. A correspondence course is not by itself a 'course of study' for this purpose.

There is no hard-and-fast rule about what constitutes a 'substantial part' of a student's time; but it can be stated as a general guide that a Commonwealth citizen is normally accepted as a student if he is able to show that he will spend at least 15 hours a week in the prescribed study of a single subject or related subjects. He might still be admitted as a student if his proposed studies occupy less than 15 hours a week so long as the immigration officer is satisfied that his *main purpose* in coming to the United Kingdom is to study and not to take full-time employment for which a Ministry of Labour voucher is required. Part-time work, or work in vacations, in order to help to pay for a course of studies is not a bar to admission as a student; but it must be the intention to start the course immediately and not at some indefinite date in the future.

In order to be admitted as a student, a Commonwealth citizen is normally expected to have plans for study for the whole of an academic year; but those proposing to take shorter courses may qualify for admission as visitors.

The decision whether or not to admit a Commonwealth citizen as a student rests with the immigration officer at the port of arrival. Where students have made advance arrangements for their studies, a letter or certificate of enrolment from the institution concerned is usually sufficient to satisfy the immigration officer that the person concerned qualifies for admission as a student. Some Commonwealth citizens are not able, for one reason or another, to enrol in advance; and some will wish to obtain a preliminary qualification before enrolling for their main course. Such people are well advised to apply for entry certificates (see below) before starting on their journey to the United Kingdom.

Entry Certificates

Any Commonwealth citizen coming to the United Kingdom for any purpose other than employment can apply for an entry certificate, which takes the form of a stamp in the passport and for which application can be made to any British post overseas. The holder of an entry certificate may not be refused admission except on grounds of criminal record, health or security, or if the immigration officer is satisfied that the certificate was obtained by fraud. Possession of an entry certificate is in no sense compulsory, but the system is widely used by Commonwealth citizens who wish to be assured before they start on their journey that they are qualified for admission to the United Kingdom. It has been found to be of particular value to students, whether or not advance arrangements for their studies have been made. A student sponsored by his own Government is usually able to obtain an entry certificate without difficulty; so, in most cases, is the holder of a certificate of enrolment for full-time studies at a bona fide educational establishment. Intending students who are not sponsored, and who have not enrolled in advance, are advised to obtain evidence from their own authorities of their ability to benefit from the study they are proposing to undertake in the United Kingdom. Entry certificates are invariably granted to those intending students who are able to satisfy the British authorities concerned of their bona fides and who produce satisfactory evidence of their ability to benefit from the study they propose to undertake.

Trainees, Apprentices, etc.

Trainees coming under sponsored schemes, for example those of the Colombo Plan, are admitted (and can, if they so wish, obtain entry certificates) on production of evidence of sponsorship. In general, other trainees and apprentices will be expected to be in possession of Ministry of Labour vouchers which may be obtained for them by the prospective employer.

Commonwealth Students in the United Kingdom

A Commonwealth student is normally admitted to the United Kingdom for a limited period; the immigration officer's stamp in his passport will show how long he may remain here. The procedure for making an application for an extension of stay is the same as for foreigners (see page 14). A Commonwealth student is normally expected to leave the United Kingdom on completion of his studies.

Customs Regulations

Although almost all articles are liable to import duty and in many cases purchase tax, duty and tax will not normally be charged on your *personal effects* including fur coats, watches, cameras, etc., which have been in your ownership and use for a considerable period or which will be re-exported at the conclusion of a visit of not more than six months' duration. If your visit exceeds six months but not twelve months, a refundable deposit to cover the duty and tax may be required for *new or little used articles*; but if your visit will exceed twelve months, outright payment of duty and purchase tax will be required.

In addition, dutiable goods (including tobacco, spirits, wine and perfume) for your personal consumption may be retained free of duty and tax, subject to the following limits:

(*a*) *Visitors permanently resident in Europe:*
    Tobacco: $\frac{1}{2}$ lb. (e.g. 200 cigarettes of normal size).
    Spirits (including liqueurs): $\frac{1}{2}$ bottle (i.e. one-twelfth of a gallon).
    Wine in bottle: 1 bottle (i.e. one-sixth of a gallon).
    Perfume and toilet waters: $\frac{1}{2}$ pint, of which not more than half may be perfume.
    If you have more than these quantities, duty (and purchase tax) will be charged on the excess.

(*b*) *Visitors permanently resident outside Europe:*
    Tobacco: 1 lb. (e.g. 400 cigarettes of normal size).

Spirits (including liqueurs): 1 bottle (i.e. one-sixth of a gallon).

Wine in bottle: 1 bottle (i.e. one-sixth of a gallon).

Perfume and toilet waters: ½ pint.

Visitors in transit through the United Kingdom are allowed to take with them, in addition to the above, up to 600 cigarettes (or the equivalent in other tobacco goods) and up to ½ litre of perfume, for use when they leave the United Kingdom.

These concessions do not apply to unaccompanied baggage not examined at the same time as accompanied baggage, and are not allowed to children and young people under the age of 17.

Film. A reasonable quantity of unexposed cine (movie) film or ordinary photographic film or plates will be passed free if the Customs officer is satisfied that it is for your personal and private use during a holiday in the United Kingdom.

Overseas Students. Overseas students who come to the United Kingdom to attend a full-time educational course at a university, technical college or hospital are allowed additional facilities. These will be explained to the student by the Customs on arrival.

Goods you take home. Whilst a licence is required for the export of some goods from Great Britain, you may take out with you, without a licence, valuables and personal belongings brought in with you, or which you have bought here out of your own currency resources. Generally, antiques, including works of art, do not require a licence for up to £1,000.

For further information you should write to the secretary, H.M. Customs and Excise, King's Beam House, Mark Lane, London, E.C.3.

Accommodation

Accommodation, especially in London and at holiday seasons, is never easy to find. This is something that a student intending to come to Britain should consider in plenty of time before he leaves home. It is generally best to arrange temporary accommodation, e.g. in a hotel, in advance, and not to make permanent arrangements until after you have arrived. Before doing so, however, it will be wise to inquire well before you leave from the university, college, school, etc., where you are going to study, whether you will be able to live in a college or hall of residence or whether there is a college, etc., lodging service which will reserve accommodation for you on arrival. You may have to arrange for yourself accommodation only for a night or two when travelling through London. The British Travel Association, 64 St. James's Street, London, S.W.1, has a comprehensive hotel guide-book which may be useful and which should normally be available through your local travel agency.

Students and trainees studying in Britain as scholars of one of the technical assistance agencies or of the British Council will probably have their accommodation arranged for them in advance. Recommended students, from those Commonwealth or other countries which operate with the British Council a system of recommendation, will also be found accommodation on arrival provided that advance notice of arrival is given to the British Council by the student's Embassy or High Commission. If you are registered with a private school, the school authorities will help you.

Prices vary from 5 gns. to 8 gns. (see under Banks and Currency, page 23) a week for bed, breakfast and evening meal. A room in a hotel will cost from 25s. to luxury hotel prices of 5 gns. to 10 gns. nightly.

Accommodation for married students is particularly difficult to find, especially where there are children. A student is well advised to come first on his own and only send for his family when he is assured of being able to make suitable provision for them. Otherwise he may be faced with extended hotel expenses while searching for accommodation.

For further details and addresses see under Accommodation in Section V, for London and other Main Centres.

If you decide to live in lodgings, you may be lucky enough to find a kindly landlady who will do far more for you than you can expect for the rent of your room. Do all you can to help her to help you. Here are a few suggestions:

(1) Tell your landlady if you are to be out for a meal or will be late.
(2) Ask if you may use the telephone and pay the charge.
(3) Consult your landlady about visitors.
(4) Keep your room tidy.
(5) Discuss arrangements for personal laundry with the landlady.

(6) Leave the bathroom and lavatory clean and tidy.

(7) Turn off lights or fires in your room when not needed.

(8) Make sure you understand how to operate appliances such as gas or electric fires, bathroom water-heaters, etc. Remember: fires and heaters can be dangerous, particularly oil-stoves.

(9) Offer to pay for any breakages or damage you may do.

The same recommendations apply to living in a hostel, but there the warden has probably also laid down certain rules.

NOTE: *Payment of Rent and Giving of Notice*

One other point to remember is that the arrangements for the payment of rent are agreed between the landlady and the student. You will usually have to pay your rent weekly, in advance, on a fixed day of the week. If you wish to leave, you will usually have to tell your landlady one week in advance, on the day of the week on which you pay your rent, but if for convenience sake you pay your rent monthly you might be required to give one month's notice, even if you are in lodgings where meals are provided. (Where rent is paid for furnished accommodation where no meals are provided, a month's notice can legally be required whether the rent is paid weekly or monthly.) It is important, therefore, to have a definite arrangement with your landlady at the beginning of your tenancy on the exact amount of notice to be given. (These arrangements also apply if the landlady wishes to give you notice.)

You should make sure you have a rent book or some sort of receipt for your rent. If the landlady does not provide a rent book, you are advised to get one yourself and ask the landlady to sign it when you pay your rent.

Sometimes students prefer to rent a flat. This may work out more cheaply, with expenses shared among three or four living together. This may involve taking a lease or contract for the flat, so be careful *before* signing any document, to read it carefully and take proper advice first if necessary.

Living with English Families

Students seeking accommodation with an English family as

paying guests where they can learn the language will find help at the offices of certain organizations, such as the Gabbitas-Thring Educational Trust, Sackville Street, London, W.1.

See also under London, Section V, for other addresses which may help in this. Weekly fees vary between $6\frac{1}{2}$ gns. and 10 gns. for full residence. Girls from other countries wishing to live in an 'au pair' capacity with an English family can also obtain information from Gabbitas-Thring and other agencies. Unfortunately, facilities do not exist for young men to be 'au pair'.

Foster-parents

Married students with children who both want to study should consider the advantage from many points of view of leaving their offspring at home with a relative. If, nevertheless, you feel that you must bring your children with you then you must be responsible for making suitable arrangements, including, if you so decide, the choice of a foster-home. Here you should note that if the child is to stay there for more than one month the foster-mother must give notice to the Children's Officer of the Local Authority for the area in which she lives two weeks before she receives the child; thus you must choose the foster-home at least two weeks before you want the child to go there. Then:

1. Agree how much money you will pay each week to the foster-mother (charges vary, but are generally £2 to £3 per week).
2. Agree who is to buy the child's clothes.
3. Give the foster-mother your name and address clearly written so that she can get into touch with you if she needs to. If you move, let her have your new address immediately.
4. Remind the foster-mother that she is required by law to give at least 14 days' notice in writing to the Children's Officer of her intention to receive your child as a foster-child. If the foster-mother does not give this notice she may be taken to Court and prosecuted.
5. Write out for the foster-mother the name, sex, date of birth and place of birth of your child as she has to give this information to the Children's Officer.
6. Arrange to visit your child regularly and agree details of these visits with the foster-mother.

Social Customs

Traditionally British people are very reserved, but you will find that underneath this is often shyness masked by a reluctance to have their motives misunderstood. London is impersonal, but elsewhere if you ask the way you will find most people very anxious to be helpful and friendly. British people are by nature polite, and you will find they appreciate it if you adopt their habit of using please and thank you at every opportunity. In shops and restaurants you will have much better service if you ask: 'Please may I have', or 'Could you help me?' rather than giving direct instructions. In a democratic country everyone feels equal to everyone else, and shop assistants, waiters, servants, and so on, are more like friends giving you a service than someone who obeys your orders. Today only the very rich people can afford servants, who are probably paid about £7 a week, and are given ample time off and their own room and television. If a British family invites you home for dinner, the hostess will have had to prepare the meal herself, and the host will probably do the washing-up. At an informal meal if you offer to help wash-up it will be much appreciated, even if your offer is declined!

All life in Britain today is keyed to labour-saving devices and cutting down housework. With women educated as well as their husbands – and sometimes even better – the British housewife resents being a slave to the kitchen sink, and with equality of the sexes among the younger generation, father probably takes his turn at bathing the baby, and even washing the clothes. Anything which uses a lot of labour is expensive, and you will make and keep many more friends while you are here if you have a better understanding of them and their problems.

Banks and Currency

Currency:

The Monetary System of the U.K. is not based on the decimal system.

The currency unit is the Pound Sterling (£1), which is divided into 20 shillings (20s.). Notes are issued to the value of £10, £5,

£1, and 10 shillings (10s.). Shillings are divided into 12 pennies. Silver coins are issued to the value of 2s. 6d. (2½ shillings – called 'half a crown'), 2s. (2 shillings – sometimes called a 'florin'), 1s., and 6d. (sixpence). There are two copper coins – one penny (1d.) and a ½ penny (½d. pronounced 'haypenny'). In addition, there is one nickel coin worth 3d. Many prices are marked in 'guineas', but there is no note or coin of this value. A 'guinea' is £1 1s.

The Money You Bring:

1. As a traveller entering the United Kingdom you may bring in sterling notes, foreign currency notes, travellers' cheques, letters of credit, etc., in any currency and up to any amount.

2. Travellers' Cheques and Foreign Currency. Your travellers' cheques or letters of credit can be exchanged into sterling at any British bank. There is no restriction on the amount of such cheques exchanged. Banks and Bureaux de Change buy American and Canadian notes freely, and will generally accept reasonable amounts of other foreign currencies.

3. As a non-resident traveller leaving the United Kingdom you may take out:

(*a*) Not more than £25 in sterling notes.

(*b*) The amount of foreign currency notes brought in by you or the equivalent of £250 whichever is the larger.

(*c*) Travellers' cheques, letters of credit, etc., issued you by authorized dealers in the United Kingdom. You may also take out travellers' cheques, letters of credit, etc., which you brought with you into the United Kingdom but which have not been cashed.

If you are about to leave the United Kingdom and are in any doubt as to the amounts you will be allowed to take with you, you are advised to consult a bank. For instance, if a traveller from overseas has more than £25 sterling notes as a result of encashing too many of his travellers' cheques, or letters of credit, the bank will exchange up to £100 into travellers' cheques, etc., available anywhere in the world.

4. Check currency before leaving. In your own interest you should make sure you do not arrive at the place of departure with excess currency since the excess cannot be deposited with Customs or Immigration Officers but is liable to be withheld with no guarantee that it will be returned. Above all, you should take

particular care to state exactly the amounts of currency in your possession; a false declaration may lead to heavy penalties.

(The above regulations do not apply to travellers journeying only between the United Kingdom and the Channel Islands, the Isle of Man or the Irish Republic.)

5. *Postal Regulations.* You may NOT send sterling notes through the post out of the United Kingdom, except to the Channel Islands, the Isle of Man or the Irish Republic.

Notes in currencies other than sterling may not be posted out of the United Kingdom unless permission has been obtained through a bank in the United Kingdom.

Finance, Scholarships and Bursaries

It is generally reckoned at the time of writing (November 1965) that it costs at the very least £500 a year for a single unmarried person of student status to live in Britain.

On top of that there are tuition fees, and these vary considerably. Oxford and Cambridge Universities are the most expensive (£750–£850 a year for minimum maintenance and tuition). London University follows (£600–£700) and other universities (£550–£650). Technical Colleges, art schools and other centres of education vary in the fees that they charge for tuition but they are normally less than the universities. For up-to-date information, write to the college itself or to the local education authority.

Overseas students may be eligible for scholarships under a variety of schemes.

(1) From their own governments. In some Commonwealth countries, government scholarships are available which are tenable in the United Kingdom. Particulars of these scholarships should be obtained from your Education Department or Ministry of Education.

(2) From the British Government or British Council funds. These are principally Commonwealth Scholarships (up to 240 annual awards for post-graduate or equivalent studies); Commonwealth bursaries (500 annual awards for studies in teacher-training institutions); British Council Scholarships (some 530 per year) open to men and women from any country for courses of advanced study or research,

normally at post-graduate level, and British Council Bursaries for shorter periods of study (3–6 months). Particulars can be obtained from your local British Council office.
(3) United Nations or similar international awards, details of which are contained in *Study Abroad*.
(4) Awards under the Colombo Plan, Special Commonwealth African Assistance Plan, and other Technical Assistance schemes, details of which should be obtained from your government.

For further information, see:

United Kingdom Post-Graduate Awards published by the Association of Commonwealth Universities, 36 Gordon Square, London, W.C.1.

Study Abroad published by UNESCO, Place, de Fontenoy, Paris, 7*e*.

Higher Education in the United Kingdom published by Longmans, Green & Co. Ltd., for the British Council.

Scholarships are also offered by individual firms and by educational foundations. These can be open to home or overseas students. Firms do not usually give University scholarships to overseas students, but concentrate on other types of course, e.g. one- or two-year 'sandwich' courses. Some firms give scholarships only to those who are recommended by their own agents and, in general, they take only those sponsored by their own governments. Occasionally firms prefer local personnel, because of accommodation difficulties, and this can apply particularly to overseas students.

For lists and further information, see:

Study Abroad as above. *Opportunities for Graduates; Opportunities for Qualified Men; Opportunities for School-leavers;* published annually by the Cornmarket Press Ltd.

Education Committee Year Book.

Grants for Higher Education compiled by Merle Hastings, published by the Cresset Press (intended for U.K. students only).

British students apply to their local education authority for grants for further education when they leave school, with the necessary General Certificate requirements and as soon as they have found a place in university or college. It may be worth noting here that if you are applying for a British Council or British Government Scholarship, you must apply from your own country, and not after arrival in Britain.

However, it should not be supposed that adult education in Britain is absolutely 'free' to all who would like to have it. State education is free to British children up to the age of 18. After that age, if they wish to continue, they can apply to their local authority who must be satisfied that, according to their means and their past scholastic achievements, they are deserving of financial help. Part-time local authority courses at evening institutes, etc., are open to all at extremely low cost to those who study there, but books and materials the students must supply for themselves. There is, in fact, a heavy hidden subsidy from Local Authorities and the Central Government to Universities and to Technical Colleges.

The British Council

The British Council exists to promote a knowledge of the United Kingdom and the English language abroad and to develop closer cultural relations with countries overseas. It is financed chiefly from Government sources but is administratively independent.

The Council maintains offices, usually with a library, in some eighty countries overseas; to these offices overseas students intending to study in Britain may turn for information and advice on educational facilities and living conditions.

The Council administers wholly or in part the educational programmes of scholarship or bursary holders studying in Britain under a number of British technical training schemes. It does the same for the holders of awards from a number of international agencies. The Council also awards annually a certain number of its own scholarships for post-graduate study. Besides having some responsibility for the well-being of those coming to Britain under such schemes the Council also has a wider concern for all overseas students studying in Britain full-time regardless of the auspices under which they come. This is effected through offices and student centres in London and in a number of other large cities outside. At these centres full-time overseas students may find a range of social and educational activities, visits, lectures, home hospitality, etc. Many of these activities are provided in co-operation with voluntary societies which are interested in overseas students.

The Council also has a special responsibility for meeting on arrival and for assistance in finding accommodation for those students recommended by the authorities of a number of specified countries, with most of which the British Government has agreements to this effect. These are mainly countries of the Commonwealth and of the Middle and Far East. The Council also operates four residences in London for students from dependent territories and from a number of other Commonwealth countries.

Headquarters: 65 Davies Street, London, W.1. Tel. GROsvenor 8011.

London Centre for Overseas Students: 11 Portland Place, London, W.1. Tel. MUSeum 6888.

Foreign and Commonwealth Representatives and Student Officers

How you approach the question whether to seek to study in Britain depends on the country you come from. The main aspects of this question are:

  (i) Where in Britain is there the sort of course of study or training I want?
 (ii) Am I qualified to follow such a course?
(iii) Can I afford the cost?
 (iv) Is my English good enough?
  (v) How can I apply?

British Council offices overseas are well placed to give guidance on how to answer these questions. In some cases, e.g. where your own place of study at home has links with corresponding institutions in Britain, you may be able to obtain information from your own college, etc., authorities. If you are from one of the Commonwealth countries or from one of the other overseas countries which award annually a number of scholarships for study in Britain you may be able to obtain information from your local Ministry of Education or other authority. Where your authorities operate a system of recommendation in conjunction with the

British Council, you may wish to take advantage of this so that
the Council may meet you on arrival and so that you may make
use of the accommodation services provided.

In Britain, there are many clubs and hostels run by overseas
nationals for their own people. It would take up too much space
to list them all here, but an inquiry to your own Embassy or
High Commission in London should tell you all you want to
know.

The following is a list of Embassies, High Commissions and
other Government representatives in London. Where no Student
Officer or Adviser is shown, the normal contact for a student is
the **Cultural Attaché** or **Counsellor.**

Commonwealth and British Dependencies:

Aden (Federation of South Arabia): Student Liaison Officer,
Suffield House, 79 Davies Street, London, W.1.

Australia: Australia House, Strand, London, W.C.2.

British Guiana: Student Officer, 28 Cockspur Street, London,
S.W.1.

Canada: Canada House, Trafalgar Square, London, S.W.1.

Ceylon: Education Officer, 13 Hyde Park Gardens, London,
W.2.

Cyprus: 93 Park Street, London, W.1.

Eastern Caribbean; Barbados; Leeward and Windward
Islands: Student Officer, 229 Kensington High Street, London,
W.8.

Gambia: Student Officer, 28 Kensington Court, London, W.8.

Ghana: Education Attaché, 102 Park Street, London, W.1.

Hong Kong: Student's Adviser, 45 Portland Place, London,
W.1.

India: Student Welfare Officer, India House, Aldwych,
London, W.C.2.

Jamaica: Student Officer, 32 Bruton Street, London, W.1.

Kenya: Education Attaché, 45 Portland Place, London,
W.1.

Malaysia; Federation of Malaya; Singapore; Sarawak and
Sabah: Education Adviser and Director, Malaya Hall, 44
Bryanston Square, London, W.1.

Malawi: Student Officer, 47 Great Cumberland Place, London,
W.1.

Malta: Student Liaison Officer, Malta House, 24 Haymarket, London, S.W.1.

Mauritius: Supervisor, Mauritius House, 16 Upper Montague Street, London, W.1.

New Zealand: New Zealand House, Haymarket, London, S.W.1.

Nigeria (Federal): First Secretary, Education, Nigeria House, Annexe, The Adelphi, John Adam Street, London, W.C.2.

Eastern Nigeria: Student Officer, Nigeria House, 9 Northumberland Avenue, London, W.C.2.

Northern Nigeria: Student Officer, Nigeria House, 9 Northumberland Avenue, London, W.C.2.

Western Nigeria; Student Officer, 178–202 Great Portland Street, London, W.1.

Mid-Western Nigeria: Student Officer, King's House, 10 Haymarket, London, S.W.1

Pakistan: 39 Lowndes Square, London, S.W.1.

Rhodesia (Southern Rhodesia): Rhodesia House, 429 Strand, London, W.C.2.

Sierra Leone: 33 Portland Place, London, W.1.

Tanzania: Director, 43 Hertford Street, London, W.1.

Zanzibar: Student Adviser, 43 Hertford Street, London, W.1.

Trinidad and Tobago: Student Officer, 51 South Audley Street, London, W.1.

Uganda: Student Adviser, Columbia House, 69 Aldwych, London, W.C.2.

Zambia: Student Officer, 7–11 Cavendish Place, London, W.1.

Bahamas; Basutoland; Bechuanaland; Bermuda; British Honduras; Brunei; Falklands; Fiji; Gibraltar; St. Helena; Seychelles; Swaziland; Western Pacific Islands: Ministry of Overseas Development, Training Department, Eland House, Stag Place, London, S.W.1.

Foreign:

Afghanistan: 31 Princes Gate, London, S.W.7.

Algeria: 6 Hyde Park Gate, London, S.W.7.

Argentina: 9 Wilton Crescent, London, S.W.1.

Austria: 18 Belgrave Mews West, London, S.W.1.

Belgium: 103 Eaton Square, London, S.W.1.

Bolivia: 106 Eaton Square, London, S.W.1.

Brazil: 32 Green Street, London, W.1.

Bulgaria: 12 Queen's Gate Gardens, London, S.W.7.
Burma: 76 Cadogan Square, London, S.W.1.
Cameroon Republic: 84 Holland Park, London, W.11.
Chile: 3 Hamilton Place, London, W.1.
Chinese Legation: 49–51 Portland Place, London, W.1.
Colombia: Flat 3A, 3 Hans Crescent, London, S.W.1.
Republic of the Congo: 26 Chesham Place, London, S.W.1.
Costa Rica: 46 Montpelier Walk, London, S.W.7.
Cuba: 22 Mount Street, London, W.1.
Czechoslovakia: 7 Kensington Palace Gardens, London, W.8.
Denmark: 29 Pont Street, London, S.W.1.
Dominican Republic: 4 Braemar Mansions, Cornwall Gardens, London, S.W.7.
Ecuador: Flat 3B, 3 Hans Crescent, London, S.W.1.
Ethiopia: 17 Princes Gate, London, S.W.7.
Finland: 66 Chester Square, London, S.W.1.
France: 58 Knightsbridge, London, S.W.1.
Federal Republic of Germany: 23 Belgrave Square, London, S.W.1.
Greece: 51 Upper Brook Street, London, W.1.
Guatemala: 30A Collingham Gardens, London, S.W.5.
Haiti: 22 Hans Road, London, S.W.3.
Honduras: 104 Great Portland Street, London, W.1.
Hungary: 35 Eaton Place, London, S.W.1.
Iceland: 1 Eaton Terrace, London, S.W.1.
Indonesia: 38 Grosvenor Square, London, W.1.
Iran: 50 Kensington Court, Kensington High Street, London, W.8.
Iraq: 21 Queen's Gate, London, S.W.7.
Israel: 2 Palace Green, Kensington, London, W.8.
Italy: 39 Belgrave Square, London, S.W.1.
Ivory Coast: 2 Upper Belgrave Street, London, S.W.1.
Japan: 44–46 Grosvenor Street, London, W.1.
Jordan: 6 Upper Phillimore Gardens, London, W.8.
Korea: 36 Cadogan Square, London, S.W.1.
Kuwait: 40 Devonshire Street, London, W.1.
Laos: 5 Palace Green, Kensington, London, W.8.
Lebanon: 21 Kensington Palace Gardens, London, W.8.
Liberia: 21 Princes Gate, London, S.W.7.
Libya: 58 Princes Gate, London, S.W.7.
Luxembourg: 27 Wilton Crescent, London, S.W.1.

Malagasy Republic: 33 Thurloe Square, London, S.W.7.
Mexico: 48 Belgrave Square, London, S.W.1.
Morocco: 49 Queen's Gate Gardens, London, S.W.7.
Nepal: 12A Kensington Palace Gardens, London, W.8.
Netherlands: 38 Hyde Park Gate, London, S.W.7.
Nicaragua: Flat 120, Roebuck House, Palace Street, London, S.W.1.
Norway: 25 Belgrave Square, London, S.W.1.
Panama: 26 Kenton Court, Kensington High Street, London, W.14.
Paraguay: Braemar Lodge, Cornwall Gardens, London, S.W.7.
Peru: 52 Sloane Street, London, S.W.1.
Philippines: 9A Palace Green, Kensington, London, W.8.
Poland: 47 Portland Place, London, W.1.
Portugal: 11 Belgrave Square, London, S.W.1.
Roumania: 4 Palace Green, London, W.8.
Salvador: 6 Roland Gardens, London, S.W.7.
Saudi Arabia: 24 Kensington Palace Gardens, London, W.8.
Senegal: 10 Gloucester Place, London, W.1.
Republic of South Africa: South Africa House, Trafalgar Square, London, W.C.2.
Spain: 24 Belgrave Square, London, S.W.1.
Sudan: 31–32 Rutland Gate, London, S.W.7.
Sweden: 29 Portland Place, London, W.1.
Switzerland: 18 Montagu Place, London, W.1.
Syria: 57 Kensington Court, London, W.8.
Thailand: 28 Princes Gate, London, S.W.7.
Tunisia: 29 Princes Gate, London, S.W.7.
Turkey: 43 Belgrave Square, London, S.W.1.
United Arab Republic: 4 Chesterfield Gardens, London, W.1.
U.S.A.: 24–32 Grosvenor Square, London, W.1.
U.S.S.R.: 13 Kensington Palace Gardens, London, W.8.
Uruguay: 48 Lennox Gardens, London, S.W.1.
Venezuela: Flat 6, 3 Hans Crescent, London, S.W.1.
Vietnam: 12 Victoria Road, London, W.8.
Yemen: 41 South Street, London, W.1.
Yugoslavia: 25 Kensington Gore, London, S.W.7.

British Government Departments
Foreign Office: Cultural Relations Department, Charles House, 5–11 Lower Regent Street, London, S.W.1. Tel. WHItehall 7810.

Commonwealth Relations Office: Downing Street, London, S.W.1. Tel. WHItehall 2323. Cultural Relations Department, 4 Central Buildings, Matthew Parker Street, London, S.W.1. Tel. WHItehall 2323.

Ministry of Overseas Development: Training Department, Eland House, Stag Place, Victoria, London, S.W.1. Tel. TATe Gallery 4366.

The Churches

If you are thinking of coming to Britain, the more you can prepare your way the better. Whether you are a Christian or not, you can approach your local Christian pastor and ask him to write to one of the Church Commendation centres in Britain. The Church authorities can arrange, on request, for you to be met when you arrive, and they can help to find you accommodation and assist you generally.

All the Churches are independent of the Government. A letter of recommendation from a church authority at home will always help to make you introductions, particularly in what is often the most difficult thing – accommodation. A letter of recommendation reassures your British hosts if they are thinking of taking you into their homes.

If you are a Christian, you may naturally want to get in touch with your Church in Britain. The Commendation Centres named below will help you in this. Otherwise, all the universities and some of the technical colleges have chaplains, who will help you whether or not you are directly under their charge.

Then there are the local parish ministers of all denominations. To find your church in the parish in which you may be staying, you can always go to the public library, whose assistants will give you the name and address of the church and its minister.

Commendation Centres:

The Overseas Students' Commendation Centre of the Church of England, 2 Salisbury Square, London, E.C.4.

The Church of Scotland, Foreign Mission Department, 121 George Street, Edinburgh 2.

The Methodist Church, The Secretary for Overseas Students, 25 Marylebone Road, London, N.W.1.

The Presbyterian Church of England, Secretary of Overseas Missions Committee, 86 Tavistock Place, London, W.C.1.

The London Missionary Society (Congregational), Livingstone House, 11 Carteret Street, London, S.W.1.

The Baptist Missionary Society, Young People's Secretary, 95 Gloucester Place, London, W.1.

The Lutheran Council of Great Britain, Lutheran Students' House, 21 Pembridge Gardens, London, W.2.

The Student Christian Movement, Student Movement House, 103 Gower Street, London, W.C.1.

Society of Friends Home Service Committee, Friends' International Centre, Courtauld House, Byng Place, London, W.C.1.

The Catholic Church in Britain: known as 'Roman' Catholic. Catholic Students' International Chaplaincy, 41 Holland Park, London, W.11.

There are also the Catholic National Churches and Societies, whose addresses you can find by applying to the International Chaplaincy or to your Embassy.

Some smaller Christian Church centres and non-Christian centres are listed below:

Buddhist: The London Buddhist Vihara, 10 Ovington Gardens, London, S.W.3.

Hindu: Hindu Centre, 5 Graham Road, Hendon Central, London, N.W.4.

Jewish: New West End (Orthodox) Synagogue, St. Petersburg Place, London, W.2. Liberal Jewish Synagogue, 28 St. John's Wood Road, London, N.W.8. West London Synagogue (Reform), Upper Berkeley Street, London, W.1.

Danish: St. Katharine's Church, Regent's Park, London, N.W.1.

German: Deutsche Lutherische St. Georgskirche, 55 Alie Street, Aldgate, London, E.1.

Norwegian: Norwegian Seamen's Church, St. Olav's Kirke, 1 Albion Street, Rotherhithe, London, S.E.16.

Swedish: Swedish Ulrika Eleonora Church, Harcourt Street, London, W.1.

Moslem: 63 Melrose Road, Southfields, London, S.W.18. (Mosque with resident Imam.) Regent's Lodge, Park Road, London, N.W.8. (Mosque of the Islamic Cultural Centre.) The

Shah Jehan Mosque, Woking, Surrey. Islamic Cultural Centre, 164 Park Road, London, N.W.8.

Orthodox: Cathedral of St. Sophia, Moscow Road, London, W.2.

Dutch: Nederlandse Hervormde Kerk, Austin Friars, London, E.C.2.

French: Eglise Protestante Française de Londres, 9 Soho Square, London, W.1.

Swiss: Eglise Suisse de Londres, 79 Endell Street, Shaftesbury Avenue, London, W.C.2.

British National and Voluntary Organizations

In addition to their ordinary social work, many organizations (the Women's Institutes, for example) run courses of instruction on their methods for overseas students and visitors generally. Individuals' or overseas bodies interested in these should apply to the British Council, or to the headquarters of the organization direct. Sponsorship by an authority is usually required.

The Africa Centre, Hinsley House, 38 King Street, London, W.C.2. Brings a Christian contribution to the study of African needs and problems and to their solution. Facilities for meetings and an international club.

Associated Country Women of the World, 78 Kensington High Street, London, W.8. To promote goodwill, friendship, understanding, between women all over the world, as well as raise their standard of living. Represented at FAO, UNESCO, UNICEF and UN.

Association for Jewish Youth, 33 Henriques Street, London, E.1. To promote the well-being of young Jews.

Boys' Brigade, Abbey House, 2 Victoria Street, Westminster, London, S.W.1. Christian International. Physical training, gymnastics, football, cricket, club-rooms, bands, first-aid, swimming, life-saving, signalling, camping, wayfaring.

Boy Scouts Association, 25 Buckingham Palace Road, London, S.W.1. To develop good citizenship. All outdoor pursuits, such as camping, hiking, climbing, caving, sailing, swimming. Branches in Scouting and close links throughout the world. International Training Centre, Gilwell Park, Chingford, Essex.

British Council of Churches, 10 Eaton Gate, London, S.W.1. Is concerned in all aspects of Christian co-operation and aid, and works in close touch with the World Council of Churches in Geneva.

British Federation of University Women Limited, Crosby Hall, Cheyne Walk, London, S.W.3. An organization representing University Women Graduates and affiliated to the International Federation of University Women.

British National Committee of the World Assembly of Youth, 57 Chalton Street, London, N.W.1. A co-ordinating body providing a means for co-operation between national youth organizations of various interests, including political youth and students.

British Red Cross Society, 14–15 Grosvenor Crescent, London, S.W.1. One of over a hundred National Red Cross Societies throughout the world. First aid, auxiliary nursing and many welfare services. First aid training and nursing and welfare training for general public. Junior Red Cross admits young people to Cadet Units and as link members in schools or other Youth organizations.

British Vigilance Association and Standing Conference of Overseas Friendship Associations, 17A King's Road, London, S.W.3. An advisory service for young workers, in particular those from Europe, and an information service about clubs and English language classes.

Camping Club of Great Britain and Ireland, 11 Lower Grosvenor Place, London, S.W.1. To encourage outdoor pastimes.

Catholic Marriage Advisory Council, Clitherow House, 15 Lansdowne Road, London, W.11. Education for marriage and family life; marriage counselling; and a medical advisory service.

Citizens' Advice Bureaux, c/o National Council of Social Service, 26 Bedford Square, London, W.C.1. – or local address from any Post Office. Provide in most towns accurate information and skilled advice on personal problems arising in daily life, such as dealing with government departments, local authorities, voluntary organizations, through the collection of evidence based on the experience of the bureaux. The provision also of emergency information services, when needed.

Co-operative Youth Movement, Co-operative Union Ltd., Education Department, Stanford Hall, Loughborough, Leicester.

Indoor and outdoor educational, social and recreational activities for young people.

Co-operative Women's Guild, Pioneer House, 348 Gray's Inn Road, London, W.C.1. To promote co-operation and help women in the Co-operative Movement.

Council for Education in World Citizenship, 25 Charles Street, London, W.1. Promotion of education for international understanding through courses, conferences and holiday-conferences abroad.

East and West Friendship Council, 101 Gower Street, London, W.C.1. Provides hospitality in British homes for non-European overseas students only, in order to promote friendship and understanding. Arranges holidays for student nurses.

Educational Centres Association, Walthamstow Educational Settlement, Greenleaf Road, London, E.17. One-day and week-end classes and courses for adults. Advice on educational settlements and centres.

Educational Interchange Council (Inc.), 43 Russell Square, London, W.C.1. Promotion of educational visits and exchanges throughout the world.

Family Planning Association, 231 Tottenham Court Road, London, W.1. Marriage and the family; advocates and promotes the provision of facilities for scientific contraception; gives postal advice.

Fellowship of Reconciliation, 9 Coombe Road, New Malden, Surrey. Youth work to promote aim of destruction of barriers between peoples. Organizes youth conferences.

Girl Guides Association, 17–19 Buckingham Palace Road, London, S.W.1. Character-training and an awareness of world citizenship. Encourages and develops international understanding.

Girls' Friendly Society, Townsend House, Greycoat Place, London, S.W.1. Branches formed of members throughout U.K. hostels and holiday homes. H.Q. open to non-members of all creeds and races.

The Grail, Waxwell Farm House, 125 Waxwell Lane, Pinner, Middlesex. Training of Roman Catholic girls and young women.

Holiday Fellowship, 142 Great North Way, Hendon, London, N.W.4. To organize open-air holidays in adult and youth guest houses in some of the most beautiful parts of Britain.

International Friendship League, Peace Haven, Creswick

Road, London, W.3. Reception of overseas visitors in holiday centres; social activities; permanent centre for accommodation of overseas and provincial members; sponsors 'People to People' week, and international correspondence service.

London Council for Welfare of Women & Girls and Central Information Bureau, 7–9 Baker Street, London, W.1. Central Information Bureau for Girls; advises on lodgings, social clubs, etc., to help settle girls in London.

National Association of Youth Clubs, 30–32 Devonshire Street, London, W.1., *or* 13 Eglinton Crescent, Edinburgh 12 (for Scotland), *or* 7 Wellington Place, Belfast 1 (for Northern Ireland). Offers advisory service on informal education; maintains holiday centres and accommodates young people in holiday houses during the summer; arranges visits and short study courses for overseas students.

National Council for the Unmarried Mother and her Child, 255 Kentish Town Road, London, N.W.5, *or* 30 Castle Street, Edinburgh 2 (for Scotland). Aims at helping the unmarried mother and her child, both by promoting public understanding of her problems and urging improved social services. It helps individual cases either directly or by referral.

National Council of Women of Great Britain, 36 Lower Sloane Street, London, S.W.1. To secure the removal of all legal, economic or social disabilities of women; to promote the establishment of human rights. Affiliated to the International Council of Women.

National Council of Young Men's Christian Associations (Inc.), 112 Great Russell Street, London, W.C.1, *or* 10 Palmerston Place, Edinburgh 12 (for Scotland). Trains local leaders overseas; arranges special courses in Britain for leaders nominated by their national Y.M.C.A.s. Provides hostel accommodation and other facilities for young men of all countries.

National Federation of Women's Institutes, 39 Eccleston Street, London, S.W.1, *or* (Scottish Women's Rural Institutes), 42 Heriot Row, Edinburgh 3, *or* N.I. War Memorial Building, Waring Street, Belfast (for Northern Ireland). Special facilities for study of the Women's Institute Movement. Provides local centres for social, educational and secretarial activities for women and girls who live and work in the country or are interested in country life.

National Federation of Young Farmers' Clubs, 55 Gower

Street, London, W.C.1, *or* 11 Rutland Street, Edinburgh 1 (for Scotland). Encourages high standards of skill in farm and farmhouse crafts; organizes exchange visits with similar organizations overseas. Clubs to promote demonstrations and competitions in farm and rural crafts, as well as lectures and courses on different aspects of agriculture.

National Marriage Guidance Council, 58 Queen Anne Street, London, W.1. Marriage counselling and education for marriage; wide range of publications.

National Union of Townswomen's Guilds, 2 Cromwell Place, South Kensington, London, S.W.7. Promotes the broad educational interests of women in art, music, drama and social studies.

Plunkett Foundation for Co-operative Studies, 10 Doughty Street, London, W.C.1. Study of methods of agricultural and industrial co-operation; library. Holds seminars and correspondence courses.

Ramblers' Association, 124 Finchley Road, London, N.W.3. Twenty area organizations arrange rambles, lectures and social activities.

Religious Society of Friends, Friends' House, Euston Road, London, N.W.10. Maintains International and Neighbourhood Centres and organizes Work Camps at home and abroad.

Rotary International in Great Britain and Ireland, Tavistock House South, Tavistock Square, London, W.C.1. World fellowship through Rotary Clubs. Rotary Clubs exist in nearly 1,000 towns in Great Britain and Ireland and are active in the field of student hospitality.

Royal College of Nursing and National Council of Nurses of the United Kingdom, 1A Henrietta Place, Cavendish Square, London, W.1. To promote the progress of Nursing Education and Professional Organization Divisions.

St. John Ambulance Association, 10 Grosvenor Crescent, London, S.W.1. Instruction, examination and issue of certificates in first-aid, home-nursing, hygiene, food hygiene, child care and kindred subjects. Textbooks in foreign languages for students overseas.

St. John Ambulance Brigade, 8 Grosvenor Crescent, London, S.W.1. A trained uniformed body of men, and cadets (11–16 years) providing a voluntary first-aid auxiliary nursing and welfare service at public functions, institutions or in the home and available to all. Many students are members.

Standing Conference of National Voluntary Youth Organizations, 26 Bedford Square, London, W.C.1 (also the National Council of Social Service), *or* 8 Rutland Square, Edinburgh 1 (for Scotland), *or* 10 Malone Avenue, Belfast (for Northern Ireland). Information centre on voluntary youth organizations; encourages co-ordination of efforts or experiments in new types of approach or research affecting youth; acts as link between these organizations and Government departments, local authorities, etc.

Student Christian Movement, Annandale, North End Road, London, N.W.11. Membership open to all students. It is concerned with the whole student community, its interests and problems. The British S.C.M. is an international movement and a member of the World Student Christian Federation.

Toc H, 15 Trinity Square, London, E.C.3. Christian foundation to build a fellowship of men through voluntary personal service. Branches throughout the U.K. and overseas, formed of members, welcome guests, seventeen residential houses for young members.

Toc H Women's Association, Crutched Friars House, London, E.C.3. A Christian fellowship of women irrespective of class and race with branches throughout U.K. and overseas. Hospitality offered to overseas students. Special scheme for student nurses to spend their leave with members in their houses organized by overseas secretary at Headquarters.

Workers' Educational Association, Temple House, 27 Portman Square, London, W.1. Organizes non-vocational evening and daytime classes, and residential courses in social studies, appreciation of the arts, and general science for adults.

Young Women's Christian Association of Great Britain, Bedford House, 108 Baker Street, London, W.1. Wide social and educational programme for all ages in club centres. Hostels for girls over the age of 16 working or studying away from home. Holiday and travel service at home and abroad.

Overseas Visitors Centre, Y.W.C.A. Central Club, Great Russell Street, London, W.C.1. Organizes Comprehensive Course in Household Management and Hostess Etiquette. Advisory Bureau.

Young Women's Christian Association of Scotland, 18 Atholl Crescent, Edinburgh 3. Clubs and hostels.

Young Women's Christian Association for Ireland, 385 Malone Road, Belfast. Clubs and hostels.

Youth Hostels Association (England and Wales), Trevelyan House, 8 St. Stephen's Hill, St. Albans, Herts, *or* Scottish Youth Hostels Association, 7 Bruntsfield Crescent, Edinburgh 10, *or* Youth Hostel Association of Northern Ireland, 28 Bedford Street, Belfast 2. Helps all young people, especially those of limited means, by providing hostels with simple accommodation for them in their travels. Summer and winter sports courses (pony trekking, ski-ing, etc.). Publications list available.

The following is a list, with very brief descriptions, of some voluntary bodies which have particular interests, responsibilities and activities overseas.

African Development Trust, 9 Hope Gardens, St. Martin's Lane, London, W.C.2. Community development projects; advice on employment opportunities in Africa within this field.

British Association of the Experiment in International Living, 'Ottesaga', Upper Wyche, Malvern, Worcestershire. 'Homestay' – living with a family for a month – an interchange scheme. Programmes arranged in co-operation with 'Experiment' offices in countries overseas. (Parent Organization in Vermont, U.S.A.)

British Society for International Health Education, 85 Central Buildings, Southwark Street, London, S.E.1. Training programmes in health education overseas; assisting development of advanced training in health education for overseas students in Great Britain.

Catholic Overseas Appointments, Hinsley House, 38 King Street, London, W.C.2. Recruits directly for educational and other posts in establishments under Catholic management in the developing countries.

Christian Aid, 10 Eaton Gate, London, S.W.1. Training and resettlement of refugees and aid for social and agricultural development.

Committee on Overseas Service, 26 Bedford Square, London, W.C.1. Co-ordination in a scheme for sending young graduates, and others with professional training, to developing countries outside Europe.

Commonwealth Society for the Deaf, 31 Gloucester Place, London, W.1. Provision of teachers and equipment for schools for deaf children, in Commonwealth territories.

Conference of Missionary Societies in Great Britain and Ireland, Edinburgh House, 2 Eaton Gate, London, S.W.1. Centre for consultation between British Missionary Societies and for information about their work.

Co-operative Union Limited, Holyoake House, Hanover Street, Manchester 4. British co-operative experience and help to countries overseas.

The English Speaking Union, 37 Charles Street, London, W.1. Concerned with inter-Commonwealth and Commonwealth-American relations. Arranges social gatherings, discussions, and study-tours to the Continent for Commonwealth students in Britain.

Freedom from Hunger Campaign, United Kingdom Committee, 17 Northumberland Avenue, London, W.C.2. Through formal and informal education, the campaign educates public opinion about the World Food Situation. Funds raised to be spent on approved projects in developing countries.

Friends Service Council, Friends House, Euston Road, London, N.W.1. Work includes missionary service; international conciliation; school; rural training; refugee relief and rehabilitation.

National Adult School Union, 35 Queen Anne Street, London, W.1. Promotes informal adult education, publishes *Study Handbook*, providing curriculum of studies for local groups.

National Association for Mental Health, 39 Queen Anne Street, London, W.1. Training for mental health social workers. A voluntary organization working outside the National Health Service to promote mental health and aid the mentally disordered. Advisory casework service. Publications on mental health problems and on child care. One- and two-year courses for teachers of the mentally handicapped.

National Institute of Adult Education, 35 Queen Anne Street, London, W.1. Advises (adult students only) and refers inquiries of a specialist nature to appropriate bodies.

Overseas Development Institute, 160 Piccadilly, London, W.1. Directs studies into development problems and facilitates the interchange of views and ideas.

Industrial Welfare Society, Robert Hyde House, 48 Bryanston Square, London, W.1. Runs training courses in human relations for personnel specialists and managers sponsored by overseas member organizations and for schemes of technical co-operation;

co-operates with U.K. bodies which serve the interests of developing countries.

Institute of Rural Life at Home and Overseas, 3 Hendon Avenue, London, N.3. Provides, through overseas 'correspondents', a clearing house of published and unpublished information on agriculture overseas.

International Social Service of Great Britain, 70 Denison House, 296 Vauxhall Bridge Road, London, S.W.1. This International Social Work agency has its headquarters in Geneva and branches of correspondents in many countries. I.S.S. gives advice and service to people with personal problems which arise from their status as immigrants, aliens or refugees, particularly when the problem requires action in another country.

International Voluntary Service, 72 Oakley Square, London, N.W.1. Voluntary service in an international context at home and abroad on a week-end, short-term (2 weeks to 6 months) or long-term (1 year plus) basis. Construction; redecoration for the elderly; water supplies and roads for remote communities; amenities work; welfare, medical and social work.

Land Settlement Association Ltd., 43 Cromwell Road, London, S.W.7. The Association can advise on land settlement problems, including marketing, arising from its experience in England and can afford facilities to study its work.

Overseas Appointments, Information and Advisory Service (Opportunities Overseas), The Castle, Farnham, Surrey. Information and advice concerning service in the developing countries in public services, private enterprise and voluntary agencies. Publishes annual guide *Work Overseas*.

Overseas Students Commendation Centre of the Church of England, 2 Salisbury Square, London, E.C.4. Receives students from overseas and channels them to Anglican Churches and homes and introduces them to the available social services of the Church of England. Acts on behalf of the Missionary Societies of the Church of England. Its services are not confined to members of the Anglican Communion.

Oxford Committee for Famine Relief, 274 Banbury Road, Oxford. Provides funds for organizations overseas in agriculture, the medical field, etc.

Practical Aids Scheme, United Africa House, 1 Blackfriars Road, London, S.E.1. Puts African women's groups in touch with British women or British women's groups so that they may obtain practical teaching aids such as clothes patterns and useful cuttings from magazines.

Royal Commonwealth Society for the Blind, 46 Victoria Street, London, S.W.1. Promotes welfare, education, employment of the blind; works for the prevention of blindness throughout the Commonwealth.

Royal Commonwealth Society, 18 Northumberland Avenue, London, W.C.2. An inter-Commonwealth forum.

The Royal National Institute for the Blind, 224 Great Portland Street, London, W.1. Provides education, rehabilitation, prevocational and vocational training and maintains a comprehensive scheme of services to the blind of Britain. Acts in an advisory capacity to overseas blind welfare organizations.

The Royal Overseas League, Park Place, St. James's Street, London, S.W.1. Has lectures, discussions, films, etc., to stimulate interest in Commonwealth affairs.

The Salvation Army, Queen Victoria Street, London, E.C.4. An evangelical Christian movement for those in need of care. Runs four eight-week training sessions and operates the Salvation Army Farm Colony.

The Save the Children Fund, 29 Queen Anne's Gate, London, S.W.1. Cares for children in need throughout the world, irrespective of race, colour or creed. Today it is working in sixteen countries, including the United Kingdom.

The Order of St. John, St. John's Gate, Clerkenwell, London, E.C.1. Teaches first-aid, etc., to members who serve voluntarily.

The Sword of the Spirit, Hinsley House, 38 King Street, London, W.C.2. A Catholic educational society that works for international understanding through conferences, publications and the exchange of information and contacts with visitors and students from overseas.

United Nations Association International Service, 93 Albert Embankment, S.E.1. Teaching, agricultural and medical projects, including work-camp programme.

United World Trust for Education and Research, 29 Great James Street, London, W.C.1. Research into issues affecting international relations. Arranges conferences for student-teachers and young people on world problems. Publications.

The Victoria League, 38 Chesham Place, London, S.W.1. Welcomes Commonwealth visitors and provides certain club facilities and hospitality. In London sponsors five committees to assist students and maintains hostel accommodation for all creeds and colours. Country branches.

Voluntary Service Overseas, 3 Hanover Street, London, W.1. Provides opportunities for school-leavers, industrial apprentices, medical students, police cadets, graduates and other qualified people to give voluntary service for a year or more in the developing countries of the world.

The Women's Council (Co-operating with Women of India, Pakistan, Ceylon, Indonesia, Malaysia, Thailand, The Philippines, Japan, Iran, Korea), 8B Ellerdale Road, London, N.W.3. Opportunities for Asian visitors in this country to visit social service institutions and to attend conferences of British Women's Organizations.

Women's Corona Society, 2 Sanctuary Buildings, Great Smith Street, London, S.W.1. Assists women going to live in a new country and after their arrival overseas or in Britain.

World University Service, 59 Gloucester Place, London, W.1. International Welfare Organization for staffs and students of universities and colleges. Provision of buildings, equipment and health service in developing countries. Advisory service for students in U.K., also small loans in case of financial hardship.

Publications

Directory for those Working Among Overseas Students, published by S. M. House, 103 Gower Street, London, W.C.1.

There are a number of other forms of Directory produced by the Islamic Cultural Centre, Regents Lodge, 146 Park Road, London, N.W.8.; The Royal Overseas League; The Victoria League, and others. Also see *A Guide to Voluntary Service* by David Hobman, from H.M.S.O.

The National Union of Students, 3 Endsleigh Street, London, W.C.1

The National Union of Students of England, Wales and Northern Ireland has a membership of over 250,000 students drawn from over 550 constituent Unions.

N.U.S. is a federal association of the Student Unions, Guilds, J.C.R.s (Junior Common Rooms) and representative councils of the institutions of higher education in England, Wales and Northern Ireland.

The objects of N.U.S. are:

(1) To represent the students of England, Wales and Northern Ireland nationally and internationally;
(2) To maintain and promote their co-operation with students of other countries and to promote the educational, social and general interests of students.

The objects shall be pursued in entire independence of all political and religious groups, and shall not permit any action which is not in accordance with the role of the National Union in the field of education.

Membership is open to recognized student organizations or to individual students at a very low fee.

N.U.S. offers travel facilities to its members, its Education and Welfare Department advises on grant problems, and its Service Department organizes work camps for students, a drama festival, a debating tournament, and vacation work.

Student News is the official newspaper of N.U.S. and many other useful publications are available on request.

The newest department within N.U.S. is Graduate Service Overseas, which places graduates and other qualified students for a brief term in the developing countries.

There is also a Scottish Union of Students with similar aims and functions, and with headquarters at 30 Lothian Street, Edinburgh 8.

The United Nations Student Association, 93 Albert Embankment, London, S.E.1.

The Association exists in over 100 colleges and universities and is a member of the International Student Movement for the UN – the only student organization with members from both sides of the Iron Curtain.

Its aims are:

(*a*) To assist in the maintenance of peace by clarifying, upholding and propagating the aims of the UN;
(*b*) To study international affairs and further international understanding;
(*c*) To create an informed body of student opinion actively interested in world co-operation.

What UNSA offers:

(1) Participation in work camps organized by the International Service Department of UNA.

(2) Cheap travel and holidays abroad.

(3) Members are informed of conferences organized on international affairs by other organizations as well as its own, and those of other national UNSAs.

(4) Free leaflets on every aspect of the UN. Briefing conferences on topical subjects are arranged regionally and nationally.

(5) An Overseas Students Secretary can arrange for new arrivals to be met and guided. Help in finding accommodation and with general problems can be given.

Membership is open to all students of colleges and universities, and can be either through a society or as an individual. Inquiries and donations should be sent to The General Secretary, United Nations Student Association, 93 Albert Embankment, London, S.E.1.

Clubs and Societies

Warning. If you are invited to join a club you know nothing about, ask one of the bodies below for advice. There are quite a few clubs (some are attached to coffee bars) which are known to the police as thoroughly undesirable.

The Citizens' Advice Bureau. (Ask Police Station for the address of the nearest Bureau.)

The Social Advisory Group for Young People Away from Home, 108 Baker Street, London, W.1.

The Standing Conference of Overseas Friendship Associations, 17A King's Road, London, S.W.3.

Employment and 'Au Pair' Situations

All student employment tends to be difficult. Education in the U.K. is not arranged, on the whole, to enable the student 'to work his way through college'. The Universities, for example, expect their students for a first degree to follow a course of fairly solid study. In addition, the student may find himself, in seeking a job, up against all kinds of prejudices and conflicting interests. His first object will be the advancement of his own experience or studies. The employer, on the other hand, naturally puts the interests of his firm – or in the case of 'au pair' posts, of her household – first. When the student has found a suitable job, and for men particularly this may not be easy, it still needs understanding and goodwill on both sides to make the arrangement work.

The following are the *official regulations* concerning both foreign and Commonwealth citizens. In outlining the main divisions it is necessary to separate regulations which apply to students from countries within the Commonwealth and those from elsewhere.

Commonwealth Students

A Commonwealth student who wishes to undertake full-time work on arrival is required to obtain before entering the country a voucher from the Ministry of Labour (see page 15). Vouchers are at present being issued only to Commonwealth students who have specific jobs to come to or who possess certain special qualifications of professional standard.

Full-time Foreign Students

Foreigners admitted to the United Kingdom as students are NOT usually allowed to take any form of employment. There are some exceptions to this general rule: they include:

(a) Students attending 'Sandwich Courses' (i.e. courses which alternate periods of practical and theoretical training) at Technical Colleges; individual authorization for the practical work involved must be obtained from the Home Office, Immigration and Nationality Department, Princeton House, 271 High Holborn, London, W.C.1.

(b) Students studying in the United Kingdom for prescribed professional qualifications involving not only the passing of examinations but periods of practical experience; individual authorization for the practical work must be obtained from the Home Office, Immigration and Nationality Department.

(c) University and college students sponsored by the International Association for the Exchange of Students for

Technical Experience (I.A.E.S.T.E.) coming to the United Kingdom for practical experience in industry during their long vacations. Students must obtain an 'I.A.E.S.T.E. (U.K.) Landing Document' issued by the Association, before coming to the U.K.

(*d*) Students attending Universities and Colleges in the United Kingdom, and remaining there during the vacations between terms of their study, are eligible to take during their vacation any employment approved by the local office of the Ministry of Labour – provided they have, beforehand, applied to the Home Office Immigration and Nationality Department and had a suitable endorsement put in their passports.

It is advisable to allow at least three weeks from the date of application to the Ministry of Labour for a vacation work permit.

Student Employees

Young people from foreign countries wishing to take short-term employment with British employers in order to improve their English and to widen their experience require a student employee permit issued by the Ministry of Labour. The permit, which has to be produced at the port of arrival, is not issued direct to the foreigner but to his employer who is responsible for sending it to the foreign worker. Except in the case of head-for-head exchanges the permits are issued on condition that the student employee is employed in a supernumerary capacity and does not receive full pay.

A number of organizations in Britain with counterparts in foreign countries sponsor schemes for finding openings for student employees. These include:

The British Hotels and Restaurants Association, 88 Brook Street, London, W.1.

The International Economic Students' Association of Great Britain (A.I.E.S.E.C.), (AIESEC) National Executive, Clare Market, London, W.C.1.

The International Exchange Committee of Social Workers and Administrators, 36 Bedford Square, London, W.C.1.

The United Kingdom Sponsoring Authority for the International Exchange of Young Agriculturists, Agriculture House, Knightsbridge, London, S.W.1.

Work Camps

  (*a*) Foreign students are admitted without labour permits for full-time employment at Volunteer Agricultural Camps. Recruitment is carried out by four organizations:

      Concordia (Youth Service Volunteers), 188 Brompton Road, London, S.W.3.

      National Union of Students, 3 Endsleigh Street, London, W.C.1.

      World University Service, Cambridge Committee, c/o Priory Farm Camp, West Walton, Wisbech, Cambridgeshire.

      Wilkin & Sons Limited, Farm Office, Tiptree, Colchester Essex.

  (*b*) Foreign students are also admitted for periods of voluntary work without labour permits, to work in camps, arranged by the following organizations:

      International Voluntary Service for Peace, 72 Oakley Square, London, N.W.1.

      The Society of Friends, Friends Work Camps Committee, Friends House, Euston Road, London, N.W.1.

      United Nations Association, 25 Charles Street, London, W.1.

      Christian Movement for Peace, 451 Battle Road, St. Leonards-on-Sea, Sussex.

Domestic Work for Women and 'Au Pair' Posts

  Here the private employment agencies can often help. Women students, mainly European, can often find full-time domestic employment or 'au pair' posts in an English family and those who have a working command of the language can often find employment in hospitals, hostels and schools, including posts as assistant matrons in boarding-schools. These jobs are residential, and board and lodging are provided in addition to the wages. Permission is obtained from the Ministry of Labour by the employer, or in the case of 'au pair' girls a letter of invitation from the host family has to be produced at the port of entry by the 'au pair' student. Opportunities are usually given to continue their English studies. The Gabbitas-Thring Educational Trust Ltd., 6 Sackville Street, London, W.1, has a list of vacancies in schools in many parts of the country and will gladly help girls to find suitable jobs. Many private agencies belong to the Employment Agents'

Federation of Great Britain, which has produced a code of conduct for its members designed to protect foreign workers and 'au pair' girls coming to this country. A list of these member agencies may be obtained from the Secretary, Employment Agents Federation of Great Britain, 133 Oxford Street, London, W.1.

Confusion sometimes arises over what exactly constitutes an 'au pair' post. As a Home Office pamphlet issued to girls on arrival has said: 'The relationship between the girl and her employer is a personal one' and 'The arrangement must not be confused with regular domestic employment for which a Ministry of Labour permit is required.'

Seasonal Employment

Unskilled employment in the hotel and catering industry is available to foreign students during the period 1st March to the end of October each year. The work usually consists of general domestic duties, portering and giving help in the kitchen of hotels, restaurants, milk bars and other catering establishments.

Students can obtain employment through private employment agencies, some of which may charge a fee for their services. Private employment agencies dealing with 'au pair' posts seldom charge a fee. Assistance in securing openings is also given by two Employers' Associations. Inquiries to the latter should be addressed to:

The British Hotels and Restaurants Association, 88 Brook Street, London, W.1.

The Caterers' Association of Great Britain, Victoria House, Vernon Place, Southampton Row, London, W.C.1.

As in the case of student employees (see pages 48–49) a permit issued by the Ministry of Labour is required by the foreign student employee before he can enter this type of employment.

Students thinking of taking a job in a hotel, restaurant or café have a good chance of getting one, particularly in the summer holiday season on the South Coast of England or elsewhere. They should apply early in May or June. They should bear in mind that the job does not usually include accommodation and that this can be expensive and far away from the place of work, with the costs of transport – jobs in the catering trade may be 'split', i.e. two shifts of work during the 24 hours – all to be set against earnings.

In fact, the student will probably feel that his need falls into one of the following categories:

(1) He needs employment as a necessary part of his training either in Commerce or in Industry. See Section 3, pages 150 and 151.

(2) He is short of money and needs to earn. Bureaux which may help in this case are:

The Ministry of Labour Offices:

(Local) See Main Centres and Central.

Central offices in London under the Ministry of Labour are:

City of London Employment Exchange, Atlantic House, Farringdon Street, London, E.C.4.

West End Employment Exchange, Kemp House, Berwick Street, London, W.1 (for women only).

Westminster Employment Exchange, Chadwick Street, London, S.W.1, *also*

The Professional and Executive Register, Atlantic House, Holborn Viaduct, London, E.C.4. (For those with a University Degree, membership of a professional body or equivalent qualification. See note on Practical Training, Section 3, page 150.)

The Hotel and Catering Trades Employment Exchange, 1–3 Denmark Street, London, W.C.1. (Deals with the full range of hotel and catering vacancies in the whole of the South of England.)

The London County Council Youth Employment Service (*Careers Advisory Section*), 9 Carmelite Street, London, E.C.4.

The National Union of Students Employment Service, Endsleigh Place, London, E.C.2.

This operates two schemes:

(*a*) Vacation work anywhere in the U.K. Lists of jobs available are issued during term time to all colleges affiliated to the N.U.S. If more than five students are required by an employer there is a charge of 7s. 6d. per job. All applications must be made through the National Union of Students.

(*b*) Daily employment scheme, London only. Casual labour as, for example, on two or three days only. A student takes an introduction card to the employer. This is arranged on a rota system for the students.

(3) He wants employment which provides a working holiday. A number of organizations specialize in this type of employment. See organizations mentioned above and also under Student Exchange (page 54).

N.B. – It is very difficult for foreign nationals to get a teaching job in Britain, particularly in private education.

Insurance

Students as such are not liable to pay National Insurance contributions for weeks of full-time education, but must pay for any weeks in which they are employed or self-employed. They should register for National Insurance when they reach age 18 if they have not already done so. Students coming from overseas who, during a vacation, take up temporary employment related to their course of studies are not normally liable for contributions until they have been in Great Britain 26 weeks.

The most important benefits from National Insurance are sickness, unemployment and widows' benefits, retirement pension and maternity benefit.

Special concessions are made in the case of students, e.g. contributions can be paid in a lump sum or by instalments at any time up to six years after the course has ended. There are special conditions also attached to students, for periods of research, 'sandwich' courses, and for employment as practical training, for married women students, full-time correspondence courses and private study, also for 'au pair' situations.

There are special provisions for exempting self-employed and non-employed persons from liability to pay contributions on the grounds of small income.

Any pensions and National Insurance Offices will be pleased to give advice. The address can be got from the local Post Office or Telephone Directory.

Private Insurance for clothing, personal effects, etc., for travelling and your stay in Britain can be arranged through most travel agencies.

Medical and Dental Treatment

The National Health Service is available to all people in the United Kingdom and to overseas visitors in an emergency. It is in no way inferior to private service, though sometimes less convenient. No insurance qualification is necessary. However, overseas residents who come to Britain in order to seek treatment are expected to pay for it.

The National Health Service provides doctors, hospital service, dentists and opticians without any charge to the patient, except for partial charges for spectacles, dentures and dental treatment, and 'amenity' beds in hospital (i.e. beds with more privacy for those who prefer it).

You should register with a doctor as soon as possible, if you are to be in Britain for any length of time; an official list of doctors in any neighbourhood is obtainable from the main Post Office or you can ask your local hospital or college authorities to give you the name and address of a suitable medical practitioner. In an emergency, go to the casualty department of any general hospital (see heading under Main Centres, Section V) but only in an emergency. Entry as a patient to a hospital is normally after consultation with a doctor.

You are usually expected to go to a family doctor's surgery during certain fixed hours, unless you are very ill. Sometimes there is no appointment system, and you must wait your turn. The receptionist may give you a form to fill in. If you are staying in Britain more than a few weeks, you should register with the doctor of your choice. Dental care is part of the National Health Service, but you may have to wait several weeks for an appointment.

Vaccination

A vaccination certificate may be needed for entry into Britain, and students should consult the British Consulate in their own country on what is required.

Publications

Medicine in Britain (published by Longmans).

'Health Services in Britain' (C.O.I. Reference Pamphlet).

Group Visits and Student Exchange Schemes

General information on opportunities for group visits and exchanges and for individual visits of all kinds is available from the Central Bureau for Educational Visits and Exchange, 55A, Duke Street, Grosvenor Square, London, W.1. This Bureau is maintained by the Department of Education and Science (formerly the Ministry of Education) and by the Scottish Education Department to provide an advisory and information service on all aspects of travel both abroad and into Britain, for educational purposes, including the study of the English language. The Bureau's advisory services are available to schools and other educational establishments, youth and student groups of all kinds and individual young people. It issues a series of information leaflets published in the early spring of each year which are available free of charge to individual inquirers, on receipt of a stamped addressed foolscap envelope. While the Bureau does not normally make practical arrangements for visits, it is prepared to do so in the case of group projects of educational value on the initiative of official or educational organizations, provided that no other suitable agency exists. It also recruits a number of individual young people for language courses, international meetings and cultural events abroad and, occasionally, in Britain in co-operation with official and voluntary bodies.

Publications

Information for Young Visitors to Britain. Lists international meetings and courses in English and other subjects, special activity holidays, holiday courses and work camps, and provides information on working holidays and exchange visits to this country for young people abroad. It also outlines facilities for foreign groups visiting Britain. (Published in March.)

Vacation Courses Abroad. A comprehensive list of short courses and study tours in Europe and North Africa for individuals over 16, cross-indexed as to subject. (Published in March.)

The following organizations specialize in arranging short-term courses or student exchanges:

The Educational Interchange Council, 43 Russell Square, London, W.C.1. The work of this body is chiefly, but not exclusively, with European countries. It arranges exchanges of teachers, students and senior pupils at school; short study visits to and from Britain for youth leaders and social workers, for young people engaged in industry and commerce, and also for professional and specialized groups, e.g. lawyers, doctors, nurses, architects and government officials. Intending organizers of groups can obtain on request the Educational Interchange Council's booklet *Study Visits to Great Britain* (available also in French and German).

The Institute of Directors, Group Visits Department, 10 Belgrave Square, London, S.W.1. The Institute of Directors organizes, throughout the year, technical study tours for organized groups of graduate and final-year students from technical faculties of overseas universities (at the moment from Europe and Latin-America). Tours, which vary from 1 to 3 weeks' duration, are specially designed to give an insight into British industrial methods; whilst comprising mainly visits to factories, research organizations and other institutions, programmes also contain cultural and sightseeing aspects when time permits.

For approved groups, an all-in subsidized fee of between 30s. and 50s. per head daily is charged which includes hotel accommodation, meals and transport whilst in Britain. Interested group organizers should apply through British Embassies or British Council representatives in their own countries.

A.I.E.S.E.C. (Association Internationale des Etudiants en Sciences Economiques et Commerciales), British National Executive, Clare Market, London, W.C.2. This is an international organization for business and economic students with headquarters in Geneva at the International A.I.E.S.E.C. Secretariat, 28 Avenue Pictet-de-Rochemont, CH 1200 Geneva (Switzerland). It arranges exchanges between students to undertake traineeships with commercial and government enterprises, but only for students at its member schools. There are thirty-eight participating member countries:

Argentina	Denmark	Greece
Australia	Ecuador	Hong Kong
Austria	Finland	Iceland
Belgium	France	Ireland
Canada	Germany	Israel
Colombia	Ghana	Italy

Japan	Peru	Tunisia
Korea	Republic of China	Turkey
Mexico	Sierra Leone	United Kingdom
Netherlands	South Africa	U.S.A.
Nigeria	Spain	Yugoslavia
Norway	Sweden	Venezuela
Portugal	Switzerland	

Anyone interested in coming to Britain or going from Britain for a business traineeship should write to his own national executive. If he does not know the address he should write for it to the headquarters in Geneva.

I.A.E.S.T.E. (U.K.)

The International Association for Exchange of Students for Technical Experience (United Kingdom), 178 Queen's Gate, South Kensington, London, S.W.7.

I.A.E.S.T.E. arranges periods of training (8–12 weeks) for technical students studying at affiliated universities and colleges on a student-for-student reciprocal basis, between member countries, and therefore for a limited number only.

Member countries are:

American University of Beirut, Lebanon	Japan
	Luxembourg
Argentina	Netherlands
Austria	Norway
Belgium	Poland
Canada	Portugal
Chile	South Africa
Colombia	Spain
Denmark	Sudan
Finland	Sweden
France	Switzerland
Germany	Tunisia
Greece	Turkey
Iceland	United Arab Republic
India	United Kingdom
Ireland	U.S.A.
Israel	Yugoslavia
Italy	

Students from abroad who wish to have technical training in the U.K. should apply to I.A.E.S.T.E.'s committee in their own country (the address of which can be obtained from the London address as shown on the previous page), well in advance of the time at which they would like to come.

U.K.S.A.

(United Kingdom Sponsoring Authority for the International Exchange of Young Agriculturists), Agriculture House, Knightsbridge, London, S.W.1.

This scheme aims at securing an interchange of young farmers, farm workers and horticultural growers between Britain and other countries – at present these are the Western European countries, Poland and the U.S. The length of visits is a minimum of 3 months, extending to 12 months. Students must be between 18–25 years and have had at least 2 years' practical experience. Anyone interested, British or foreign, should apply, well in advance, in order to enable arrangements to be made with the employer and the work permit to be issued.

Publications

UNESCO, 'Handbook of International Exchanges'.
UNESCO, *Vacations Abroad.*
Holiday Courses in Europe by Peter Latham (published by Blackie & Co. Ltd.).

Travel and Holidays in Britain

Information for Visitors to Britain

Information about travel to Britain can be obtained in the major cities of the world from any travel agent, airline, railways or shipping company's office, or by writing direct to The British Travel Association, 64–65 St. James's Street, Piccadilly, London, S.W.1, England. In the *U.S.A.* apply to The British Travel Association, 680 Fifth Avenue, New York, 10019 N.Y.; 39 South La Salle Street, Chicago, 60603 Illinois; and 612 South Flower Street, Los Angeles, 90017 California. In *Argentina* to The British Travel Association, Avenida Cordoba 645, Buenos Aires. In *Brazil* to The British Travel Association, Rua Aurora 960, Salas 2–3, São Paulo. In *Canada* to The British Travel

Association, 151 Bloor Street West, Toronto 5, Ontario; and 661 Howe Street, Vancouver 1, B.C. In *Australia* to The British Travel Association, Swire House, 8 Spring Street, Sydney, N.S.W. In *New Zealand* to The British Travel Association, 207 Vivian Street, Wellington. In *South Africa* to The British Travel Association, Union Castle Building, 36 Loveday Street, Johannesburg; 12 Queen Victoria Street, Cape Town; Aliwal House, Aliwal Street, Durban; and Pearl Assurance House, Jameson Avenue, Salisbury. In *France* to The British Travel Association, 6 Place Vendome, Paris 1er. In *Belgium* to The British Travel Association, 41 Boulevard Adolphe Max, Brussels 1. In *Germany* to The British Travel Association, Neue Mainzer Strasse 22, Frankfurt-am-Main. In *Holland* to The British Travel Association, Leidseplein 29, Amsterdam. In *Italy* to The British Travel Association, 21A–21B Via Torino, Rome. In *Sweden* to The British Travel Association, Norrmalmstorg 1, Stockholm C. In *Japan* to the British Travel Association, Room 246, Tokyo Club Building, 4, 3-chome, Kasumigaseki, Chiyoda-ku, Tokyo. In *Spain* to the British Travel Association, Torre de Madrid 11°–2, Plaza de España, Madrid 13.

Upon arrival in Britain all overseas visitors are invited to make use of The British Travel Association's Tourist Information Centre at 64–65 St. James's Street, Piccadilly, London, S.W.1 (Tel. MAYfair 9191), where an information staff is available to give advice concerning travel, itineraries, and current events.

Similar services are available at The Scottish Tourist Board, 2 Rutland Place, West End, Edinburgh 1; The Welsh Tourist and Holidays Board, 7 Park Place, Cardiff; and The Northern Ireland Tourist Board, 10 Royal Avenue, Belfast (*Branch Office:* 13 Lower Regent Street, London, S.W.1, England).

Tourist Information

Many towns in Britain have local Information Bureaux where visitors can obtain further help and advice. When touring through Britain watch out for the special sign which indicates where this service is available.

TOURIST INFORMATION CENTRE ⚕

Useful Addresses (some of these, which are clubs, require a small membership fee).

The following addresses are additional to those of many commercial Travel Agents who will also supply advice and assistance free on request:

Automobile Association, Fanum House, Leicester Square, London, W.C.2. Tel. WHItehall 1200.

Boy Scouts Association, Scout Headquarters, 25 Buckingham Palace Road, London, S.W.1. Tel. VICtoria 6005.

British Canoe Union, 147A Station Road, London, E.4. Tel. SILverthorn 8456.

British Cycling Federation, 21 Blackfriars Road, London, S.E.1. Tel. WATerloo 3827.

British European Airways, Dorland Hall, Lower Regent Street, London, S.W.1. Tel. GERrard 9833.

British Railways: British Railways Travel Centre, 4 Regent Street, London, S.W.1. Tel. TRAfalgar 4343. Eastern Region, Liverpool Street Station, London, E.C.2. Tel. BIShopsgate 7600. London Midland Region, Euston Station, London, N.W.1. Tel. EUSton 1234. Southern Region, Waterloo Station, London, S.E.1. Tel. WATerloo 5151. Western Region, Paddington Station, London, W.2. Tel. PADdington 7000. North Eastern Region, York. Tel. York 53022. Scottish Region, 302 Buchanan Street, Glasgow C.2. Tel. DOUglas 2900. For all information on Rail Travel, Runabout Tickets, Party Tickets, Cheap Day Excursions, and other special concessions.

Camping Club of Great Britain and Ireland, and Canoe Camping Club, 11 Lower Grosvenor Place, London, S.W.1. Tel. TATe 9232.

Caravan Club Ltd., The, 46 Brook Street, London, W.1. Tel. MAYfair 6441.

Central Bureau for Educational Visits and Exchanges, 55A Duke Street, Grosvenor Square, London, W.1. Tel. MAYfair 5477.

Central Council of Physical Recreation, The, 26–29 Park Crescent, W.1. Tel. LANgham 6822.

Cyclists' Touring Club, 3 Craven Hill, London, W.2. Tel. PADdington 8271.

En Famille Agency, 1 New Burlington Street, Regent Street, London W.1. Tel. REGent 8868.

English-Speaking Union (American and Commonwealth only), 37 Charles Street, Berkeley Square, London, W.1. Tel. MAYfair 7400.

Franco-British Society, 1 Old Burlington Street, London, W.1. Tel. REGent 0815.

Holiday Fellowship, The, 142 Great North Way, Hendon, N.W.4. Tel. SUNnyhill 3381.

Inland Waterways Association Ltd., 114 Regent's Park Road, London, N.W.1. Tel. JUNiper 2556.

International Friendship League, Peacehaven, Creswick Road, Acton, London, W.3. Tel. ACOrn 4303.

National Association of Boys' Clubs, 17 Bedford Square, London, W.C.1. Tel. MUSeum 5357.

National Association of Youth Clubs, 30–32 Devonshire Street, London, W.1. Tel. WELbeck 2941.

National Federation of Permanent Holiday Camps, 10 Bolton Street, Piccadilly, London, W.1. Tel. GROsvenor 2002.

National Federation of Young Farmers' Clubs, 55 Gower Street, London, W.C.1. Tel. MUSeum 9944.

National Union of Students, Travel Department, 3 Endsleigh Street, London, W.C.1. Tel. EUSton 2184.

Northern Ireland Tourist Board, 10 Royal Avenue, Belfast, Northern Ireland, Tel. Belfast 31222–5.

The Ramblers' Association, 124 Finchley Road, London, N.W.3.

Royal Automobile Club, 85 Pall Mall, London, S.W.1. Tel. WHItehall 4343.

Royal Commonwealth Society, Northumberland Avenue, London, W.C.2. Tel. WHItehall 6733.

Royal Overseas League, Overseas House, Park Place, St. James's, London, S.W.1. Tel. HYDe Park 5051.

School Journey Association of London, 23 Southampton Place, London, W.C.1. Tel. CHAncery 4854.

Scottish Council of Physical Recreation, 4 Queensferry Street, Edinburgh. Tel. CALedonian 3117.

Scottish National Camps Association Ltd., 57 Melville Street, Edinburgh, 3. Tel. CALedonian 6392.

Scottish Tourist Board, 2 Rutland Place, West End, Edinburgh 1. Tel. FOUntainbridge 1561.

Scottish Union of Students, Travel Department, 30 Lothian Street, Edinburgh 8. Tel. CALedonian 2061.

Scottish Youth Hostels Association, 7 Bruntsfield Crescent, Edinburgh 10. Tel. MORningside 4755.

Student Movement House, 103 Gower Street, London, W.C.1. Tel. EUSton 1640.

Welsh League of Youth, Swyddfa'r Urdd, Aberystwyth, Wales. Tel. Aberystwyth 579.

Welsh Tourist and Holidays Board, 7 Park Place, Cardiff, Wales. Tel. Cardiff 27281.

Workers' Educational Association, Temple House, 27 Portman Square, London, W.1. Tel. WELbeck 0491.

W.T.A. (Galleon Holidays), Eccleston Court, Gillingham Street, London, S.W.1. Tel. VICtoria 6688.

World Assembly of Youth, British National Committee, 57 Charlton Street, London, N.W.1. Tel. EUSton 7559.

World University Service, 59 Gloucester Place, London, W.1. Tel. WELbeck 3921.

Young Men's Christian Association, Holiday and Travel Department, 37 Bedford Square, London, W.C.1. Tel. MUSeum 3744.

Young Women's Christian Association, Holidays and Travel Service Department, 108 Baker Street, London, W.1. Tel. WELbeck 6591.

Youth Hostel Association of Northern Ireland Ltd., 28 Bedford Street, Belfast, Northern Ireland. Tel. Belfast 24733.

Youth Hostels Association (England and Wales), Trevelyan House, St. Albans, Herts. Tel. St. Albans 55215. Travel Department at: 29 John Adam Street, London, W.C.2. Tel. TRAfalgar 1722 or 3210.

Other useful addresses in London include the following: British Railways Travel Centre, Lower Regent Street, London, S.W.1. Victoria Coach Station, 164 Buckingham Palace Road, London, S.W.1. West London Air Terminal, Cromwell Road, London, S.W.7. B.E.A., Dorland House, Lower Regent Street, London, S.W.1; Terminal House, Grosvenor Gardens, London, S.W.1.; and 102 Cheapside, London, E.C.2. B.O.A.C., Airways Terminal, London, S.W.1.

See also *Young European's Guide* and *Holiday Courses in Europe*, by Peter Latham (published by Blackie & Co. Ltd.).

Camping

Tourists who bring their own camping equipment should join the Camping Club of Great Britain and Ireland; if, however, they are already members of a club affiliated to the International Federation of Camping and Caravanning they are eligible for temporary and free membership of the Camping Club of Great

Britain and Ireland. Members are provided with a list of over 2,000 inspected camping sites, in all parts of the British Isles, where they can camp, at an average cost of between 2s. and 2s. 6d. per person per night. No licence to camp is required.

Lists of sites can be obtained only from camping organizations and from the offices of The British Travel Association.

Farming and Work Camps

There are a number of such camps in various parts of the country where volunteers may help with general farming, forestry, harvesting, etc. The work is paid, but a charge is made for food and accommodation. Details may be had from The Farm Camps Organizer, National Union of Students; Concordia (Youth Service Volunteers), Ltd.

Youth Hostels ('Y.H.A.')

The Youth Hostels Association of England and Wales (see also page 40), the Scottish Youth Hostels Association and the Youth Hostel Association of Northern Ireland have nearly five hundred hostels where Association members, or members of an overseas youth hostels association, can obtain simple accommodation normally at 3s. 6d. per night (2s. for persons aged under 16 years). All hostels have separate dormitory accommodation for men and women and facilities for members cooking their own meals. Some hostels provide inexpensive meals. Visitors are expected to take part in the domestic duties of the hostel. Accommodation should generally be booked well in advance during July and August, at Easter and Whitsun, and throughout the summer in London and Edinburgh, where accommodation is particularly hard to obtain at short notice.

Information leaflets and itineraries can be obtained from The British Travel Association offices and from the individual Youth Hostels Association's offices.

Y.M.C.A. and Y.W.C.A. Hostels

These organizations have large hostels in London and other parts of Britain; they can often help visitors with accommodation, particularly during university vacations. Since 25th March, 1963, a new Youth Hostel, administered by the Y.W.C.A., is offering individuals and youth parties accommodation in London's West End at all times of the year. (Applications to: The Recep-

tionist, Y.W.C.A., Hyde House, Bulstrode Street, London, W.1.
Tel. WELbeck 7887.)

Inns and Private Accommodation

There is a large number of country inns which have one or two
bedrooms to let at modest rates (about 25s. to 30s. per night
including breakfast during the summer months) and in most
villages accommodation can be obtained in private houses.
Cyclists' and ramblers' organizations issue to their members
useful lists of this type of accommodation (see pages 59–61).

Boarding-houses

Accommodation, which is simpler than that offered by hotels,
but which is nevertheless comfortable, is provided by boarding-
houses. The average cost is 25s. for bed and breakfast in London,
and from 20s. outside London.

No list is available covering the whole of Britain, but offices of
The British Travel Association can supply lists of addresses in
most major towns and resorts.

University Hostels

During the Long Vacation certain of the university residential
hostels are made available to educational and school tour parties
at favourable rates. Party organizers should waste no time in
making their arrangements with the relevant College or University.

Holiday Centres and Guest Houses

Many large and attractively situated country houses have been
organized as holiday centres and guest houses. These centres
provide opportunities for meeting British families. The costs,
which are inclusive of all meals, vary according to locality and
season from 95s. to 280s. per week. Advance booking is necessary,
and bookings of less than one week are rarely possible during
July and August.

Holiday Camps

A holiday camp in Britain is an estate organized to provide
holidays for a large number of people on a communal basis. The
estate is usually situated on a popular stretch of the coast, and
consists of a central block, containing general dining-room,

sitting-rooms, dance-hall and games rooms, surrounded by a number of small chalets providing sleeping accommodation for two or four people. Rates are inclusive of all meals, and cover almost all entertainments, sports and other activities. The average camp accommodates between 200 and 300 visitors, though some hold over 1,000.

Costs vary according to the camp and season and range from 130s. to 360s. per week. Booking must be made in advance. Details can be obtained from The National Federation of Permanent Holiday Camps (see address on page 60).

TRANSPORT

By Car. For the motorist who wishes to bring his own car to Britain, special facilities are offered by The Royal Automobile Club and The Automobile Association to those who are already members of motoring organizations within the Commonwealth. Both organizations maintain road services in every part of the country, and at their London and area offices give advice of all kinds to their members.

Intending purchasers of motor-cars, exempt from purchase tax subject to export within a specified period, may place their orders in their own home town by contacting the distributor of the car favoured. Delivery can be taken on arrival in Britain.

The British Travel Association or any area office of the A.A. can supply names of experienced and reliable organizations from which cars may be hired. Cars of all sizes, with and without drivers, can be supplied.

The use of trailer caravans is widespread, and information about hiring and sites may be obtained from The Caravan Advice Bureau or from any area office of the A.A. Useful advice is given to its members by The Caravan Club of Great Britain and Ireland (see address on list on page 59). See also Driving Licences in this Section on page 72.

By Rail. British Railways facilities are subject to modification and students should obtain up-to-date information prior to planning itineraries by rail. Such facilities include *Circular Tour* Tickets, obtainable by prior notice, which cover any desired route which is made up of at least three stages in continuity, a break of journey being allowed at any place en route; Holiday '*Runabout*' Tickets which allow unrestricted travel for periods varying from six to seven days in a specified area; *Party Tickets* which offer special concessions for parties of eight and over; and the popular '*Railrover*' Ticket, obtainable in the summer season. Further information about these, and other special facilities, can be obtained when in London, from The Travel Centre, British Railways, Lower Regent Street, London, S.W.1.

Return Tickets, available for three months between any two places, except for journeys within the Greater London area which are valid two days, or at week-ends from Friday to Monday inclusive, allow a break of journey at intermediate stations. They can be obtained on demand from railway stations and travel agencies. The cost is usually double the normal single fare. *Day and Half-day Excursion Tickets* at prices much below the normal return fares are at times available between certain places, and where in operation offer a convenient and inexpensive way of visiting a place of interest. Day excursion tickets cost about $1\frac{1}{2}$d. per mile for the double journey, and half-day excursions something less than for the day excursions. Inquiries and bookings must be made at railway stations and travel agencies after arrival in Britain. There are also sometimes mid-week reductions.

There are only first- and second-class carriages on British trains. Second-class is the one generally used by British travellers. *Thrift Coupons*, obtainable only in North America, cost $30 second-class and $45 first-class in the U.S.A. and $32.50 second-class and $48.75 first-class in Canada, where approximately 1,000 miles of travel in Great Britain and Ireland will be undertaken within six months. The coupons are in convenient form, exchangeable only at British Railways stations and offices in Great Britain and Ireland for all types of travel tickets and reservations (except for road journeys and for Continental boat train and steamer services).

Guest Passes, obtainable in North America, Australia, New Zealand, France, Belgium, Holland, Germany, Switzerland, Italy, Denmark, Finland, Norway and Sweden, allow unlimited journeys for seven days or more over British Railways in England, Wales and Scotland. For the prices at which they may be purchased, inquire from The British Travel Association's office in your own country.

By Air. Regular services between the major cities of England, Scotland, Northern Ireland and the Channel Islands are operated

T—c

by British European Airways and British United (C.I.) Airways. Full information from your local B.E.A. office, travel agent, or from B.E.A., Dorland House, Lower Regent Street, London, S.W.1., Terminal House, Grosvenor Gardens, London, S.W.1, 102 Cheapside, London, E.C.2, and West London Air Terminal, Cromwell Road, London, S.W.7. For particulars of facilities provided by British United (C.I.) Airways apply to Victoria Air Terminal, Victoria Station, S.W.1, *or to* 35 Piccadilly, London, W.1.

British European Airways offer reduced fares for off-peak periods and night flights on United Kingdom services. Special off-peak flights operate between London and Belfast, Edinburgh, Glasgow and Manchester. School-children, and students travelling between home and their place of study in the United Kingdom or the Continent, can benefit by up to 25 per cent reduction on normal adult fares; rebates also apply to most fares for parties of ten or more persons.

For particulars of the services provided by independent airlines, apply to your travel agent or to the offices of The British Travel Association.

By Bicycle. Cyclists from overseas are recommended to join either The Cyclists' Touring Club or The British Cycling Federation (addresses on page 59), unless they are already members of The Alliance Internationale de Tourisme, membership of which confers honorary membership of the above organizations.

There is no restriction on bringing a bicycle to Britain, provided the cyclist gives a verbal assurance to the Customs Officers that he intends to take his machine with him on return to his own country. No documents are required, and no deposit has to be paid. The only regulation affecting bicycles is one which requires cyclists using the roads at night to show on the front of their cycles a white light; and, at the rear, a red light as well as a red reflector.

Bicycles may be hired by the day or week, or alternatively a visitor can purchase a cycle upon his arrival and sell it before departure.

Many cyclists extend their range by travelling by train to a convenient centre. Reduced railway fares for both passenger and cycle are available on presentation of tour vouchers supplied by cycling organizations.

Motor-cycling. A lightweight motor-cycle offers an economical method of extensive touring at a reasonable cost. The motor-cyclist can bring his own machine to Britain or one of the British lightweight motor-cycles can be bought on arrival.

In either case, the tourist should first get in touch with a motoring association in his own country or with one of the two British motoring organizations listed on page 72 (The Automobile Association and The Royal Automobile Club). These organizations will advise on the formalities and customs requirements. It should be noted that any bicycle fitted with a motor (e.g. velomoteurs and mopeds) is subject to the same regulations as motor vehicles.

On Foot. Walking tours are possible in many beautiful parts of the British Isles: Wales, the Lake District, the Cotswolds, the Pennines, Devon and Cornwall, etc.; so also is mountaineering in Scotland and Wales; pot-holing and caving in the Peak District in Derbyshire, and elsewhere. For further information on caving, apply to: The Speleological Society, 15 Westgrove Lane, London, S.E.10.

For mountaineering in Britain: The British Mountaineering Council, 6 Belmont Grove, London, W.4. The Mountaineering Association, 102a Westbourne Grove, London, W.2. Scottish Mountaineering Club, Synod Hall, Castle Terrace, Edinburgh.

A walking holiday usually starts with a rail or bus journey to the area which the visitor wishes to explore. Reduced fare rail-tickets are obtainable from railway stations as advertised, available on day of issue, for specific tours. Maps, known as Ordnance Survey Maps, are obtainable at most bookshops. The most convenient scale for walking is one inch : one mile.

Britain is probably the best country in the world for walking in, for not only is there a great variety of scenery, but there exist innumerable paths and tracks, extending throughout the countryside and through all types of country. The Youth Hostels Association (England and Wales), The Scottish Youth Hostels Association, and The Youth Hostel Association of Northern Ireland (addresses see page 61) open their memberships to all, and provide inexpensive accommodation and simple meals. There are nearly five hundred hostels in Britain, and it is said that nowhere is there a greater distance than 30 miles between any two of them. Owing to the great popularity of walking holidays in the summer months, advance booking at that time of the year is a wise precaution. For information on walking or rambling in the countryside, apply to: The Ramblers Association, 124 Finchley Road, London, N.W.3.

By Inland Waterways. Great Britain and Ireland are intersected with rivers and canals. In addition, there are, particularly in Northern Ireland, Scotland and Wales, large lakes, to say nothing of the less numerous but nevertheless extensive stretches of water in the English Lake District. Inland waterways of a different type are offered by the Norfolk Broads. All particulars about canoeing, hiring canoes, and camping, may be obtained from The Camping Club of Great Britain and Ireland, Canoe Camping Section. Further information can also be obtained from The Inland Waterways Association, 114 Regent's Park Road, London, N.W.1, and from The British Travel Association who publish the booklet *Holidays on Britain's Inland Waterways*. Membership of overseas canoe associations carries with it the right to facilities offered by the British Canoe Union.

Steamer Service. There are fast, comfortable steamer services which run every night except Sundays from Heysham, Liverpool and Glasgow to Belfast, and between Stranraer and Larne to Northern Ireland. In the summer months there is also a night service on Sundays between Heysham and Belfast, and daylight services operate on some routes. Also there are frequent air services daily between the main cities of Britain and Belfast.

At week-ends during certain summer months and at the Christmas, Easter and Whitsun holiday times, sailing tickets must be obtained in advance through British Railways offices or accredited travel agencies.

No separate passport is required, and as Northern Ireland is part of the United Kingdom there are no customs formalities. British currency is used and there is no restriction on the amount that can be brought in.

There are also short-distance steamer services between the larger holiday resorts on the coast. The most spectacular of these services are those which sail from Glasgow down the River Clyde and to the Western Isles.

Details of the many services can be obtained from travel agencies or from The British Travel Association's offices.

Regular Motor Coach Services. Regular long-distance motor-coach services run to almost all parts of Britain. They afford a comfortable and interesting way of combining travel with a new view of the countryside. It usually takes longer to reach a destination by motor-coach than by rail.

Coach travel costs a little more than 1d. per mile, and advance booking is essential on most services. Detailed information can be obtained through travel agencies or The British Travel Association offices.

Private Coach Hire. It is often convenient and sometimes economical for an organized party to travel by private motor-coach. The organization or agency handling the party in Great Britain can usually make the necessary arrangements.

Local Bus Services. It is possible to reach any part of the country by using local bus services, but changes from one local bus service to another may be necessary, according to the nature of the journey. The fares on these services are just under 3d. per mile, and in some cases the bus tickets may be exchanged for local railway tickets.

In all large towns and tourist centres the local bus companies run day and half-day excursions at very reasonable fares to points of interest.

GENERAL ADVICE ON TRANSPORT

Buses are clean, and in towns fairly frequent, but the high level of wages means that fares are not cheap. You should always form a queue at a bus-stop and take your turn. Smoking is not generally permitted downstairs on a double-deck bus. *Trains* generally leave and arrive on time. There is usually no need to book in advance for trains, except at peak holiday periods. *Long-distance coaches* are cheap but take longer than trains, and you should book in advance. The railways, coach companies and pleasure boats generally run day excursions which are cheaper than original fares, and are a very good way of seeing the country reasonably. Cars may be hired for a day or more, but most proprietors ask for a large deposit from students and foreigners.

Taxis are plentiful in London, and they must have a meter with the fare clearly shown. They are less frequent in the provinces, except outside railway stations. It is usual to telephone one of the local taxi-hire companies, whose numbers can be found in a telephone book. Fares are usually limited by law, and you should look at the meter if you are in any doubt, but trips beyond 5 miles or ⬩outside city limits are usually not governed by the meter, and you should ask the taxi-driver in advance how much it will cost approximately. The taxi-driver usually expects about 15 per cent or 20 per cent tip.

In most cities, the last bus is about 10.30 p.m., but check in advance. In London the easiest and quickest way to get about is by underground train – the 'Tube' – the last Tube is around midnight. There are clear route maps at every station, and a good simple guide on finding your way around London can be bought at any Underground ticket office.

Traffic. Do not forget that traffic drives on the left – very alarming when you are crossing the road at first! The British drivers are usually courteous, and will give way to you if you use a 'zebra' pedestrian crossing.

LEFT LUGGAGE AND LOST PROPERTY

Any luggage can be left, locked, at main railway stations in the 'Left Luggage' office or 'cloakroom'. A small fee is charged and a receipt is given which you must keep in order to reclaim your luggage. In London there are coin-operated 24 hour left-luggage lockers.

There are Lost Property Offices at all ports and railway stations, also in most large stores or shops. For property lost elsewhere inquire from the Police or Transport Office (see under Main Centres).

The Weather

There can be, it is true, long periods of rain or drizzle at all times of the year but these are rare, as are long periods of 'set fair' weather. Intense cold or intense heat are also very exceptional, the main feature being a rather temperate inconstancy. Usually, in fact, it is very difficult to know exactly what the weather is going to do and that is why it figures so much in all British conversation.

The average temperature for London (Kew Gardens) and Edinburgh, over a normal year, is quoted here as a guide:

Month	London	Edinburgh
January	40·1°	38·7°
February	40·4°	38·8°
March	43·8°	41·3°
April	48·3°	44·5°
May	54·3°	49·1°
June	60·2°	54·9°
July	63·8°	58·5°
August	62·8°	57·6°
September	58·3°	54·1°
October	51·2°	48·4°
November	44·5°	42·8°
December	40·8°	40·1°

Centigrade		Fahrenheit
100	· · ·	212
30	· · ·	86
25	· · ·	77
20	· · ·	68
15	· · ·	59
10	· · ·	50
5	· · ·	41
0	· · ·	32
17·8	· · ·	0

The Fahrenheit scale is used for measuring temperatures. Both Fahrenheit and Centigrade are now quoted in weather forecasts. Comparison between the Fahrenheit and Centigrade scale may be seen from the diagram.

In London the average daily duration of bright sunshine is six to seven hours in summer (June to August) and five hours in spring (March to May). It exceeds seven hours daily during the summer at nearly all British South Coast resorts.

Britain's Public Holidays

In England, Wales and Northern Ireland: Good Friday, Easter Monday, Whit-Monday, last Monday in August, Christmas Day and Boxing Day (first weekday after Christmas). Also (*Northern Ireland only*) 17th March and 13th July (in 1964).

In Scotland: New Year's Day, Good Friday, first Monday in May, first Monday in August and Christmas Day. There are also spring and autumn holidays in Edinburgh and Glasgow. Only New Year's Day is universally a holiday; other public holidays vary from place to place.

Driving Licences

If you intend to remain in the United Kingdom for less than 12 months, you may drive during that period on your national current licence or any other valid licence you may have. If you intend driving after having been in the United Kingdom for more than 12 months you must obtain a provisional licence and be accompanied by a person holding a full and valid licence until you successfully pass the Ministry of Transport driving test. An International Driving Permit issued abroad is acceptable in the U.K.

For further details and advice on particular cases apply to: The Automobile Association, Fanum House, Leicester Square, London, W.C.2, or to: The Royal Automobile Club, 85 Pall Mall, London, S.W.1.

Students registered at a University or Training College for more than one year must take steps to take their driving test immediately, if they wish to drive a car in Britain.

There is a four-months' waiting list for driving tests in the London area. It is generally quicker to arrange to take the test in less populated parts of the country. A form for a provisional licence can be obtained from any Post Office which you should send, when filled in, to the local Taxation Office.

It is important to abide by the regulations, as failure to do so will affect insurance in the event of an accident. Driving your own, or any other person's car, it is essential to have third party insurance in accordance with the requirements of the Road Traffic Act.

Publication

'The Highway Code' (obtainable from any Post Office or H.M.S.O.)

The Police

Organized on a local basis, the Police Force in the U.K. is in no way a military force. The maintenance of law and order is the chief care of the police officer who performs his duties unarmed and with a long-established tradition of training and organization behind him. In any emergency, a road accident, traffic dislocation, a case of sudden illness, as well as in instances of crime or rioting, the public normally first turns to the police officer for help and he is trained 'to render all the comfort and aid in his power'.

The Police have all the facilities for specialized advice and are expert in local knowledge. They can usually direct the stranger on his way and will also advise on roads and 'off-street' car-parks. As a last resort, by going to the nearest police station, it is always possible to learn where to find a bed for the night.

By dialling '999' in London on the nearest telephone, private or call-box, you may summon the police, fire-brigade or ambulance.

(*Note:* When dialling the Emergency Service always give your address and the service required as the first thing you say.)

The Headquarters of the London Metropolitan Police: New Scotland Yard, London, S.W.1. Tel. WHItehall 1212.

Post Office

Letters and parcels in the U.K. are addressed by putting the name of the addressee first, then the street followed by the town, and last the county: e.g. John Slaithwaite Esq., 126 Commercial Street, HALIFAX, Yorkshire.

Postage Rates within the U.K: The charge for letters weighing not more than 2 oz. is 4d. Postcards, 3d.

Postage Rates to Countries Abroad: (a) Surface. For letters weighing not more than 1 oz. the charge is 4d. to the Commonwealth and 6d. to other countries. Postcards, 3d. to the Commonwealth, 4d. to other countries. *(b)* Air. There are no special air mail rates to Europe. Letters and postcards prepaid at surface postage rates are sent by air whenever this will give quicker delivery. Air mail labels should *not* be used.

Air mail rates to countries outside Europe vary according to destination. Air mail labels *must* be used.

Air letters, postage 6d., on special letter forms obtainable from the post office may be sent to all countries outside Europe.

For full details of inland and overseas postage rates, inquire at any post office. There are special regulations for packing, especially for parcels abroad, prohibitions on the articles sent, etc. The *Post Office Guide*, a thick volume (price 2s. 6d.) obtainable through any post office or from H.M.S.O. (see page 83) gives all information on parcel rates as well as on all other post office services.

Generally speaking, letters take 1–2 days for delivery within the U.K., 2–3 days to Europe, and 1–3 days by air and 6–11 days by surface to the United States of America.

Among the many special services which the post office gives are:

Poste Restante: For travellers and for 3 months only in any one town. A letter or packet may be addressed to any post office marked 'Poste Restante' or 'to be called for' provided that the addressee's name is properly given. Evidence of identity must be given. In some foreign countries the addressee is charged a special fee. In Belgium, France and Spain parcels should be addressed to the railway station *En Gare* not *Poste Restante*.

Express Post, Inland: A letter or parcel may be sent all the way by special post office messengers at a charge of 3s. per mile.

Postal packets sent under this service may be registered or sent by recorded delivery service.

Inland Registered Post: A letter or parcel may be registered for a minimum fee of 1s. 9d. with compensation for loss not exceeding £20. This requires special sealing and must be handed in at a post office. Nothing intended for registration should be dropped into a letter-box.

Overseas Registration: Fee, in addition to postage, 1s. 9d., carries compensation up to £2 18s. generally in the event of total loss. Not applicable to parcels.

Overseas Insurance: Letters and parcels may be insured against loss or damage for sums up to £400. The service extends to most countries but in many the limit is less than £400. There is a charge for advice of delivery at 6d. For all conditions and charges, inquire at the larger post offices.

Sending Money: Currency must not be sent outside the British Isles.

Money Orders: These may be sent to most overseas countries. The limit is £40, but in some countries is less. Poundage from 2s. to 10s. according to value of order. Telegraph orders may be sent to certain countries, poundage 3s. 6d. to 11s. 6d. according to value of order, plus cost of official telegram of advice.

Postal Orders: An order addressed to the payee for any sum up to £5 may be sent to most territories within the British Commonwealth.

Savings: The post office runs a useful savings bank service, which is available during post office hours. An account may be opened with 5s. or more by going to any savings bank post office and withdrawals may be made from any of these offices on production of a signature and savings book.

Licences: Post offices issue the various kinds of licences which people are required by law to hold for the use of motor vehicles, guns, and broadcast receiving sets, etc.

Telegrams: Telegrams may be dictated over the telephone or handed in on a special form at the post office. The charge for an inland telegram of 12 words or less (including name and address) is 5s., 5d. for each extra word. Overnight telegrams may be sent between 8 a.m. and midnight for delivery normally by first post next morning; charges 12 words or less 2s. 6d., 2½d. for each extra word.

There are also decorative greetings telegrams, priority telegrams, and multiple address telegrams and pre-paid reply telegrams at small extra charges.

Advice for the addressing of a telegram will be given by the post office authorities.

Telephone

How to Make a Call

Most telephone exchanges in the United Kingdom are of the automatic type and trunk calls can be dialled without the assistance of an operator from approximately half of all telephones. The British Post Office is working towards the replacement of all manual exchanges and the extension of 'Subscriber Trunk Dialling' to all telephones by 1970.

If the telephone you are using has no dial, then, for all calls, you simply lift the receiver and when the operator answers tell her the exchange and number of the person to whom you wish to speak.

If the telephone has a dial and you want to speak to a number on the same exchange, you lift the receiver, wait for dialling tone (a continuous purring sound) and when you hear it dial the number you want.

If you wish to make a call from a telephone with a dial to a number that is not a local number then you should refer to the more detailed instructions contained in the front of the telephone directory.

If the telephone has a coin-box, the instructions displayed beside it should be studied carefully before a call is made.

The detailed instructions referred to will tell you if you can dial the call for yourself and if so, how to do it. If you cannot dial the call yourself the instructions will indicate how to obtain the services of an operator.

Tones

Apart from 'dialling tone' which is described above, there are four tones which you should learn to recognize:

Ringing tone (a repeated 'burr-burr') – tells you that the called number is being rung.

Engaged tone (a repeated high-pitched note) – means that

the number you have dialled (or, occasionally, the exchange equipment) is engaged. When you hear this you should replace the receiver and try the call again later.

Number unobtainable tone (a steady high-pitched note) – usually means that the number you have called is temporarily out of service, but it may mean that you have dialled a spare line. You should check the number and then dial the call again.

Pay-tone (rapid pips) – on calls from certain coin-box telephones indicates that money should be inserted by the caller.

Services

Details of charges and services available are shown in the front of the telephone directory but a few of the more important items are given below:

There is a *cheap rate* period for inland calls between 6.0 p.m. and 6.0 a.m. each night and all day Sunday.

Telegrams may be handed in by telephone.

Telephone numbers may be obtained from '*Directory Inquiries*'.

Overseas Calls, *Weather Forecasts*, and *Time* can be obtained – by dialling in some cases, otherwise with the help of an operator (see Directory Preface).

Personal Calls (person-to-person) and *Transfer Charge Calls* (on which the operator will ask the called person to accept and pay for the call) are also available.

Newspapers and Periodicals

No British newspaper or periodical is subject to State control or censorship. There are the national newspapers, daily and on Sunday, which are circulated throughout the British Isles; and there are the provincial newspapers, which, with one or two exceptions such as the *Yorkshire Post*, and the Scottish or Irish national papers, have a mainly local reputation.

The national press is read for news of national and world affairs. Some national newspapers, such as *The Times*, the *Daily Telegraph* and the Sunday papers, also carry advertisements of entertainment, mainly for London, educational establishments and employment vacancies. The London evening papers also give advertisements for the London area; these include jobs and accommodation. The same is true of provincial evening papers.

The great majority of provincial papers do not set out to compete with the national press in giving world news, political comment, etc. They are, however, a useful means of advertising, and notices of local events, colleges, accommodation and job vacancies can usually be found on their pages.

There are all kinds of weekly, monthly and quarterly journals which cover every sphere of interest. They include the B.B.C. and Television periodicals and many women's magazines.

NATIONAL NEWSPAPERS

Daily Express (Independent Conservative)
The Sun (Independent)
Daily Mail (Independent Conservative)
Daily Mirror (Independent Labour)
Daily Sketch (Independent Conservative)
Daily Telegraph (Conservative)
Daily Worker (Communist)
Financial Times (Independent)
Guardian (Independent Liberal)
The Times (Independent Conservative)

EVENING PAPERS (London)

Evening News (Conservative)
Evening Standard (Conservative)

SUNDAY PAPERS

News of the World (Independent)
Observer (Independent)
People (Independent)
Sunday Citizen (Labour)
Sunday Express (Independent Conservative)
Sunday Mirror (Independent Labour)
Sunday Telegraph (Conservative)
Sunday Times (Conservative)

MISCELLANEOUS

Christian Science Monitor
Overseas Daily Mirror and Sunday Mirror

N.B. – *The Times* can be obtained at half-price by bona fide, full-time students who are resident in the United Kingdom; registration forms with details of the scheme can be obtained from the Subscription Manager, Printing House Square, London, E.C.4.

SOME PERIODICALS OF INTEREST

The Times Educational Supplement (all aspects of education).
The Times Literary Supplement (book reviews).
Economist (public affairs).
The Statist (public affairs).
The Spectator (reviews of politics, literature and the arts).
New Statesman (independent review of politics and literature).
Coming Events in Britain (British Travel and Holidays Association).
Commonwealth Development (news of the Commonwealth).
Country Life (English country pursuits and culture).
Dalton's Weekly (advertisements of accommodation).
Encounter (current affairs).
The Listener (British Broadcasting Corporation, reprints of broadcasts, reviews survey of world radio, TV, etc.).
Time and Tide (political review).
Punch (humour and satire).
Illustrated London News (news items in pictorial form).
This is London (guide and review).
Reader's Digest (international articles).
Asia and Africa Review (trade, politics, culture).
Catholic Herald (international affairs and religious matters).
New Scientist (applied science for the layman).
London Magazine (the arts, literature, music, painting, theatre).
Twentieth Century (literature and current affairs).

The names and prices of most of the various professional journals are given in *Guide to Current British Periodicals*, edited by Mary Toase, published by the Library Association. Some are mentioned in Section IV, in this Guide under 'The Principal

Professions and Vocations'. Where names are missing under headings in Section IV, you may inquire from the relevant professional bodies.

Libraries

Most educational institutions have their own libraries, to which you should apply first. These may be able to supply all your needs, but in addition every borough and county in the United Kingdom has a public library which can be used by any student or other person, free of charge, who lives, works or studies in the area. Some form of guarantor is always required; e.g. the signature of the Principal of the student's school or college, and as this regulation varies from library to library, so the student should go to the library and inquire first from the librarian what he has to do.

The larger branches and most central public libraries are usually open every morning and afternoon except Sunday, and on Monday to Friday evenings, but some close for one half or whole day during the week. Books are mostly arranged under subject. The librarian will show the student how to use the library or will get the books for him on request. If the book requested is not on the shelves, the library may be able to undertake to get it for him. This may take anything from one day to several weeks, depending on the availability of the book. Whenever a book is needed for some special purpose – e.g. for preparing an examination – notice as long as possible should be given and absolutely accurate details of title, author and publisher. Lists of books for vacation study, with the order of priorities marked, should be sent to a local library well in advance and the date when the books are needed should be stated.

Public libraries also have up-to-date newspapers and periodicals, pamphlets, manuscripts, maps, railway and coach guides, sheet-music. Many also have gramophone records, and sometimes tape recordings, film-strips, etc.

Reference books such as encyclopaedias are not usually allowed out, but most libraries offer facilities for study, even if this may be only one or two tables and chairs in the smaller branch libraries. They also run concerts, exhibitions, lectures, etc., and sometimes arrange classes.

There are many special libraries of industrial and commercial firms, universities, government departments, research establishments, technical and professional institutions. Special libraries are, of course, maintained for their own clientele, but can arrange sometimes for outsiders to use them. The learned societies also maintain specialist libraries and it is not generally known that membership is often open to students. This may be useful, not only for the sake of their library and publications services but also to make contact with ideas and with people working in the same field. To some extent the functions of the learned societies overlap with those of the professional bodies, who also maintain their own libraries (see also Professional Bodies, page 145). For information on the Learned Societies see the handbook *Scientific and Learned Societies* (published by Allen & Unwin for the British Council).

For information on all these, on the great National Libraries like the British Museum (see under London and in other main centres) and on the public libraries, there is a Directory to Sources of Information published by Aslib, which is available at most libraries of all kinds. This is especially useful, as it is arranged by towns, with a subject index.

The same organization, Aslib, 3 Belgrave Square, London, S.W.1, also runs an information service and library, a research department and consultative and translation services, particularly valuable on technical subjects. Aslib is maintained for the benefit of its membership, which may be institutional or individual.

See also *The Libraries, Museums and Art Galleries Year Book*, ed. E. V. Corbett (published by James Clark, 33 Store Street, London, W.C.1).

Bookshops

There are good bookshops for students in the larger University towns. The most famous are probably Foyles and Dillon's in London, Blackwell's in Oxford, Bowes & Bowes and Heffer's in Cambridge and Hudson's in Birmingham. But all of the shops in the following list carry large stocks which you can inspect without any obligation to buy and they will also make inquiries, advise from their specialized knowledge and order for you any books currently in print. Any good bookshop will gladly mail details of new publications to customers in Britain and overseas alike.

The Shops to look out for in London are:

Collett's Holdings Ltd., 45 Museum Street, London, W.C.1.
Dillon's University Bookshop, 1 Malet Street, London, W.C.1.
Foyles Ltd., 119 Charing Cross Road, London, W.C.2.
Claude Gill Books, 481 Oxford Street, London, W.1.
Hatchards, 187 Piccadilly, London, W.1.
Modern Book Co, 19–21 Praed Street, W.2.
The Times Book Shop, 42 Wigmore Street, London, W.1.

the Book Departments of the principal Department Stores:

Harrods Ltd., Knightsbridge, London, S.W.1.
Selfridges Ltd., Oxford Street, London, W.1.
Army and Navy Stores Ltd., 105 Victoria Street, London, S.W.1.

and Specialist Shops such as:

H. K. Lewis & Co. Ltd. (Medical), 136 Gower Street, London, W.C.1.
The Economists' Bookshop Ltd., Clare Market, Portugal Street, London, W.C.2.

In University towns outside London:

Galloway & Morgan, 21 Pier Street, Aberystwyth.
Bookland & Co. Ltd., 326–8 High Street, Bangor, Caernarvon.
Hudson's Bookshops Ltd., 116 New Street, Birmingham 2.
Bredon's Bookshop (Bredon & Higinbotham Ltd.), 10 East Street, Brighton.
W. George's Sons Ltd., 89 Park Street, Bristol.
Bowes & Bowes (Cambridge) Ltd., 1 Trinity Street, Cambridge.
Galloway & Porter Ltd., 30 Sidney Street, Cambridge.
W. Heffer & Sons Ltd., 4 Petty Cury, Cambridge.
Students' Bookshops Ltd., Cambridge and Keele.
Lear's University Bookshop (H. J. Lear Ltd.), 59 Park Place, Cardiff.
Grant Educational Co. Ltd., 91 Union Street, Glasgow C.2.
James Thin, 53–9 South Bridge, Edinburgh.
Pitt's Bookshop, 22 Cathedral Yard, Exeter.

A. Brown & Sons Ltd., 24 George Street, Hull, Yorkshire.

Austick's University Bookshop Ltd., 172 Woodhouse Lane, Leeds 2.

Midland Educational Co. Ltd., 17 Market Street, Leicester.

Philip, Son & Nephew Ltd., 7 Whitechapel, Liverpool.

A. E. Parry & Co., 49 Hardman Street, Liverpool 1.

Percivals, Peter House, Oxford Street, Manchester 1.

W. H. Willshaw Ltd., 16 John Dalton Street, Manchester 2.

University Bookshop, Norwich.

Sisson & Parker Ltd., 2 Wheeler Gate, Nottingham.

Mawson, Swan & Morgan, Grey Street, Newcastle.

I. R. Maxwell Ltd., Oxford and Edinburgh.

Blackwell, B. H., 50 Broad Street, Oxford.

George Over Ltd., 22 Market Place, Rugby.

Seed, W. Hartley Armstrong Duffield (Booksellers) Ltd., 171 West Street, Sheffield.

A. B. Ward, 1 Leavygreave, Sheffield 3.

W. C. Henderson & Son Ltd., University Press, 80 Market Street, St. Andrews, Fife.

Thomas C. Godfrey, York.

The chain stores, principally W. H. Smith, stock books for casual readers, e.g. mainly popular novels and biographies, paper-backs, guide-books etc., but will always get any kind of book on order even at a small book-stall.

There are many good small bookshops in provincial towns, particularly small-sized second-hand booksellers. These are well worth finding, and students will benefit by getting to know them and spending some of their leisure hours in them.

Her Majesty's Stationery Office

H.M.S.O. publishes and sells books for the British Parliament, government departments, and many museums and public bodies. They issue pamphlets and reports on food, finance, education, building and innumerable other authoritative and inexpensive publications. A useful one of a general nature is *Britain, an Official Handbook*, 30s. in the U.K., 17s. 6d. limp-covered edition overseas (1966), 584 pages.

It publishes one newspaper, *The London Gazette*, periodicals, booklets on careers for young people, and guides to Britain's monuments and parks.

It also acts as a distributor for the publications of the following:

Council of Europe.
Customs Co-operation Council.
European Communities (ECSC, EEC, EURATOM).
European Free Trade Association (EFTA).
Food and Agriculture Organization (FAO).
International Atomic Energy Agency (IAEA).
International Civil Aviation Organization (ICAO).
International Court of Justice.
International Customs Tariffs Bureau.
International Monetary Fund.
General Agreement on Tariffs and Trade (GATT).
Organization for Economic Co-operation and Development (OECD).
Organization of American States (OAS).
United Nations Education, Scientific and Cultural Organization (UNESCO).
United Nations (UN).
Western European Union.
World Health Organization (WHO).

It is an agent for the sale of the publications of the United States Government Printing Office, the Canadian Government, the Instituto Poligrafico Dello Stato (Italian Government), and certain other organizations.

In London, there are two bookshops which the visitor may inspect with no obligation to buy: H.M.S.O., 49 High Holborn, London, W.C.1; *and* 423 Oxford Street, London, W.1.

There are also Government Bookshops in six other cities:

Edinburgh 2, 13A Castle Street.
Cardiff, 109 St. Mary Street.
Belfast 1, 80 Chichester Street.
Manchester 2, Brazenose Street.
Birmingham 5, 35 Smallbrook, Ringway.
Bristol 1, 50 Fairfax Street.

H.M.S.O. publications may be obtained through any bookseller; many leading booksellers are agents and keep a selection of these publications in stock.

H.M.S.O. has agents in many countries overseas including: Argentina, Australia, Belgium, British Guiana, Canada, Ceylon, Denmark, France, Germany, Ghana, India, Irish Republic, Italy, Jamaica, Kenya, Netherlands, New Zealand, Nigeria, Norway, Pakistan, Peru, Portugal, Sierra Leone, Singapore, Sweden, Switzerland, Trinidad, U.S.A., Yugoslavia.

Catalogues

H.M.S.O. issues daily, monthly and annual catalogues for a small charge and supplies 'Sectional Lists' free. These are catalogues of current non-parliamentary publications, with a selection of parliamentary publications, presented in separate lists according to the Government Departments sponsoring the publications included, e.g. Ministry of Agriculture, Fisheries and Food, Department of Education and Science, Medical Research Council. A leaflet giving full details of all Catalogue Services can be obtained from H.M.S.O.

If you are making an inquiry to H.M.S.O. it is best to be as specific as possible, for example, by asking: 'What books have you on Economics?' and not by asking for a general list of publications. With over 6,000 items published per year, it is difficult to satisfy a vague inquiry.

Names of books and prices can be obtained by looking through catalogues, by writing to H.M.S.O., or by calling at a Government Bookshop or agent. A standing order service is available, providing automatic supply of certain classes of publications.

Careers Booklets

Over 100 booklets on careers are available at prices ranging from 6d. to 2s. 6d. They cover such professions as Accountancy, Architecture, Law and Medicine and a free list of titles can be obtained from H.M.S.O. Many are named in this book under 'The Principal Professions and Vocations', Section IV.

Historical Monuments and Museums

There are more than nine hundred museums and galleries in the United Kingdom; and even the smallest town usually has on show some records of local interest. London, largely owing to the great private collections of the nineteenth century, is perhaps the most significant single centre in the world for the display of objects of art. The following are the main galleries and museums:

The British Museum. Collections of archaeological and ethno- graphical material from ancient Greece, Rome, Egypt, the Eastern civilizations, South America, and Pacific, etc.; also its world-famous library (where Karl Marx studied) and Department of Prints and Drawings.

National Gallery. Examples of all the great European masters from the beginning of Western European civilization to the close of the nineteenth century.

The Victoria and Albert Museum. Furniture, tapestries, objects of art of every age and from all nations.

Tate Gallery. British School of Painting from the eighteenth century and Modern French Schools from 1850.

The London Museum; Kensington Palace (illustrating the history of the capital); the *National Portrait Gallery*; *Imperial War Museum; National Maritime Museum, Greenwich; Public Record Office* (Doomsday Book and other historical documents); *Guildhall Museum* (City treasures); *Wallace Collection* (a magnifi- cent private collection of French seventeenth- and eighteenth- century furniture, armour, paintings, *objets d'art* handed over to the nation in the last century); *Tower of London* (historic armour- ies); the superb *Buckingham Palace Gallery* (paintings from the Queen's important private collection); also the *Science Museum*, the *Geological Museum*, the *Natural History Museum*, the *Dulwich Art Gallery* and many smaller ones besides.

The Commonwealth Institute, with social facilities and a students' club as well, holds exhibition film shows and has a permanently open gallery.

The Royal Academy, *Piccadilly*, holds temporary exhibitions during the winter and summer seasons, often of paintings and treasures from other countries, as do also the Tate Gallery, the Victoria and Albert and the Whitechapel Art Gallery. There are also many private exhibitions in the galleries of art dealers.

There are other really great museums in the provincial cities (e.g. the City Museum and Art Gallery, Birmingham; the Fitz- william at Cambridge; the Ashmolean at Oxford).

There is the Royal Scottish Museum and the National Museum

in Edinburgh, others in Glasgow and Dundee, the Folk Museum of Wales in Cardiff and that of Northern Ireland in Belfast.

In addition, there has been considerable development recently throughout the country of 'historic house' museums – i.e. the private collections of paintings, furniture, etc., now open to the public in the many great country houses or 'stately homes' as they are called (in fact, the palaces of the ancient aristocracy). The gardens of England, Scotland and Wales are also world-famous and a list of those on view in the summer can be obtained from the publication named below.

Thanks to the National Trust, the National Arts Collection Fund, the Carnegie United Kingdom Trust and other similar organizations, the treasures of the past, much-loved in Britain, are usually well displayed, and accessible to the public free or at little cost. For the museums and monuments named here and many more besides, the following publications may be useful:

Historic Houses, Castles and Gardens in Great Britain and Ireland (published yearly by Index Publishers Ltd. for the British Travel Association).

The Ancient Monuments and Historic Buildings in the Care of the Ministry of Public Buildings and Works (free to purchasers of the Ministry Season Ticket).

England, Wales, Scotland, Ireland (four volumes) by R. L. Muirhead (Blue Guide Series published by Benn).

Sport

Many sports in Britain are rigidly divided into amateur and professional, and in some these two elements only mix at the highest level, that of open championship; in others, notably cricket, the distinction has ceased or is ceasing, amateurs and professionals alike becoming merely 'players'; in horse-racing, amateurs often ride alongside professional jockeys; and in certain other sports it is possible for an amateur to compete on equal terms with professionals.

Overseas students will be interested in sports at all levels of attainment, though few will be in a position to compete professionally while in this country. Overseas athletes have made their mark in international competitions while studying here, but most students will be looking for games at club levels. They would be well advised, in the first place, to participate in the sporting activities of their colleges and universities; through the affiliation of these to national bodies, overseas students may be able to compete at a high level without going outside the student field. The first step is, therefore, to join a college or university club covering a particular sport, or an amalgamated club or union. However, some students look for games near their own lodgings, some like sports for which their college or university does not cater, and some want opportunities for mixing with people who are not fellow-students.

The following information may help all these, and also the many overseas students who share the enthusiasm of the British public for spectating.

Certain national organizations are concerned with sport and physical recreation. Among these are the Central Council for Physical Recreation (26–29 Park Crescent, London, W.1. Tel. LANgham 6822) whose many activities include coaching courses in various sports as well as the administration of national recreation centres – Bisham Abbey on the Thames, near Marlow; Lilleshall Hall, Shropshire; Crystal Palace in London and Plas y Brenin, a mountain-activities centre in Snowdonia. The National Playing Fields' Association (71 Eccleston Square, London, S.W.1, Tel. TATe Gallery 8151) helps to provide and improve facilities in hundreds of parks and playing-fields throughout the country. In addition, certain centres provide facilities for a number of different sports at a high level: Wembley Stadium, for example, with its adjacent Empire Pool, was the venue for the Olympic Games of 1948 and here you can watch the Cup Final of the Football Association, the Cup Final of the Rugby League, international athletics both outdoor and indoor, badminton, indoor lawn tennis, and greyhound racing.

The information that follows relates to 25 sports and may not include a particular student's favourite sport, as there are several times that number of sports. However, our list will probably cater for interests of about 99 students out of every 100. If others require further information, they can contact, mostly in London, the headquarters of the national bodies governing sports in England, Great Britain, the Commonwealth, or in one or two cases the world. The list starts with the name of the governing body, continues where necessary with a few notes and gives main centres for the game in the London area, and the names of journals.

Association Football

The Football Association, 22 Lancaster Gate, London, W.2.
Amateur Football Alliance, 19 Ludgate Hill, London, E.C.4.

Main events of the professional game in England and Wales are the competition for the F.A. Cup and the Football League Championship. For the latter, professional sides are divided into four divisions. The main teams having their grounds in or very near London are:

Arsenal, Highbury (U., Arsenal).
Brentford, Griffin Park (U., Boston Manor, thence by bus).
Charlton Athletic, The Valley (B.R., Charlton).
Chelsea, Stamford Bridge (U., Fulham Broadway).
Crystal Palace, Selhurst Park (B.R., Selhurst).
Fulham, Craven Cottage (U., Putney Bridge).
Leyton Orient, Osborne Road (B.R., Leyton).
Millwall, The Den (U., Newcross Gate).
Queen's Park Rangers, Loftus Road (U., Shepherds Bush).
Tottenham Hotspur, White Hart Lane (B.R., White Hart Lane).
Watford (U., Watford High Street).
West Ham United, Upton Park (U., Upton Park).

   (U—Underground. B.R.—British Railways.)

Fortunately, for students who are keen spectators, the League First Division teams (1965–66) happen to coincide very well with the main centres of study. Anyone in these cities or towns will know the way to their grounds; League fixtures are in the national daily press and (well in advance) in the F.A. official year-book (4s., from bookstalls).

They are:

Manchester United	West Ham United	Aston Villa
Leeds United	Blackburn Rovers	Blackpool
Chelsea	Stoke City	Leicester City
Everton	Burnley	Sheffield United
Nottingham Forest	Arsenal	Fulham
Tottenham Hotspur	West Bromwich	Newcastle United
Liverpool	Albion	Northampton Town
Sheffield Wednesday	Sunderland	

There are also amateur leagues, an F.A. Amateur Cup competition and an A.F.A. Cup competition. The Isthmian, Spartan, Athenian and London Leagues are centred on London and provide the chance of watching good amateur football; the London League includes the teams of Woolwich Polytechnic and Northern Polytechnic. But amateur football is ubiquitous, and the overseas student who wishes to participate can always find a team that will welcome his membership.

The main professional events of the year are the F.A. Cup Final in May, and the Amateur Cup Final in April, both at Wembley.

England professional internationals are held at Wembley and amateur internationals at leading club grounds in the London area.

F.A. Year Book, annual; *F.A. News*, monthly – and a variety of football weeklies published on Saturdays during the season.

Athletics

Amateur Athletic Association, 54 Torrington Place, London, W.C.1. Tel. LANgham 3498.

Women's Amateur Athletic Association. *Secretary:* 41 Hayward Court, Levehurst Way, London, S.W.4.

The British Games and the A.A.A. Championships are held annually at the White City at Whitsun and in July respectively. Other important meetings are held at the Polytechnic Stadium, Chiswick (W.4), and Motspur Park, Malden, Surrey.

A new track forms part of the facilities of the National Recreation Centre at the Crystal Palace, and has been used for international events. A number of London clubs and colleges have their own tracks of a high standard, and the location of public tracks and facilities for field events can be ascertained from the National Playing Fields Association.

Athletics Weekly, Saturdays.

Badminton

Badminton Association of England. *Secretary:* 4 Madeira Avenue, Bromley, Kent.

The national championships are held at the Empire Pool, Wembley, in March.

B.A. of E. Official Handbook, annual; *Badminton Gazette*, October, November, December, February, March and April.

Billiards

Billiards Association and Control Council, Maxwell House, Arundel Street, London, W.C.2. Tel. TEMple Bar 7887.

The national championships are held at Burroughes Hall, Soho Square, London, in February–March.

Billiards and Snooker, monthly.

Boxing

Amateur Boxing Association, 69 Victoria Street, London, S.W.1. Tel. ABBey 3295.

British Boxing Board of Control, 1–9 Hills Place, London, W.1.

Top-class bouts are held at the Royal Albert Hall, Earls Court Arena and Seymour Hall.

Boxing News, Fridays; *Boxing News Annual.*

Cricket

Marylebone Cricket Club, Lord's Ground, London, N.W.8.

Cricket is played under the 'Laws of Cricket' and is governed by the Committee of the M.C.C. A high proportion of the population either plays or watches this national game. Test matches are played between members of the Imperial Cricket Conference, in a somewhat irregular rotation. The Tests in England in 1966 will be against the West Indies, and in 1967 against India and Pakistan.

Seventeen 'major counties' participate in the County Championship. The major counties close to London are Surrey, Middlesex, Kent and Essex, which have their headquarters respectively at the Oval (Kennington), Lord's (Marylebone), Canterbury and Chelmsford. There is also a 'minor counties' championship.

The thirteen major counties away from London, with their grounds, are:

Derbyshire, Nottingham Road, Derby.
Glamorgan, St. Helens, Swansea.
Gloucestershire, County Ground, Bristol 7.
Hampshire, County Ground, Southampton.
Lancashire, Old Trafford, Manchester 16.
Leicestershire, Grace Road, Leicester.
Northants, Wantage Road, Northampton.
Nottinghamshire, Trent Bridge, Nottingham.

Somerset, St. James' Street, Taunton.
Sussex, Eaton Road, Hove 3.
Warwickshire, Edgbaston, Birmingham 5.
Worcestershire, County Ground, Worcester.
Yorkshire, Headingley, Leeds 6.

Test Matches are played at Lord's, the Oval, Old Trafford, Trent Bridge, Edgbaston and Headingley.

The Club Cricket Conference (*Secretary:* 64c Wimbledon Hill Road, London, S.W.19, Tel. WIMbledon 3586) assists in the organization of amateur club cricket, particularly in the Home Counties and the Midlands. It should be remembered that membership of cricket clubs, as of many other sporting clubs, is often restricted by the number of players that can be accommodated and requires personal introductions. Students will normally find good facilities at their university or college clubs, but may well be able to obtain introductions from these to outside clubs.

Cricketer, fortnightly: May–September; monthly: October–April.

Times, cricket fixtures.

Fencing

Amateur Fencing Association, 83 Perham Road, West Kensington, London, W.14.

Ladies Amateur Fencing Union. *Secretary:* 58A Ridgmount Gardens, London, W.C.1.

Golf

More a way of life of the Scots than a national sport of the English.

Headquarters: Royal and Ancient Golf Club, St. Andrews, Fife, Scotland.

There are several courses in or near London; some public and others requiring membership.

Main public courses: Beckenham; Brent Valley (Hanwell); Enfield; Richmond Park; Ruislip.

Main clubs: Ealing (Greenford); Fulwell (Hampton); Wimbledon (Wimbledon Common, London, S.W.17); Home Park (Hampton Wick); London Scottish and Royal Blackheath (Eltham, London, S.E.); Royal Mid-Surrey (Richmond);

Shirley Park (Croydon); Sudbury (Wembley); Sundridge Park; Surbiton.

Golf Illustrated, Thursdays; *Golf Monthly*; *Golf News*, weekly; *Golf World*, monthly; *Golfing*, monthly; *Golfer's Handbook*, annual.

Greyhound Racing

Greyhound Racing Association Limited, 20 Berkeley Square, London, W.1.

Principal tracks in or near London: Catford, Clapton, Hackney Wick, Harringay, Hendon, New Cross, Romford, Wembley, White City.

Greyhound Owners and Breeder, Thursday.

Greyhound Racing in London, annual, free. (Tel. CLIssold 6991.)

Sporting Life, daily.

Midday editions of London evening papers.

Hockey

Hockey Association, 26 Park Crescent, London, W.1.

All-England Women's Hockey Association. *Secretary:* 45 Doughty Street, London, W.1.

Main club centres in or near London: Bromley, Chiswick (W.4), Richmond, Southgate (N.1), Surbiton, Teddington, Tulse Hill (S.W.2).

Horse Racing

Flat Racing and Steeplechasing are controlled by separate authorities.

Flat Racing: The Jockey Club. *Secretary:* 15 Cavendish Square, London, W.1.

Steeplechasing: The National Hunt Committee. *Secretary:* 15 Cavendish Square, London, W.1.

Race-courses in the London area are: Alexandra Park (N.22), Ascot, Epsom, Kempton Park (Sunbury), Sandown Park (Esher).

Outside the London area, main race-courses (with at least four meetings a year) in or within easy reach of main education centres are:

Birmingham
Cheltenham

Chepstow	Cardiff 28 m. Bristol 16 m.
Doncaster	Leeds 28 m. Sheffield 18 m.
Leicester	
Liverpool (Aintree)	
Newbury	Oxford 27 m. Reading 17 m.
Newcastle upon Tyne	
Newmarket	Cambridge 13 m. Thetford 20 m.
Newton Abbot	Exeter 16 m. Torquay 7 m.
Nottingham	
Plumpton	Brighton 7 m. Lewes 5 m.
Stratford upon Avon	Birmingham 24 m. Warwick 8 m.
Warwick	
Wetherby	Leeds 13 m. York 14 m.
Windsor	London 23 m. Reading 18 m.
Wolverhampton	

(m. — miles.)

Flat Racing between May and the beginning of October and Steeplechasing between September and May. Main Flat event: 'The Derby' at Epsom in June. Main Steeplechase: 'The Grand National' at Aintree in March.

Point-to-Point Racing, organized by individual Hunts, is also a popular spectator sport.

Racing Calendar, Thursday; *Racehorse*, Wednesday.
Dailies: *Sporting Life*, *Sporting Chronicle*.
Horse and Hound, Saturdays.

Judo

British Judo Association, 68 Chandos House, Palmer Street, London, S.W.1.

Judo, monthly.

Lacrosse

English Lacrosse Union. *Secretary:* 92 Chelmsford Road, London, N.14.

All-England Ladies' Lacrosse Association. *Hon. Secretary:* 108 Dereham Road, Barking, Essex.

Ladies' Amateur International matches are held on the Guinness sports ground at Park Royal.

Ladies' journal: *Lacrosse*, monthly during the season.

Lawn Tennis

Lawn Tennis Association. *Secretary:* Palliser Road, Barons Court, London, W.14.

Widely played on public and club grass courts between May and September and hard courts throughout the year; and (at its highest amateur level) watched by many thousands at the Wimbledon Championships each June–July. Main public tennis courts in London:

Battersea Park, London, S.W.11.
Bishop's Park, Fulham Palace Road, London, S.W.6.
Clapham Common, London, S.W.4.
Finsbury Park, London, N.4.
Greenwich Park, London, S.E.10.
Lincoln's Inn Fields, London, W.C.2.
Parliament Hill, Hampstead, London, N.W.3.
Queen's Park, Kilburn, London, N.W.6.
Ravenscourt Park, Hammersmith, London, W.6.
Regent's Park, London, N.W.1.

Covered courts are available at the National Recreation Centre at the Crystal Palace.

There are membership clubs in London and the suburbs. Clubs where open tournaments are held to which the public are admitted as spectators include:

All-England Lawn Tennis Club, Wimbledon (London, S.W.19).
Beckenham.
Cumberland (Finchley Road, London, N.W.6).
Lowther (Ferry Road, London, S.W.13).
Queen's (West Kensington, London, W.14).
Roehampton (London, S.W.15).
Surbiton.
Sutton.

In England, and outside London, main open tournaments and months when they are usually held are:

April	Hard Court Championships of Great Britain	Bournemouth
May (early)	Open tournament	Guildford

May–June	Open tournament	Wolverhampton
	,, ,,	Northern (Manchester)
June	Open tournament	Cardiff
	,, ,,	Merseyside (Liverpool)
	,, ,,	Sutton Coldfield (Birmingham)
	West of England Championships	Bristol
	Open tournament	Nottingham
July	East of England Championships	Felixstowe
	Midland Counties Championships	Edgbaston
	Welsh Championships	Newport
August	Open tournament	Moseley (Birmingham)
	Under-21 Championships	Northern (Manchester)
	North of England Championships	Scarborough
	Open tournament	Budleigh Salterton
September	South of England Championships	Eastbourne

In Scotland

June	Under-21 Championships of Scotland	Edinburgh
July	Scottish Championships	Edinburgh
August	Scottish Hard Court Championships	St. Andrews

In Ireland:

| May | Fitzwilliam (Dublin), Hard Court Championships of Ireland | |
| July | Fitzwilliam (Dublin), The Championships of Ireland | |

August	Fitzwilliam (Dublin),
	The Junior Cham-
	pionships of Ireland

British Lawn Tennis, monthly; *Lawn Tennis and Badminton*, twice a month; *L.T.A. Handbook*, annual.

Motor Racing

Royal Automobile Club, Pall Mall, London, S.W.1.

British Racing and Sports Car Club, 6 Buckingham Street, London, W.C.2. Tel. TRAfalgar 1351.

The principal tracks in the London area are Brands Hatch and Crystal Palace. In 1964 the British Grand Prix, which was also the European Grand Prix, was held at Brands Hatch (21 miles S.E. of London on the Maidstone Road). Principal tracks in the provinces are:

Oulton Park (Tarporley, Cheshire).
Silverstone (Towcester, Northants).

Motor Racing, monthly; *Motor Rally and Racing Review*, monthly; *Motor Sport*, monthly.

Motor-Cycle Racing

Auto-Cycle Union, 31 Belgrave Square, London, S.W.1. Tel. BELgravia 7636.

The main spectator events – the Senior 'Tourist Trophy', the Junior 350 c.c. Race and the Manx Grand Prix – are held in the Isle of Man.

Motor Cycle, Thursday; *Motor Cycling with Scooter Weekly*, Wednesday; *Motor Cyclist Illustrated*, monthly; *Motor Cycle News*, Wednesday.

For *Mountaineering* and *Caving*, see page 67.

Riding

British Horse Society, 16 Bedford Square, London, W.C.1. Tel. LANgham 7206.

British Field Sports Society, 53 Victoria Street, London, S.W.1. Tel. ABBey 5407.

British Show Jumping Association, 16 Bedford Square, London, W.C.1. Tel. LANgham 7206.

There are a number of riding stables in London and the suburbs where horses can be hired and lessons taken.

T—D

Riding, monthly; *Horse and Hound*, Saturdays; *Horse and Hound Year Book*, annual.

Rowing

Amateur Rowing Association. *Secretary:* The Tower, The Terrace, Barnes, London, S.W.13.

The most popular spectator event is the University Boat Race between Oxford and Cambridge, held in late March or early April over a four-mile course between Putney and Mortlake. This can be watched at many points from the public towpath.

The main international regatta is in June–July, also on the Thames, 36 miles W. of London at Henley (Oxfordshire), where in 1964 the finalists in the main event, the Grand Challenge Cup, were London University and a Russian club. There are several clubs on the Thames, the Serpentine in Hyde Park and the Welsh Harp, Hendon.

Rowing, monthly.

Rugby Football

Rugby Football Union, Whitton Road, Twickenham, Middlesex.

'Rugby Union' is a wholly amateur sport; the professional version is 'Rugby League'. There are numerous first-class clubs in the London area which provide excellent spectating on Saturdays in the season, and welcome new playing members. Among them are:

Club	Ground	Nearest Station
Blackheath	Rectory Field, London, S.E.3	Blackheath
Harlequins	Whitton Road	Twickenham
London Irish	Sunbury-on-Thames	Sunbury
London Scottish	Athletic Ground	Richmond
London Welsh	Old Deer Park	Richmond
Richmond	Athletic Ground	Richmond
Rosslyn Park	Roehampton	Barnes
Rugby Union	Whitton Road	Twickenham
Saracens	Pavilion Green Road, London, N.14	Cockfosters
Wasps	Eaton Avenue, Sudbury	Sudbury Town

The headquarters ground at Twickenham is the scene, every winter, of two of the four England International matches against Wales, Scotland, Ireland and France; and, most winters, of an international match against a touring team from Australia, New Zealand or South Africa.

Sailing

Royal Yachting Association, 171 Victoria Street, London, S.W.1. Tel. TATe 4197.

Royal Ocean Racing Club, 20 St. James's Place, London S.W.1. Tel. HYDe Park 5252.

Yachting Monthly; Yachting World, monthly; *Yachts and Yachting*, fortnightly; *Yachtsman*, monthly.

Skating

National Skating Association of Great Britain. *Secretary:* Charterhouse, London, E.C.1. Tel. CLErkenwell 3824.

Main public rinks in the London area: Queen's Ice Skating Club (Queensway, London, W.2), Streatham, Richmond and Wembley.

Skating World, monthly (excluding July and August).

Skating on Ice, annual.

Squash Rackets

Squash Rackets Association. *Secretary:* 26 Park Crescent, London, W.1. LANgham 1345.

Women's Squash Racket Association. *Secretary:* 22 Childebert Road, London, S.W.17.

Most squash is played at members' clubs but the public can play at the National Recreation Centre (Crystal Palace), Ealing Squash Courts and Club, St. Marylebone Public Baths and Wanstead Squash Rackets Club, London, E.11. The Open Championship is held at the Lansdowne Club, Royal Automobile Club and Royal Aero Club in January.

British Lawn Tennis and Squash, monthly.

Swimming

Amateur Swimming Association, 64 Cannon Street, London, E.C.4. Tel. CENtral 4868.

Public swimming baths in London include:

Chelsea, King's Road, London, S.W.3.

Clapham, Clapham Manor Street, London, S.W.4.
Fulham, Walham Green, London, S.W.6.
Hampstead, Finchley Road, London, N.W.3.
Hyde Park (open air), Serpentine, London, W.2.
Oasis (indoor and open), Endell Street, London, W.C.2.
Roehampton (open air), Priory Lane, London, S.W.15.
Wandsworth, Elmfield Road, London, S.W.17.
Westminster, Buckingham Palace Road, London, S.W.1.
Great Smith Street and Marshall Street.

The A.S.A. Championships are held at the Crystal Palace in August, also the Diving Championships.

Table Tennis

English Table Tennis Association. *Secretary:* 26 Park Crescent, W.1.

Main Centres: Wembley (Empire Pool), Royal Albert Hall.

Table Tennis, eight times a year, October–May.

Tenpin Bowling

British Tenpin Bowling Association. *Secretary:* 212 Lower Clapton Road, London, E.5. Tel. AMHerst 2115.

Main London centres: Top Rank Bowl, Golders Green; Leytonstone Bowl, Leytonstone; Streatham Bowl, Streatham Hill; ABC Bowl, East Acton; Tenpin Lanes, Upper Clapton Road, Stamford Hill; ABC Bowl, Harrow; Top Rank Bowl, Southall.

Tenpin Pictorial, monthly.
Tenpin Bowling Yearbook.

Entertainment

Theatre, Music and Cinema

THE THEATRE

Plays of outstanding merit can always be seen at the London theatres. Indeed, there are usually more first-class productions running in London than anywhere else in the world. The provinces are visited by London companies on tour, and many towns, particularly Birmingham, Liverpool, Norwich (the Maddermarket Theatre), Sheffield, Nottingham, Bristol (Old

Vic Company), and Guildford have permanent repertory companies. Shakespeare's plays are given by the Royal Shakespeare Company at Stratford-upon-Avon and in London at various times throughout the year at the Aldwych Theatre, together with new plays and non-Shakespearean classics. Famous too among theatres in London are the National Theatre at the Old Vic (under the direction of Sir Laurence Olivier), Covent Garden (National Opera House and home of the Royal Ballet Company), Sadler's Wells (home of the Sadler's Wells Opera Company), Drury Lane (for musicals), the Savoy (well-known for operas of Gilbert and Sullivan), the Palladium (music-hall) and many others.

Some of the small theatres in London, such as the Arts Theatre are theatre-clubs. To become a member usually entails no more than the payment of a small fee before booking seats, or at the most a 48-hour interval. Most give special terms for overseas visitors.

A recent innovation at some theatres is the provision of simultaneous translations into a number of languages while the play is being performed. Regular translations are now provided at Wyndham's Theatre in French, German, Italian, Spanish and Arabic.

How to obtain tickets: Theatre tickets can be obtained from any of the numerous theatre booking agencies such as Keith Prowse Ltd., or direct from the theatre, by personal application or reservation by telephone. Tickets are often available on the day of the performance, but advance booking is usually advisable whenever possible. Theatre ticket agencies invariably show clients a plan of the theatre in which the exact location of the seats offered can be seen. If the inquiry is made by telephone, the booking clerk will generally give details. The price of seats varies according to their location. A box containing four seats will usually cost between £3 and £6, a comfortable seat in a good position should not cost more than 25s., the best seats at the National Theatre are 27s. 6d. Gallery seats cost from 5s. to 7s. 6d. When, as is often the case, all advance booking for a popular show is taken, the determined theatre-goer can still, in many cases, see the show of his choice by using the gallery or by queueing for standing room.

The Gallery. At some theatres the method of booking is to reserve a place in the gallery queue in the morning; a small wooden stool, with the reservation number on it, will be found on returning in the evening, placed on the pavement leading to the gallery entrance. There are more seats than are represented by the number of stools, so one can join a gallery queue even at a late hour with some hope of success. Details of time and procedure should be checked when booking.

Standing Room (only available when every other seat has been sold). For those who have the necessary stamina and enthusiasm, it is possible at the majority of London theatres to stand and see a show that has been 'sold out'. Prices range from 2s. 3d. to 7s. 6d. depending on location and the nature of the production. It is necessary to arrive at the theatre well before the performance. More exact information may be obtained from the theatre box offices.

MUSIC IN LONDON

There are five permanent orchestras in the capital, each giving its own series of concerts – The Royal Philharmonic; The London Philharmonic; The B.B.C. Symphony; The New Philharmonia; and The London Symphony.

In addition to the front-rank symphony orchestras, there are several excellent small combinations, such as Philomusica of London, the London Mozart Players and the English Chamber Orchestra, which play music not requiring the extended resources of a modern symphony orchestra. Besides these, there are frequent visits from famous orchestras, conductors and soloists from abroad and from other cities in Britain.

The two chief concert halls are: The Royal Festival Hall, owned by the London County Council, which was inaugurated in 1951 on the opening day of the Festival of Britain; The Royal Albert Hall, facing Kensington Gardens and considerably older and larger. Here for two months each summer (17th July–11th September, 1965, except Sundays) are held the nightly 'Promenade' Concerts. In the Albert Hall, too, such choirs as that of The Royal Choral Society perform oratorios and other works in their annual series of concerts. There are several smaller halls in London for the performance of chamber music and recitals. Perhaps the best-known of these is the Wigmore Hall. Only 30 minutes' from Charing Cross or Victoria by train is London's latest and most modern concert and theatre building, The Fairfield Halls, Croydon, which incorporates the Ashcroft Theatre.

But concerts in London are by no means confined to concert-halls. In the summer months, music can be heard in all manner of settings – in the parks or by the lake or in the orangery at Kenwood House in North London, and, to the south, at the Crystal Palace Concert Bowl. Concerts are also given in the Victoria and Albert Museum, in the hall hung with the famous Raphael Cartoons.

MUSIC AND DRAMA OUTSIDE LONDON

Apart from the festival centres, by no means all of which are listed on pages 106–107, the great cities of Britain – and many of the smaller towns – are the scene of a musical and dramatic life of a very high order. Glasgow, for example, apart from symphony concerts, can also claim the Glasgow Citizens' Theatre. Perth and Dundee also have first-class repertory theatres, while for those who visit Edinburgh out of festival time there are regular concerts by the Scottish National Orchestra in the Usher Hall, and several excellent theatres which frequently show plays prior to their London production.

In Northern Ireland, the great centre of music and drama is, of course, Belfast. The Belfast Philharmonic Society organizes an annual series of concerts with guest artists and the theatrical life of the city centres round the Opera House and the Group Theatre which is noted for its characteristic plays of Ulster life. These and other companies tour Northern Ireland during the summer.

One of Manchester's proudest possessions is the old-established Hallé Orchestra, under the direction of Sir John Barbirolli. It has its headquarters in the Free Trade Hall. Liverpool also possesses two musical centres in St. George's Hall and the Philharmonic Hall, in which are held the concerts given by the Liverpool Philharmonic Orchestra. The Town Hall at Birmingham is the home of the City of Birmingham Symphony Orchestra, another of Britain's leading orchestras. The Birmingham Repertory Company ranks with the best theatrical companies in the U.K. A musical and dramatic festival is staged at Wolverhampton, in the Civic Hall. Then there are the Bradford Citizens' Theatre closely associated with the work of J. B. Priestley; the Yorkshire Symphony Orchestra, which has its home at Leeds; and the Huddersfield Choral Society.

The leading musical and dramatic centre of the south-west is the ancient seaport city of Bristol, which possesses in the Theatre Royal the finest surviving example of a Georgian playhouse still in regular use, the headquarters of the Bristol Old Vic Company, an offshoot from the original 'Vic' in London.

It is worth noting that many London productions make their début in provincial theatres – in Brighton, Oxford, Cambridge, Edinburgh and Bristol, for example.

LITTLE THEATRES

There are a number of picturesque Little Theatres to be found in all parts of the kingdom, besides those in London. In the east, the cathedral city of Norwich, besides being the scene of the great Triennial Music Festival, is famous in the world of drama for the productions given at the Maddermarket Theatre. There is a good example of a Little Theatre at Bangor, on the coast of Northern Ireland; and many visitors to St. Andrews spend an evening at the little Byre Theatre. There is also a Georgian Theatre at Richmond in Yorkshire, and another at Bury St. Edmunds.

Near Land's End in Cornwall is the unusual Minack Theatre at Porthcurno, and Lake District visitors would find a visit to the Rosehill Society's Theatre at Moresby, Whitehaven, Cumberland, an enjoyable experience; here opera, recitals and plays are included in the repertoire.

Touring the provinces is the mobile 'Century Theatre', which can be dismantled and moved from place to place.

The plays given by the students in the college halls and gardens at Oxford and Cambridge and other Universities may also be regarded as part of the Little Theatre movement.

IN THE HOLIDAY RESORTS

Britain's holiday towns are strong rivals to the large cities as dramatic and musical centres. The Theatres and Concert-halls of well-known spas and health resorts like Harrogate, Buxton, Leamington, Malvern and Tunbridge Wells are among the chief attractions for visitors, and similar entertainment is to be found at seaside resorts such as Bournemouth, Torquay, Eastbourne and Hastings. Brighton, on the Sussex coast, is the headquarters of the Southern Philharmonic Orchestra. The Festival Theatre at Chichester has the first permanent arena-style stage to be built in Europe. Bournemouth has its Symphony Orchestra which was the first to be formed in the country. Southampton is also noted for the quality of its concerts. Worthing, on the Sussex coast, supports its own all-the-year-round Municipal Orchestra, a Municipal Choir and a Citizens' Orchestra. Scarborough, the biggest seaside resort in Yorkshire, has an open-air theatre with seating for 8,000 spectators and an island stage which is used for opera and other spectacular musical productions.

FESTIVALS IN BRITAIN

Outside London, from early spring until late autumn, festivals of various kinds are held up and down the country; most of them last for a week or two, but there are a few, such as Glyndebourne, Pitlochry and the Stratford-upon-Avon Shakespeare Season, which run for several months. In addition to the attraction of the festivals themselves, the towns in which they are held have their own interest and charm.

Space does not allow the inclusion of the many smaller festivals which take place throughout the country every year. In London, apart from the Southwark Shakespeare Festival, there is the St. Pancras Arts Festival. Outside London there are festivals at Hintlesham, Harrogate, Edington (cathedral music), Stroud (religious drama; October), Wharfedale and Little Missenden.

It is not usually possible for the smaller festivals to give detailed information about their programmes, dates and prices more than a month or two in advance, but the British Travel Association, through their offices at home and abroad, will provide programmes for major festivals as soon as they are received (usually early in the year) and exact information about the smaller ones nearer the time of their taking place.

Not included here are the series of concerts given in National Trust properties throughout the country by the National Trust Concert Society (whose president is Yehudi Menuhin). Claydon House, 55 miles from London and home of the Verney family since the thirteenth century, is an example with its summer Sunday concerts of this combination of music and historic setting. National Trust concerts are held between May and September; details of dates, locations, artistes and programmes will be available from the B.T.A.

The following is a list of major festivals:

Aldeburgh, Suffolk. Festival of Music and Arts, presided over by Benjamin Britten.

Bath, Somerset. Festival of the Arts.

Braemar, Aberdeenshire. Scottish Festival: music and dancing.

Broadstairs, Kent. Dickens Festival.

Bromsgrove, Worcestershire. Bromsgrove Festival: music, drama and art.

Buxton, Derbyshire. Buxton Festival of Music: Concerts by Hallé Orchestra.

Cambridge. Cambridge Festival: concerts, recitals and opera.

Canterbury, Kent. Cathedral Festival: music and poetry.

Cheltenham, Gloucestershire. The Cheltenham Festival: mainly presentation of new British musical works, and Festival of Literature.

Chester, Cheshire. Miracle Plays: every five years, next in 1967.

Chichester, Sussex. Drama Festival.

London, *Cardiff*, *Glasgow*, *Liverpool*. Commonwealth Arts Festival: music and dance; performances of jazz and light entertainment; arts and crafts exhibitions; films, and also many other events; processions, fireworks, etc. Conferences for artists, students and teachers.

Coventry, Warwickshire. Festival of Music and other Orchestral Concerts are held in the new cathedral at regular intervals throughout the year.

Edinburgh, Scotland. International Festival and International Film Festival. The International Festival includes presentations of opera, drama, symphony concerts, chamber music, recitals, art exhibitions, late-night entertainments and the military tattoo, held nightly, except Sundays and Thursdays, on the esplanade of Edinburgh Castle.

Glyndebourne, Sussex. Opera Festival.

Harrogate, Yorkshire. Hallé Music Festival.

Haslemere, Surrey. Festival of Early Music.

King's Lynn, Norfolk. Festival of the Arts.

Lake District (National Park). Lake District Music Festival.

Llangollen, Denbigh, Wales. International Musical Eisteddfod. (Singing and dancing.)

London. St. Pancras Arts Festival: opera, music and art; usually stages some notable first British performances.

Ludlow, Shropshire. Festival of the Arts, in Ludlow Castle.

Norwich, Norfolk. Triennial Festival of Music. This festival due to be held next in 1967.

Pitlochry, Perthshire, Scotland. Drama Festival. Beginning in early April, this festival runs for 6 months.

Southwark, London, S.E.1. Shakespeare Festival.

Stour, Kent. Festival of Music and Painting. Church concerts, medieval music, religious drama and organ recitals.

Stratford-upon-Avon, Warwickshire. Shakespeare Season.

Swansea, Glamorgan, Wales. Festival of Music and the Arts.

Three Choirs Festival. Worcester, Hereford and Gloucester. Main events take place in the cathedral.

Wales. Royal National Eisteddfod. At a different centre each year. A competitive festival of music, drama, literature, arts and crafts, but its chief feature is the singing of the choirs for which Wales is world-famous.

York. Mystery Plays: every three years, to be held next in 1966.

Entertainment and Festivals Generally

In fact, there are all kinds of other annual shows and festivals in Britain, such as town festivals, jazz festivals, steam fairs, motor rallies, agricultural shows, etc. For all information apply to The British Travel Association (see page 57) or to local Tourist Information Bureaux (see Section V).

AT THE CINEMA

There are over 4,000 cinemas in Great Britain; many belong to the three major circuits – ABC, Odeon and Granada. Each circuit tends to show the same programme throughout the country, although the independent cinemas show far more varied programmes.

Prices of admission differ according to the cinema and location. The first-run theatres in London and the other major cities tend to be expensive – 7s. 6d. to 21s. – when compared with local cinemas where prices range from 3s. to 7s. Some first-run cinemas operate on a reserved seat system with set times for shows, whilst the local cinemas run a continuous performance pattern with shows at 1 p.m., 4 p.m., 6 p.m., 8.30 p.m. A number of cinemas in London's West End arrange late-night shows.

Exact times and programmes are advertised in the newspapers.

There are an increasing number of specialized cinemas. The Everyman, Hampstead, The Academy, Paris-Pullman, Cameo Polytechnic and many others in London as well as cinemas in Glasgow, Newcastle, Leeds, Manchester and other major cities.

They show largely continental films, reissues and films which have not been chosen for screening to circuit audiences. The Classic Cinemas Group is a pioneer in this field, and can always be relied upon to offer varied programmes. Apply to the Classic Cinema, Baker Street, London, W.1, for mailing list.

Where there is no specialized cinema there is usually a film society. Details may be obtained from The British Film Institute, 81 Dean Street, London, W.1; The Secretary, Federation of Film Societies, 55A Welbeck Street, London, W.1 (England and Wales); or The Secretary, Federation of Scottish Film Societies, Film House, Randolph Crescent, Edinburgh (Scotland).

The National Film Theatre is a unique movie museum showing over 600 feature films a year in its cinema under Waterloo Bridge, South Bank, London, S.E.1. Programmes reflect achievement in the cinema from the earliest days to the latest productions from every part of the world. Associate Membership is 10s. per year. Prices of admission 3s., 5s., 7s. 6d. Details from The British Film Institution, 81 Dean Street, London, W.1 (Tel REGent 0061). Many student organizations, universities, colleges and schools are Corporate Members, which gives students free membership of the National Film Theatre.

Hotels and Restaurants, etc.

These close much earlier in Britain than in most overseas countries because of the strict laws governing the hours of workers. Some small hotels and guest-houses serve meals only at fixed hours; even the bigger hotels insist on rigid hours for meals, and even if they promise that dinner is served between 7 to 8.30 p.m., it is unwise to walk into the dining-room at 8.25 p.m. and expect good service. Cafeterias, snack-bars and coffee-bars will provide meals outside normal hours on a self-service basis – you collect the food on a tray yourself – but most of these close around 10.30 p.m. In bigger towns there are often Indian and Chinese restaurants which may stay open until midnight, but outside London it is well to check in advance.

Drink. Alcohol may be served in 'pubs', bars and restaurants only in strict licensing hours, usually from 11.30 a.m. to 3 p.m. and 5.30 p.m. to 10.30 p.m. These hours are, however, restricted on Sundays, and in some parts of Wales Sunday opening is prohibited. But wines, spirits and beer for consumption at home may now be purchased throughout normal shopping hours from wine-shops and grocers with 'off-sales' licences.

Tipping. Unless a service charge is included on the bill, you should give the waiter or waitress between 10 and 12 per cent. The taxi-driver expects about 15 to 20 per cent and if a hotel or railway porter carries your bags, 2s. is the usual minimum. Most other people do not need tipping, except about 2s. 6d. for a woman's hairdresser, and about 1s. for a man's hairdresser.

Food. Most overseas visitors complain that food in Britain lacks seasoning, although salt, pepper, mustard and bottled sauces are provided on the table. You will probably be given a lot of bread and potatoes rather than rice. Vegetables are limited in variety, and fresh fruit, which is generally expensive and not very sweet, is not usually served with a meal. Most restaurants do not provide water on the table, except on request, and you must be prepared for no ice in drinks. In our climate we fill up with starchy foods to keep warm, and feel no need to cool down! Outside London, 'night-life' is very quiet and does not go on late.

See also 'Eating Out in London' – Section V.

Shopping and Miscellaneous

The hours of opening and closing are controlled by law to make sure that shop-assistants work only a reasonable number of hours. Most shops are open only from about 9 a.m. to 5.30 p.m. and, except in big cities, most close for lunch for an hour. Almost all close for either a complete day or a half-day each week in addition to Sunday. For the overseas visitor, the big stores and supermarkets like Woolworth's, Marks & Spencers, British Home Stores and C. & A. are usually most popular because all their prices are clearly marked. If you are not sure about clothing sizes you will find the assistants very helpful if you ask their advice. Some small shops stay open until about 8 p.m. and for a few hours on Sundays, but there are laws which govern what they can sell in these times. Chemists close at much the same time as other shops, but take it in turn to open for an hour in the evenings and on Sundays for the sale only of drugs urgently needed. Banks close at 3 p.m. daily, and are closed from 11.30 a.m. on Saturdays, plus all day Sundays. There is no free market in money, and any bank will give you the official rate of exchange, less a small commission for your currency or travellers' cheques. Shops in the West End of London are closed on Saturday afternoons but are open in other districts.

As an overseas visitor you have special Purchase Tax concessions. Purchase Tax, at varying rates, is levied on most luxury class articles and on a number of non-luxuries, including clothing. Many items are not subject to Purchase Tax.

These are the ways to obtain relief from Purchase Tax:

(a) Many of the principal stores are able to send goods direct to an address abroad free of British Purchase Tax.

(b) Under the Personal Export Scheme, if the tax-free value of the goods bought at any one time is £5 or more, you may, as a visitor, have them delivered free of tax direct to the seaport or airport by which you are leaving the country, for exportation as baggage. Such purchases should be made a few days before departure to allow time for delivery. Alternatively, goods purchased under this scheme may be exported by post or as freight. There is usually a small delivery charge made by the shop.

Shops operating the concessions generally display a notice in their windows. Most of the large stores offer these facilities.

When selling taxable goods free of tax under these arrangements the shopkeeper will normally ask to see your passport.

Laundry. This is very expensive, and many people in Britain do their own. This is why drip-dry shirts, dresses, etc., are very popular.

Cigarettes. Cost at the time of writing about 4s. 10d. for a packet of twenty, but many people today smoke filter-tips at 4s. 2d. for twenty. Both cigarettes and alcoholic drinks are heavily taxed.

Clothes. These are generally of very good quality, and usually no dearer than overseas. If you come from a hot country you will find Britain cold and damp, and very often the summer temperatures average only 65° Fahrenheit. If you come from the tropics you will seldom need what you use as summer clothing at home. Raincoats are essential but can be bought quite cheaply in Britain, as can overcoats. A duffle-coat is cheap and hard-wearing, and excellent for students. June, July and August are the warmest months; January, February and March the coldest.

Shoes. Men's shoes, and women's also, should not be thrown away when they are worn, but can be taken to be mended at a shoe repairer.

Electrical Equipment. If you bring electrical equipment you should ensure that any electric irons, radios, etc., which you may take to Britain can be used on British voltages. The most general are 200–250 v. A.C., 50 cycles. Notices are generally displayed in the few areas where D.C. is used.

Section II

English Language

Section II

English Language

Special Facilities for learning English as a Second or Foreign Language and Examinations

Many students come to Britain primarily in order to improve their knowledge of the English language.

To cater for such students, regular courses in English language are arranged by some local education authorities; there are a number of private schools which specialize in teaching English; there are summer schools in which study is combined with a holiday; and, for advanced students and teachers of English, there are special summer schools and courses, e.g. in phonetics or literature, some of them at universities. A useful annual publication which includes brief details of most types of courses is the leaflet 'Information for Young Visitors to Britain', obtainable from the Central Bureau for Educational Visits and Exchanges, 55A Duke Street, London, W.1.

Most of the regular classes in English are designed to enable students to take one or more of the following examinations in English:

Examinations

University of Cambridge: The Secretary, Examinations in English, 17 Harvey Road, Cambridge. Lower Certificate in English; Certificate of Proficiency in English; Diploma of English Studies.

Institute of Linguists, 3 Craven Hill, London, W.2. Student I, II and III; Associate; Fellow.

London Chamber of Commerce; The Secretary, Department of Commercial Education, 69 Cannon Street, London, E.C.4. English Examination at Elementary, Intermediate and Higher Stages, *and* English for Commerce for Overseas Students; Intermediate and Higher Stages.

Royal Society of Arts: The Secretary, 18 Adam Street, Adelphi,

London, W.C.2. Examinations in English; Elementary, Intermediate and Advanced Stages. (Entries must be made through a centre and not direct to R.S.A.)

London University: The Director, Department of Extra-Mural Studies, Room 254, University of London, Senate House, London, W.C.1. Certificate of Proficiency in English (held only in London).

The Pitman Institute. Communications about Pitman's Examinations should be addressed to: The Secretary, Pitman Examinations Institute, Godalming, Surrey. (1) English Language for Overseas Candidates (Elementary, Intermediate, Advanced); (2) Certificate in Spoken English (held only in London).

Arrangements are made for candidates for the Cambridge and London Chamber of Commerce Examinations to sit the examinations at centres overseas (in Hong Kong, for example, or Hamburg) as well as in London and elsewhere in the United Kingdom. Students abroad wishing to sit for one of these examinations should inquire at the local British Council Office or British Consulate for details.

In Britain, application should be made to the Secretary of the appropriate Examining Body, as listed above.

English Courses Provided by Local Education Authorities

Many Local Education Authorities in London and in the provinces provide English courses for students from overseas. These vary from full-time courses to part-time and evening courses. Classes are sometimes large (average 20 students a class) but fees are low. Terms run from September each year, and entry is not possible after the course has started.

Minimum fee: Evening classes, £2 a term; Day-time classes, £5 a term.

Maximum fee: £30 a session, or £10 a term, for attendance of 20 hours a week or more.

In London, seven Colleges under the Inner London Education Authority teach English to overseas students and provide full-time courses leading up to examinations of the University of Cambridge Local Examinations Syndicate, as well as part-time and evening courses. These are:

City of London College, Moorgate, London, E.C.2. Tel. MONarch 8112/3/4.

Holborn College of Law, Languages and Commerce, Red Lion Square, London, W.C.1. Tel. HOLborn 2889.

Kennington College, West Square, St. George's Road, London, S.E.1. Tel. RELiance 5597.

The Polytechnic, 309 Regent Street, London, W.1. Tel. LANgham 2020.

Princeton College, Princeton Street, London, W.C.1. Tel. HOLborn 1048.

Pulteney College, Peter Street, Wardour Street, London, W.1. Tel. GERrard 8381.

West London College, Airlie Gardens, Campden Hill Road, London, W.8. Tel. PARk 4550.

Details of the courses at these seven colleges, and of part-time courses at other colleges in the London area, may be obtained from:

The Education Officer, County Hall, Westminster Bridge, London, S.E.1.

Information concerning the many Technical Colleges, Colleges of Commerce and other local authority colleges outside London which provide English teaching and special courses for overseas students can be obtained from the British Council, the Central Bureau for Visits and Exchanges or from the Local Education Authorities (see under Section III, pages 136–142). See also under Technical Colleges, Section V, Main Centres.

Most local education authority colleges maintain lists of addresses for local accommodation.

Publication

Classes in English for Students from Abroad, published by the Inner London Education Authority (which gives details of all courses of English for foreigners run by the Inner London Education Authority).

Private Schools for Adults

Private Schools which teach English as a foreign language may, if they wish, be inspected by the Department of Education and Science. These inspections cover the work of members of the teaching staff, methods of study, premises, arrangements for students' accommodation and out-of-school activities. Schools which satisfy the inspectors are formally 'recognized as efficient' by the Department of Education and Science, and may become members of the Association of Recognized English Language Schools.

A list of such schools can be obtained from any British Council Office, The British Travel Association, or from The Secretary, Association of Recognized English Language Schools, 43 Russell Square, London, W.C.1. Tel. LANgham 7665. A.R.E.L.S. will advise on the choice of a suitable recognized school.

There are still many unrecognized schools, varying in size and quality.

Overseas students can obtain help, without any fee, from the agencies or consultants which specialize in offering advice on private education generally, e.g. The Gabbitas-Thring Educational Trust, 6 Sackville Street, Piccadilly, W.1. Tel. REGent 0161; *and* The Truman and Knightley Educational Trust Ltd., 93 Baker Street, London, W.1. Tel. HUNter 0931.

Most of the existing private schools of English are known to these consultants. Points to ask about in seeking advice are size of classes, qualifications of teachers, arrangements for accommodation and out-of-school activities.

The private schools provide classes both for beginners and those who wish to study at a more advanced level and to take examinations such as Cambridge Certificate of Proficiency in English or, in some cases, the General Certificate of Education. The schools are situated in cities such as Oxford, Cambridge and London or in seaside resorts or the countryside. Some schools are residential; the other schools normally find accommodation for their students with local families. The fees for board and tuition in a residential school are about £150 to £200 for a twelve-week term; tuition fees in a non-residential school for a twelve-week term range, according to the number of lessons provided and other amenities, from about £18 to £70.

A private school generally has small carefully graded classes (average 14 students to a class) and is able to give considerable care and attention to individual students both inside and outside their school life. Many schools are open throughout the year; students are normally admitted only at the beginning of a term, except in the case of short courses.

Tutorial Establishments

A student who wants to study other subjects as well as English at a private school can attend a tutorial or, as it is usually called in England, a coaching establishment. These establishments specialize in giving individual tuition to small groups of pupils. Fees range from £170 to £220 inclusive for a 12-week term for boarders. Day pupils are charged between £80 and £100 a term.

Private English Lessons

If a student wishes to have private tuition in English, the consultants and agencies can supply the names and addresses of suitable tutors. Fees for private coaching are from 12s. 6d. an hour.

English Courses at the Universities

In addition to the many university degree courses in English studies in Britain which are attended by British and foreign students alike there are courses at some universities specially designed for overseas students. They are all advanced courses for students who are able to follow lectures and converse easily in English; some of them are intended for teachers of English wishing to study the principles and methods of teaching English as a foreign or second language. One-year courses for overseas students are at present provided by the following universities: Edinburgh, Exeter, Leeds, Liverpool, London, Manchester, Nottingham, Wales (University College of North Wales, Bangor) and York, and by the Welsh College of Advanced Technology in Cardiff. These courses begin in October of each year and application for admission should be made 6 to 12 months beforehand.

Several universities provide summer courses during the vacation for overseas students who have a good knowledge of the English language. Birmingham, Edinburgh, London and Oxford run a joint summer schools programme, with courses in English history, literature and drama. Other universities provide courses outside this programme in linguistics, phonetics, language or literature.

For information about university courses apply to the university direct; to the British Council; or to the Central Bureau for

Educational Visits and Exchanges, 55A Duke Street, London W.1.

Schools for Children

The local education authority colleges and most of the private schools of English do not accept pupils under the age of 18 or, in some cases, 16. Parents who wish to send a child to Britain at an earlier age to learn English can either arrange for him to take part in one of the school exchange schemes or enrol him in an ordinary British school. There are no special courses in English for foreign children in ordinary schools, except classes for the young children of immigrants into Britain; if a child attends an ordinary school he will have to take the full range of subjects which it offers.

School Exchanges and Links

Most arrangements for exchanges of school-children are made through the 'school-linking' scheme and links registered under this scheme usually benefit from financial assistance in other countries. This scheme is administered by the Central Bureau for Educational Visits and Exchanges, 55A Duke Street, London, W.1, which is also responsible for some individual placings of young people in term-time exchanges. The Educational Interchange Council, 43 Russell Square, London, W.C.1, arranges some specific projects for home-to-home exchanges.

See also Group Visits and Student Exchange Schemes, pages 54–57, Section I.

Enrolment in a School

The schools within the State system of education run by the local education authorities do not admit children from overseas unless their parents are normally resident in the United Kingdom. If a parent wishes his child to attend a State school, he should apply to the local education authority in the area in which he lives.

Private Schools for Children

There is a large number of private fee-paying schools for children in Britain, both day and residential, all the best of which are recognized as efficient by the Department of Education and Science. The most well known of these are the so-called 'Public Schools'. These take in girls from the age of 11 and boys from the age of 13½. Children below these ages attend what are called Preparatory Schools. Very few of the Private Schools are co-educational.

Inquiries about private schools for children can be made to the educational consultants such as: The Gabbitas-Thring Educational Trust, 6–8 Sackville Street, London, W.1, *and* The Truman and Knightley Educational Trust Ltd., 93 Baker Street, London, W.1.

It is extremely difficult to gain admission into boys' Public Schools. Owing to pressure for places, in many cases the name has to be registered for entry soon after the child is born. Very occasionally a place may be found for a boy of 17 for one year, if he has exceptional ability. Entry into the girls' schools is not so difficult and a place can usually be found.

There is a second category of school for children of secondary school age known as Independent Schools. These are not so difficult to get into and a vacancy can usually be found. They are run on similar lines to the Public Schools.

Vacancies can occasionally be found for foreign boys or girls during July in Preparatory Schools and, very occasionally, in Public Schools. The majority of Boarding (i.e. residential) Schools in England are Protestant but there is no discrimination against Roman Catholics and facilities can usually be made available for Roman Catholic children. There is a limited number of purely Roman Catholic schools. There are also the 'aided' schools (Direct-Grant, receiving money direct from the Government: Grant-Aided, receiving money from the Government via the L.E.A.) which occasionally have places vacant.

There are residential and non-residential 'Finishing Schools' for girls of 16 or 18 both in London and in the country. Some English Finishing Schools or Colleges offer specialized training in domestic science subjects, others give a vocational training, including shorthand and typing, and sometimes drama or dancing, especially ballet. Many offer an all-round education. All Finishing Schools in England assist foreign students to improve their knowledge of English. Fees in England for non-residential schools vary between £150 and £200 a year; at a residential school, fees range from £300 to about £500. (Swiss Finishing Schools charge about £600 for a year's course.) There are no entrance examinations, but some knowledge of English and some educational qualifications are desirable.

Summer Schools for older children are run occasionally by English Language Schools and Local Education Authorities are also starting them up.

Correspondence Courses in English

English can also be studied through a Correspondence Course, either generally or in preparation for one of the recognized examinations (such as G.C.E. or one of the examinations in English for overseas students as mentioned earlier in this section). There are a number of organizations in England which specialize in teaching by correspondence. The cost of a short course is about £6. A complete course, which includes lessons on Commercial English, costs about £12.

The names and addresses of colleges which provide correspondence courses in English and in other subjects are given on page 147, Section III.

Students are reminded, however, that a correspondence course organization, by its nature, cannot be responsible for its pupils in the same way as a school or college authority. Such courses are the student's own responsibility.

Audio-Visual Aids

For information on audio-visual methods of learning the English language, i.e. by using pictures, film-strips and other mechanical aids, the following addresses will help: Overseas Visual Aids Centre, 31 Tavistock Square, London, W.C.1, *and* British National Film Catalogue Ltd., 55A Welbeck Street, London, W.1.

Many schools and colleges have, or are about to start, using language laboratories as one method of teaching English to foreigners.

English by Radio and Television

In its broadcasts to the world in English and 40 other languages the B.B.C. includes English by Radio Courses. There are courses with explanations in other languages for beginners and students at the elementary level, and courses in English only for advanced students. These courses reach listeners abroad direct from London and by re-broadcasting in many other countries. Special textbooks are published and there are also gramophone records for school and home use.

The B.B.C. also produces English by Television Courses such as the well-known 'Walter and Connie' series, for showing in other countries.

The B.B.C. publishes a magazine, *English by Radio and Television*, which is designed to assist teachers and students of English. Subscriptions to this magazine may be taken out through B.B.C. Publications, 35 Marylebone High Street, London, W.1, at an annual rate of £1, or through overseas subscription agents at the local equivalent.

The B.B.C. is glad to provide information about its broadcasts and about its English by Radio and Television courses. If interested, write to: B.B.C. English by Radio and Television, Bush House, Strand, London, W.C.2.

Section III

Educational Institutions Explained

Educational Institutions Explained

The following is a short list of terms which sometimes have a different meaning in Britain than in other countries:

Student: usually means a young person, not in employment, who is following a course of study at University or College.

Apprentice or Trainee: a young person in employment whose employer undertakes to instruct or to allow training.

Sandwich Course: a course in which periods of academic study alternate with practical training.

Post-graduate Student: a student who has already obtained a first degree, and who is taking a more advanced course of study.

Degree: a title conferred by a University (Bachelor's Degree: the first degree – Master's Degree: the second degree – There are some exceptions to the status of these titles, e.g. at Oxford, a Bachelor of Science is a second degree, in Scotland 'Master's' is first degree).

Doctor: a rare and higher degree, conferred by a University usually for an original piece of work. In everyday speech, it usually means a family doctor of medicine.

Professor: usually the head of a University department of study.

Diploma: a document testifying that a candidate has passed an examination in some subject; a University diploma course is usually shorter than a degree course.

Certificate: a document testifying to a standard of attainment usually lower in value and more specialized than a diploma standard except for professional membership.

The 'academic year' runs from September or October to June or July; that is to say, a year's course of study for almost all U.K. educational institutions begins at the end of September or the beginning of October and covers approximately nine months, ending for the long summer holiday. It is as well to remember this when making plans in advance.

Publication
  A Handbook of British Educational Terms by Barnard and Lauwerys (published by Harrap).

Preliminary Requirements for Higher Education and Training

Generally speaking, all candidates, British or overseas, for Higher Education in the United Kingdom are required to have passed the General Certificate of Education ('G.C.E.') – or equivalent, usually with a specified number of passes in specified subjects at 'Ordinary' (O) and 'Advanced' (A) Levels.

The recognition of equivalence of overseas qualifications is the responsibility of individual institutions. The Cambridge Overseas School Certificate and Higher School Certificate and the Cambridge Proficiency in English qualification (for 'Proficiency' see also page 129) are generally recognized.

Each application for a College of any kind is considered on its merits. Entry to all forms of Higher Education is, in fact, on merit only, i.e. mainly on examination performance.

Any overseas candidate seriously wishing to take a course in Britain should apply for advice first to his own Ministry of Education, to the Student Office of his Embassy or High Commission in London, or to any British Council Office in the U.K. or overseas.

The General Certificate of Education ('G.C.E.') and the Cambridge Overseas School-leaving Certificate

Many school-children in England, Wales and Northern Ireland take G.C.E. as their school-leaving examination. In Scotland there is the Scottish Certificate of Education which is used by all State schools in Scotland and recognized by Scottish Universities, though some independent schools in Scotland prefer to enter their pupils for the English G.C.E. examinations. In Northern Ireland there have been until the present time two separate examinations, the Junior and Senior Certificate, corresponding to the G.C.E. at Ordinary and Advanced Levels, but more and more schools, both in the State and Independent sectors, are currently going over to the G.C.E.

G.C.E. is open to candidates not attending school and up to any age. The standard is high and for many people it may be unnecessary to take any other formal examination for the purposes of employment or career.

It is arranged on the basis of individual subjects, which you may take in June or December examinations, in any number or approximately any grouping, concurrently or at different times. Subjects are set at Ordinary ('O') Level and Advanced ('A') Level. If you intend to go on after G.C.E. to a course of further formal education, you should bear in mind the date at which you hope to enter university or technical college and should seek advice and make your plans well in advance. In particular, you should choose your subjects for G.C.E. to suit the ultimate qualifications and career you have in mind; the subjects you have taken and passed in will very probably be taken into account.

In addition, there is the Overseas School-leaving Certificate of Cambridge University, c/o the Secretary, Syndicate Buildings, Cambridge.

This examination, unlike G.C.E., is arranged on the basis of not less than five subjects taken together at the same sitting. Credits equate with passes at Ordinary Level G.C.E. Passes at Principal Standard in the Cambridge Higher School Certificate equate with passes at Advanced Level G.C.E.

The Cambridge Proficiency in English qualification generally gives exemption from the English Language Paper of G.C.E.

There are eight examining boards for G.C.E.:

Oxford and Cambridge Schools Examination Board, Brook House, 10 Trumpington Street, Cambridge.

Oxford Delegacy of Local Examinations, 12 Merton Street, Oxford.

Cambridge University Local Examinations Syndicate, Syndicate Buildings, Cambridge.

Southern Universities Joint Board for School Examinations, 22 Berkeley Square, Bristol 8.

University of London, University Entrance and School Examinations Council, Senate House, London.

Joint Matriculation Board of the Universities of Manchester, Liverpool, Leeds, Sheffield and Birmingham, Devos Street, Oxford Road, Manchester 15.

T—E

Welsh Joint Education Committee, 30 Cathedral Road, Cardiff.

Associated Examining Board for the General Certificate of Education, Hesketh House, Portman Square, London, W.1.

All these bodies, except the Joint Matriculation Board and the Southern Universities Board, conduct their examinations also in certain countries overseas. Inquiries about centres abroad are best made to your local British Council Office.

Details of syllabus, past examination papers, all regulations and information on centres can be obtained by writing to the Secretary of the appropriate board at any of the above addresses.

Each of the examining boards offers its own list of subjects. Lists of subjects set by the different examining boards for G.C.E. can also be obtained on application. These vary a good deal. For example, the Associated Examining Board sets a wide range of vocational subjects, while the University of London offers over 60 specially approved languages, in addition to the principal European ones. A pamphlet, 'The General Certificate of Education', which lists the Examining Boards and all the subjects offered, can be obtained from H.M.S.O.

The Universities

There are, at the time of writing (November 1965), twenty-five universities in England. They are: Birmingham, Bristol, Cambridge, Durham, East Anglia (at Norwich), Essex (at Colchester), Exeter, Hull, Keele, Kent at Canterbury, Lancaster, Leeds, Leicester, Liverpool, London, Manchester, Newcastle upon Tyne, Nottingham, Oxford, Reading, Sheffield, Southampton, Sussex, Warwick (at Coventry), York. In Wales there is one, the University of Wales, with Colleges at Aberystwyth, Bangor, Cardiff and Swansea. In Scotland there are five: Aberdeen, Edinburgh, Glasgow, St. Andrews, Strathclyde (at Glasgow); and there is one in Northern Ireland at Belfast. See also under Section V, Main Centres, in this book.

Three new universities are to be set up at Stirling, Dundee, and Coleraine. Ten Colleges of Advanced Technology, and Heriot-Watt College, Edinburgh, will achieve university status in the immediate future.

Trinity College, Dublin, and the National University of Ireland are outside the U.K. For information on these, see Appendix I of the *Commonwealth Universities Yearbook, 1965*, or write to the Registrars in Dublin.

British universities do not come under government administration, either central or local, and are autonomous. Admission does not depend upon the nationality of the student but on his academic qualifications and on his previous education. Each university has its own minimum entrance requirements, but its students are selected from applicants for admission possessing these qualifications up to the limited number of places available for both first degree and post-graduate study. Both first degree level candidates and post-graduates are considered in relation to the very limited number of places available. Personal testimonial is also taken into consideration.

Each university has its own rules of practice about the recognition for entrance purposes of qualifications held by overseas candidates for admission. In general, a person applying on the basis of examinations passed overseas must be able to produce evidence that these qualifications entitle him to enter a university in his own country (if it has a university). The possession of such qualifications does not entitle a candidate to actual admission to a university in Britain since, as mentioned above, the students are selected in competition on their merits. However, overseas students who obtain awards from bodies like the Rhodes Trust, the Fulbright Commission, the British Council, etc., can usually rely on the particular body concerned assisting them with their applications for admission to universities.

Full information about entrance requirements and about courses can be obtained by writing direct to the Registrar of the university of the student's choice (not to the U.C.C.A.).

A university sometimes consists of a number of colleges and has central lecture rooms for faculties or 'schools'. Individual teaching is an essential characteristic of British universities and this, among other factors, makes the number of places extremely limited. Pressure for places may enable colleges to insist on more then the minimum university entrance requirements. Some universities, for example Oxford and Cambridge, require two languages other than the candidate's own native tongue to be included among his entrance requirements in all except Science subjects.

Application for any university (except Belfast) should be made to: The Universities Central Council for Admissions, 29–30 Tavistock Square, London, W.C.1.

Agencies may apply to this address for copies of the current U.C.C.A. handbook and application form for the use of their students. Individual candidates who apply from abroad will be charged a postage fee towards the cost of dispatch of the handbook and of decisions from universities to them by airmail.

The Universities Central Council on Admissions does not handle applications for admission to degree courses in technical colleges. However, a list of available degree and degree equivalent courses and a week by week vacancy list are available from the Advisory Centre for Education (ACE), 57 Russell Street, Cambridge during August and September. The current vacancy list is reprinted in the *Sunday Times* each week in September. Enfield College of Technology, Queensway, Enfield, Middlesex also runs an advisory service on degree courses at technical colleges.

One point may be of special interest if you are an overseas candidate. You stand a better chance of admission to a British university if you make your application from your own country and, if possible, with official sponsorship. Roughly 10 per cent of university places are, in fact, held by overseas people. If you apply as an overseas national staying in Britain you may have to compete with British nationals also applying for the place.

First Degree Courses

On the whole, the academic authorities in Britain and overseas do not favour a student taking his first degree in Britain, if he can do so at a university in his own country. Many overseas students therefore take a first degree at home and later on a second degree in Britain. In this case, his home degree will normally be accepted as qualification for admission here, provided it has been taken in a suitable subject.

For information on first degree requirements at universities (U.K. qualifications only), see *A Compendium of University Entrance Requirements for First Degree Courses in the United Kingdom* (published by the Association of Commonwealth Universities, price 11s. 6d.).

Post-graduate Courses

There is a stronger case for students from overseas taking post-graduate courses in Britain and indeed for the interchange of students at post-graduate level between countries generally.

For detailed information on British universities and their courses, see the *Commonwealth Universities Yearbook, 1965* (published by the Association of Commonwealth Universities, price £5 5s. plus postage and packing), and *Higher Education in the United Kingdom* (published for the Association of Commonwealth Universities and the British Council by Longmans, Green & Co.).

What are the advantages of a university? To the British mind, it is intended to give an education, rather than a training. All universities are engaged in research as well as in teaching and it is generally recognized that they provide the most favourable environment for learning and opportunities for the widest studies.

The authorities do not expect university students in Britain to take employment during their courses. A university degree is a helpful general qualification for the higher posts in any walk of life; but it should also be realized that further specialist training, practical as well as academic, is often needed before a university graduate can really start earning or take his place in the world.

Colleges of Advanced Technology

There are ten of these which provide the most advanced courses in technical education, including post-graduate and research work, and which are disposed now to widen the range of their subjects in the direction of social studies, economics, psychology, etc. Recently it was decided that they should have university status with power to award both first and higher degrees. The minimum age of entry is 18 and normal qualifications for admission are at least 2 passes in G.C.E. at Advanced Level and passes in three different subjects at Ordinary Level, including English Language.

All the 'C.A.T.s' are in England and Wales. They are:

The Birmingham College of Advanced Technology.
The Bradford Institute of Technology.
The Bristol College of Science and Technology.
Battersea College of Technology, London.
Brunel College of Advanced Technology, Acton, London.
Chelsea College of Science and Technology, London.
Northampton College of Advanced Technology, St. John Street, London, E.C.1.
Loughborough College of Technology.

The Royal College of Advanced Technology, Salford.
The Welsh College of Advanced Technology, Cardiff.

Two C.A.T.s, Battersea and Brunel, have in principle become universities already.

Regional Technical Colleges

These also provide advanced technological work, including full-time and sandwich courses. Each offers preparation for some or all of the following awards:

Ordinary and Higher National Diplomas and National Certificates ('O.N.D.', 'H.N.D.', etc.) (awarded jointly by the professional body concerned and the government).

Diplomas in Technology, (now being replaced by the B.Sc. degree awarded by the Council for National Academic awards).

External degrees of London University; *and*
The examinations of the professional bodies.

They are:

Brighton College of Technology.
Lanchester College of Technology, Priory Street, Coventry.
S.E. Essex Technical College and School of Art, Dagenham.
Hatfield College of Technology, Roe Green, Hatfield.
Huddersfield College of Technology, Huddersfield.
Kingston-upon-Thames College of Technology.
Leeds College of Technology, Calverley Street.
Leicester College of Technology.
City of Liverpool College of Technology, Byrom Street, Liverpool.
City of Liverpool College of Building, Clarence Street, Liverpool.
Borough Polytechnic, Borough Road, London, S.E.1.
Brixton L.C.C. School of Building, Ferndale Road, London, S.W.4.
Northern Polytechnic, Holloway Road, London, N.7.
The Polytechnic, 309 Regent Street, London, W.1.
Sir John Cass College, Jewry Street, London, E.C.3.
Woolwich Polytechnic, Thomas Street, London, S.E.18.
Rutherford College of Technology, Newcastle upon Tyne.

Nottingham and District Technical College, Nottingham.
Plymouth College of Technology, Plymouth.
Portsmouth College of Technology, Portsmouth.
Rugby College of Engineering Technology, Rugby.
North Staffordshire College of Technology, Stoke-on-Trent.
Sunderland Technical College, Sunderland.
Glamorgan College of Technology, Treforest.
West Ham College of Technology.

AREA TECHNICAL COLLEGES IN ENGLAND AND WALES

There are about 160 of these, providing courses in technical education up to the Higher National Certificate, but occasionally also for O.N.D. and H.N.D., for external degrees of London University, and for the examinations of the professional bodies.

Apply to the Local Education Authority (see list on pages 136–142) in this Section for addresses and particulars of each college.

LOCAL TECHNICAL COLLEGES IN ENGLAND AND WALES

There are about 350 of these, intended to cater for local people. They offer courses, according to demand, in general education for G.C.E., etc.; in craft-training for the examinations of the City and Guilds of London Institute and for the less advanced examinations of the professional bodies; and in technical training for O.N.C.

EVENING INSTITUTES IN ENGLAND AND WALES

There are almost a thousand smaller educational establishments, open in the evenings only, run by local educational authorities for part-time studies in languages, the arts, crafts, etc., both vocational and non-vocational, and subject to demand. For addresses and particulars of these, apply to the local education authorities.

SCOTLAND

In Scotland, technical education is arranged rather differently. There are seventeen central institutions, linked to some extent with the universities, doing advanced work, and offering many of the same examinations as those offered in England and Wales.

Six of these give their own diploma and associateship as well. They are:

Robert Gordon's Technical College, Aberdeen.
Dundee Institute of Art and Technology, Dundee.
Heriot-Watt College, Edinburgh.
Scottish Woollen Technical College, Galashiels.
Leith Nautical College, Leith.
Paisley College of Technology, Paisley.

The remaining eleven central institutions are specialist colleges in Agriculture, Art, Commerce, Domestic Science and Music.

There are about ninety supporting local technical colleges with more expected in the near future. Evening classes are provided at local centres.

NORTHERN IRELAND

Technical Education in Northern Ireland is arranged similarly to that in England and Wales. There are two principal colleges doing advanced work, Belfast College of Technology and the Municipal Technical College, Londonderry. Other centres are at Larne, Lisburn, Ballymena and Bangor.

For a complete list of technical and other colleges, including those in Scotland and Northern Ireland, arranged by county and giving general particulars of subjects offered, etc., see the *Year Book of Technical Education and Careers in Industry* (published by A. & C. Black.)

See also *Higher Education in the United Kingdom* (published by Longmans for the British Council and the Association of Universities of the Commonwealth).

N.B. – Application for admission to a course at a technical college has to be made to the college direct or through the Local Education Authority.

Local Education Authorities

Local Education Authorities are either administrative counties or county boroughs (cities or large towns). In London it is the Inner London Education Authority, formerly called the London

County Council. It is to the Local Education Authority that you should apply for all information (what courses are given, where, etc.) concerning non-university colleges and institutes within the area. It is also the authority to which the British student (and, very rarely, an overseas student with more than two years' residence in Britain) can apply for a financial grant to complete his education.

Some Local Education Authorities publish handbooks, setting out the facilities they offer. In each case, enquiries should be addressed to the Education Officer.

For a complete list of the addresses of Local Education Authorities, see 'Department of Education and Science', List 8, obtainable from H.M.S.O., but in simplified form they are as follows:

County Council Education Offices in England
Bedfordshire, Shire Hall, Bedford.
Berkshire, Shire Hall, Reading.
Buckinghamshire, County Offices, Aylesbury.
Cambridgeshire, Shire Hall, Cambridge.
Cheshire, County Hall, Chester.
Cornwall, County Hall, Truro.
Cumberland, The Courts, Carlisle.
Derbyshire, County Offices, Matlock.
Devonshire, County Hall, Exeter.
Dorset, County Hall, Dorchester.
Durham, County Hall, Durham.
Essex, County Hall, Chelmsford.
Gloucestershire, Shire Hall, Gloucester.
Hampshire, The Castle, Winchester.
Herefordshire, County Offices, Bath Street, Hereford.
Hertfordshire, County Hall, Hertford.
Huntingdonshire, Gazeley House, Huntingdon.
Isle of Ely, County Hall, March.
Isle of Wight, County Hall, Newport.
Kent, Springfield, Maidstone.
Lancashire, County Hall, Preston.
Leicestershire, Grey Friars, Leicester.
Lincolnshire (Holland), County Hall, Boston.
Lincolnshire (Kesteven), County Offices, Sleaford.
Lincolnshire (Lindsey), County Offices, Lincoln.
London, The County Hall, Westminster Bridge, London, S.E.1.

Norfolk, Stracey Road, Norwich.
Northamptonshire, County Hall, Northampton.
Northumberland, County Hall, Newcastle upon Tyne.
Nottinghamshire, County Hall, West Bridgeford.
Oxfordshire, County Offices, New Road, Oxford.
Rutland, County Offices, Oakham.
Shropshire, Shire Hall, Shrewsbury.
Somerset, County Education Office, Trull Road, Taunton.
Staffordshire, County Buildings, Martin Street, Stafford.
Suffolk (East), Rope Walk, Ipswich.
Suffolk (West), 5–6 St. Mary's Square, Bury St. Edmunds.
Surrey, County Hall, Kingston on Thames.
Sussex (East), County Hall, Lewes.
Sussex (West), County Hall, Chichester.
Warwickshire, 22 Northgate Street, Warwick.
Westmorland, County Hall, Kendal.
Wiltshire, County Hall, Trowbridge.
Worcestershire, 17 Castle Street, Worcester.
Yorkshire E.R., County Hall, Beverley.
Yorkshire, N.R., County Hall, Northallerton.
Yorkshire, W.R., County Education Office, Bond Street, Wakefield.

County Council Education Offices in Wales
Anglesey, Shire Hall, Llangefni.
Breconshire, County Offices, Brecon.
Caernarvonshire, 4 Castle Street, Caernarvon.
Cardiganshire, Swyddfa'r Sir, Marine Terrace, Aberystwyth.
Carmarthenshire, County Hall, Carmarthen.
Denbighshire, Ruthin.
Flintshire, County Education Offices, King Street, Mold.
Glamorgan, County Hall, Cardiff.
Merioneth, County Offices, Penarlag, Dolgelley.
Monmouthshire, County Hall, Newport, Mon.
Montgomeryshire, County Offices, Newtown.
Pembrokeshire, County Offices, Haverfordwest.
Radnorshire, County Hall, Llandrindod Wells.

English and Welsh County Borough Education Offices
Barnsley, Town Hall.
Barrow in Furness, Town Hall.

Bath, Guildhall.
Birkenhead, 63 Hamilton Square.
Birmingham, Margaret Street, Birmingham 3.
Blackburn, Library Street.
Blackpool, 3 Caunce Street.
Bolton, Nelson Square.
Bootle, 53 Balliol Road,
Bournemouth, Town Hall.
Bradford, Town Hall.
Brighton, 54 Old Steine.
Bristol, The Council House, College Green.
Burnley, Town Hall.
Burton upon Trent, Town Hall.
Bury, Town Hall.
Canterbury, Municipal Buildings, Dane John.
Cardiff, City Hall.
Carlisle, Civic Centre.
Chester, Town Hall.
Coventry, Council House.
Croydon, Town Hall.
Darlington, North Lodge.
Derby, Becket Street.
Dewsbury, Halifax Road.
Doncaster, Whitaker Street.
Dudley, 3 St. James's Road.
Eastbourne, Grove Road.
East Ham, Town Hall Annexe, Barking Road, London, E.6.
Exeter, Southerhay West.
Gateshead, Prince Consort Road South.
Gloucester, Belsize House, Brunswick Square.
Grimsby, Eleanor Street.
Halifax, West House, King Cross Street.
Hastings, 20 Wellington Square.
Huddersfield, Ramsden Street.
Ipswich, 17 Tower Street.
Kingston-upon-Hull, Guildhall, Hull.
Leeds, Municipal Buildings, Calverley Street.
Leicester, Newarke Street.
Lincoln, 4 Lindum Road.
Liverpool, Municipal Buildings, Dale Street.
Manchester, Deansgate.

Merthyr Tydfil, Pontmorlais.
Middlesbrough, Municipal Buildings.
Newcastle-upon-Tyne, Town Hall.
Newport, Mon., Education Office, Civic Centre.
Northampton, Springfield, Cliftonville.
Norwich, Education Office, City Hall.
Nottingham, Exchange Buildings, Smithy Row.
Oldham, Union Street West.
Oxford, Education Office, City Chambers, Queen Street.
Plymouth, Municipal Offices.
Portsmouth, 1 Western Parade, Southsea.
Preston, Municipal Building.
Reading, Blagrave Street.
Rochdale, Fleece Street.
Rotherham, 21 Moorgate Road.
St. Helens, Town Hall.
Salford, Chapel Street, Salford 3.
Sheffield, Leopold Street.
Smethwick, 215 High Street.
Southampton, Civic Centre.
Southend-on-Sea, Warrior Square.
Southport, 99–105 Lord Street.
South Shields, Westoe Village.
Stockport, Town Hall.
Stoke on Trent, Town Hall, Hanley.
Sunderland, 15 John Street.
Swansea, The Guildhall.
Tynemouth, 14 Northumberland Square, North Shields.
Wakefield, 27 King Street.
Wallasey, Town Hall.
Walsall, Darwall Street.
Warrington, Sankey Street.
West Bromwich, Highfields.
West Hartlepool, Park Road.
Wigan, Municipal Buildings, Library Street.
Wolverhampton, Town Hall.
Worcester, 5–6 Barbourne Terrace.
Yarmouth, 22 Euston Road.
York, 5 St. Leonard's Place.

Education Offices in the Channel Islands, etc.
  Jersey, 5 Library Place, St. Helier.
  Guernsey, Elm Grove, St. Peter Port.
  Isle of Man, Strand Street, Douglas.
  Isles of Scilly, Town Hall, St. Mary's.

Education Offices in Scotland
  Aberdeen (City), Castle Street.
  Aberdeenshire, 22 Union Terrace, Aberdeen.
  Angus, 50 East High Street, Forfar.
  Argyll (County), Education Offices, Dunoon.
  Ayrshire, County Buildings, Ayr.
  Banff (County), Education Offices, Keith.
  Berwick (County), Education Office, Southfield, Duns.
  Bute (County), Education Office, Colbeck Place, Rothesay.
  Caithness, Education Office, Rhind House, Wick.
  Clackmannan (County), Education Offices, Ludgate, Alloa.
  Dumfriesshire, Huntingdon, Moffat Road, Dumfries.
  Dundee, 14 City Square.
  East Lothian, Education Offices, Haddington.
  Edinburgh, St. Giles Street.
  Elgin. See Moray and Nairn.
  Fife, County Offices, Wemyssfield, Kirkcaldy.
  Glasgow, Education Offices, 129 Bath Street, and 25 Bothwell
Street.
  Inverness (County), Ardross Street.
  Kincardineshire, Education Office, Stonehaven.
  Kinross. See Perthshire.
  Stewartry of Kirkcudbright, Castle Douglas.
  Lanarkshire, 118 Queen Street, Hamilton.
  Midlothian, 9 Drumsleigh Gardens, Edinburgh.
  Moray and Nairn, County Buildings, Elgin.
  Orkney (County), Albert Street, Kirkwall.
  Peebles (County), County Buildings, Peebles.
  Perthshire and Kinross-shire, County Offices, York Place,
Perth.
  Renfrewshire, 16 Glasgow Road, Paisley.
  Ross and Cromarty, High Street, Dingwall.
  Roxburgh (County), Newtown Street, Dingwall.
  Selkirk (County), Technical College, Galashiels.
  Stirling (County), Spittal Street.

Sutherland (County), Brora.
West Lothian, Linlithgow.
Wigtownshire, 10 Market Street, Stranraer.
Zetland (County), Brentham Place, Lerwick.

Education Offices in Northern Ireland
Antrim County, Education Office, 475–7 Antrim Road, Belfast 15.
Armagh County, Education Office, Courthouse, Armagh.
Belfast (County Borough), Education Office, Academy Street.
Down County, Education Office, 18 Windsor Avenue, Belfast 9.
Fermanagh County, Education Office, East Bridge Street, Enniskillen.
Londonderry County, Education Office, New Row, Coleraine.
Londonderry (County Borough), Education Office, Brooke Park.
Tyrone County, Education Office, Omagh.

Colleges for the Training of Teachers, now called Colleges of Education

Responsibility for the academic teaching and practical training of teachers is taken by the University Institutes of Education. They examine the candidates and give certificates to those who are successful. The Department of Education and Science (formerly called Ministry of Education) then registers the candidates as qualified teachers.

There are a number of teacher-training institutes. These are: Institutes (or Schools) of Education (which are also area training organizations for co-ordination of initial training and refresher courses of teachers already in service); University Departments of Education; General Training Colleges; and (for specialist training) Home Economics Colleges; Physical Education Colleges; Training Departments of Colleges of Art; and Technical Training Colleges. Some colleges are for men or for women only; others are mixed. Some give post-graduate courses. A few London Colleges offer four-year degree and training courses for B.A. and B.Sc. Now the opportunity of taking four-year B.Ed. degree courses is being offered by colleges (in conjunction with the Universities) to a proportion of their students.

The historical background to teaching gives it a special character. Until the twentieth century, all training for teaching was in the hands of the Churches. Over 30 per cent of British teacher-training colleges have a denominational foundation; that is, Church of England, Roman Catholic, Methodist and other religious foundations. The remainder are the more recent foundations of the Local Education Authorities.

For a complete list of colleges, apply to The Registrar, Central Register and Clearing House, 151 Gower Street, London, W.C.1, or see *Whitaker's Almanack*, or *Higher Education in the U.K.* (published for the British Council and the A.U.C.).

Publication
Handbook on Training for Teaching by the Association of Teachers in Colleges and Departments of Education (published by Methuen).

Specialist Colleges

There are eight National Colleges which provide advanced courses for specialized techniques. They are managed by independent bodies and are as follows:

> National College for Heating, Ventilating, Refrigeration and Fan Engineering, Borough Polytechnic, Borough Road, London, S.E.1.
> National College of Rubber Technology, Northern Polytechnic, Holloway Road, London, N.7.
> National College of Food Technology, St. George's Avenue, Weybridge, Surrey.
> National Foundry College, Stafford Street, Wolverhampton.
> National Leathersellers College, Tower Bridge Road, London, S.E.1.
> National College of Agricultural Engineering, Silsoe, Bedford.
> Royal College of Art, Kensington Gore, London, S.W.7.
> College of Aeronautics, Cranfield, Bedfordshire.

There are also a number of other specialist colleges in Britain, principally in Agriculture, Engineering, Aviation, Art and in branches of one or two other professions, e.g. for wireless training in Seafaring. Many of these are already attached either to the

Universities or they come under the Local Education Authorities. But there are some which are managed by independent bodies or are purely private schools. A large number of private schools specialize in languages or commercial and secretarial training for girls.

For information on courses in *Private Schools and Colleges* apply to consultants in the field of private education. The best known of these are:

The Gabbitas-Thring Educational Trust Ltd., 6 Sackville Street, London, W.1.

Truman and Knightley Educational Trust Ltd., 93 Baker Street, London, W.1.

J. & J. Paton Ltd., Ormond House, 63 Queen Victoria Street, London, E.C.4.

For information on professional courses in general, apply to the appropriate Professional Body under headings for the Principal Professions and Vocations, Section IV.

University Teaching Hospitals

These provide practical training for doctors and are attached to medical schools. As hospitals, they are under the responsibility of the Ministry of Health, but they are also partly administered by University authorities.

Training Hospitals for Nurses

These include the University Hospitals, but are larger in number. For names and addresses, apply to the General Nursing Council for England and Wales, 23 Portland Place, London, W.1, and the General Nursing Council for Scotland, 5 Darnaway Street, Edinburgh 3.

Training Schools and Courses for Professions Allied to Medicine

For the details of these schools and courses, apply to the Professional Bodies as listed on pages 183–186. Section IV. A student should not undertake any training in an occupation allied to Medicine without inquiring from the relevant Professional Body first.

The Inns of Court

There are four Inns of Court – Gray's Inn, Lincoln's Inn, The
Middle Temple and the Inner Temple. For centuries past it has
been a feature of the English legal system that anyone wishing to
become a member of the Bar must first be admitted as a student
of one of these Inns. In many ways the Inns of Court resemble a
legal university situated close to the Law Courts in London. They
have their own halls, libraries, churches, chambers, common
rooms and gardens. The chambers are, in fact, the offices in
which barristers work when they are not in Court. Each Inn has
residential chambers as well, where some of its members can live.
When students have 'kept terms' by eating a set number of
dinners in their halls and have also passed the necessary legal
examinations, they may become barristers by being called
to the Bar by their respective Inns. The executive body of each
Inn of Court consists of its Benchers who are naturally enough
appointed by its most senior and most respected members,
including Judges of the High Court.

See also page 186, The Law, under Section IV, The Principal
Professions and Vocations.

Professional and Examining Bodies

In Britain, most occupations are organized and standards of
professional competence and conduct are maintained by the
membership and rules of an association, or 'professional body'.
There is sometimes more than one association to a profession
and the bodies concerned then often specialize, as their titles
often show, in a particular branch or area of the profession – for
example, there are several professional bodies in Accountancy.
Most of these professional bodies are also examining bodies and
their members have to qualify before they are accepted. Various
services are provided for the members; for example, news and
views about developments within the profession are often
supplied by means of a journal, meetings are held, and some
professional bodies also maintain an employment register for
members (see page 46, under Employment).

The professional bodies are not to be confused with the learned societies. The latter exist to further the study of a subject; their functions often overlap those of professional bodies, but they do not hold examinations. See under 'Libraries', General Information, Section I, and also the handbook *Scientific and Learned Societies of Great Britain* (published by George Allen & Unwin for the British Council).

A professional body must not be confused, again, with a college – which is often, like some of the professional bodies, called an 'Institution' or 'Institute'. Nor is it, in any sense, a trade union or trade association.

The professional body may be distinguished, for the purposes of this book, as a qualifying association.

The first step towards joining a professional body is usually to become a registered student. Requirements for registration depend upon the body concerned. There is some variation between bodies as to what is required – for example, in the number of subjects required at G.C.E. Ordinary or Advanced Level.

After registration, qualification for membership is by examination often divided into two parts. The first stage of membership is usually Associateship and the second stage is Fellowship. University degrees and other qualifications, sometimes also overseas qualifications, give exemption according to the rules of the professional body concerned. Each professional body has its own system and makes its own rules according to the demands of its profession.

For a further definition of the professions and a fairly comprehensive list of bodies, see *The Qualifying Associations* by Geoffrey Millerson (published by Routledge & Kegan Paul Ltd.); also *Trade Associations and Professional Bodies* by Patricia Millard (published by David Fanning Associates). *Whitaker's Almanack* gives a shorter list of professional examining bodies, as does also the *Education Committee Year Book*.

Many professional bodies are named in this guide under 'The Principal Professions and Vocations', Section IV.

N.B. – Some of these professional bodies have branches overseas, or there are local institutions in alliance with the U.K. body. A number of professional bodies set and conduct examinations overseas or may recognize some local examinations as exempting from their own examinations as mentioned above. You should inquire first from your own Ministry or Department of Education.

There are also a number of examining bodies (apart from those for G.C.E., etc.) with centres overseas, which examine in a number of vocational subjects and which are not professional bodies, e.g.:

The City and Guilds of London Institute (Technical Education), 76 Portland Place, London, S.W.1.

The London Chamber of Commerce, Department of Education, 69 Cannon Street, London, E.C.4.

The Royal Society of Arts, John Adam Street, Adelphi, London, W.C.2.

Correspondence Courses and Colleges

Many students find that, for one reason or another, they want to take a course by correspondence. Quite apart from other considerations it may serve as a useful way of practising the English language. Learning this way consists mainly of guided reading, questions set and corrected by post, with model answers.

With a correspondence course, the responsibility is the student's own. He must bear in mind that, in the absence of the physical presence of teacher, classroom and fellow-students, more self-discipline and determination is needed to cope with the pressure of work and to get to the end of his course. To save disappointment, he might pay attention to the following points:

(1) He can make a careful choice of the college to which he will belong, writing first to the college authorities (some colleges have an advisory officer) and deciding on it only after a study of the courses and of the details of all his undertakings.

(2) In writing to the college, he should understate his present level of education rather than overstate it. Many students fail to complete the course, because they have tried to start at too high a level. Similarly he should also understate the time he can allow for studying. Another cause of frequent failure is that the student finds he cannot keep up with the time-table expected by his tutors.

(3) He should make sure that the course to which he applies fully prepares him for the examination he wishes to take. Some examining bodies do not accept students who have prepared by correspondence course only. For example, if

he is required to take practical training in addition to his theoretical studies, he will have to arrange for this himself. He should write to the examining body for details of the syllabus, independently, and make sure a correspondence course is accepted as preparation.

(4) He should also ascertain that this examination will be recognized for the purposes of the job he may want to achieve with it afterwards.

There are a number of correspondence colleges in the United Kingdom giving such courses, particulars of which are best seen in the professional journals. The following is a list of some of the largest ones, with the courses they give. Some, as marked, have branches abroad, which prepare special courses to meet local needs.

British College of Accountancy, 20 Milton Road, Harpenden. Accountancy.

British Institute of Engineering Technology, College House, 29–31 Wright's Lane, Kensington, London, W.8. Architecture and Building; Auctioneering and Estate Agency; Automation; Civil Service; Cost Accountancy; Draughtsmanship; Engineering (all branches); General Certificate of Education; Instrument Technology; Management; Radio and Electronics; Surveying; Telecommunications; University Degrees.

College of Estate Management, St. Alban's Grove, Kensington, London, W.8. Auctioneering; Estate Management; Land Agency; Municipal Engineering; Sanitary Science; Surveying; Town Planning.

H. Foulkes Lynch & Co., 4–7 Chiswell Street, London, E.C.1. Accountancy.

International Correspondence Schools, Intertext House, Parkgate Road, London, S.W.11, branches in overseas countries. Advertising; Art and Lettering; Architecture and Building; Chemistry; Civil Service; Coal Mining; Commerce; Engineering; Farming; General Education; Horticulture; Management; Plastics; Radio and Electronics; Salesmanship.

Metropolitan College, St. Albans, Hertfordshire. Accountancy; Advertising; Banking; Building Society Work; Civil Service; Export; General Certificate of Education; Insurance; Local Government; Salesmanship and Sales Management; Secretaryship; University Degrees.

Nalgo Correspondence Institute, 8 Harewood Row, London, N.W.1. Accountancy; General Certificate of Education; Hospital Administration; Housing Management; Local Government; Medical Records; Municipal Engineering; Public Administration; Public Health Engineering; Secretaryship; Weights and Measures Inspection.

National Extension College, Shaftesbury Road, Cambridge. English and Maths 'O' Level; Spanish and French for beginners; Practical Radio and Electronics; and other subjects.

National Institute of Engineering, 148–50 Holborn, London, E.C.1. Building; Civil Service; Draughtsmanship; Engineering; General Certificate of Education; Housing; Radio; Surveying.

Pitman Correspondence College, Pitman House, Godalming, Surrey. Accountancy; General Certificate of Education; Hospital Administration; Local Government; Salesmanship and Sales Management; Secretaryship; Transport.

Rapid Results College, Tuition House, London, S.W.19. Accountancy; Banking; Civil Service; General Certificate of Education; Law; Local Government; Secretaryship; University Degrees.

The School of Accountancy, Regent House, 2 West Regent Street, Glasgow, C.2. Accountancy; General Certificate of Education; Law; Taxation; Local Government; Management; Secretaryship.

Skerry's College, 13 Bath Street, Glasgow, C.2. Civil Service; University Entrance; Commercial Subjects; General Certificate of Education; University Degrees.

University Correspondence College, Shaftesbury Road, Cambridge (part of National Extension College). General Certificate of Education; 'O' Level and 'A' Level and University Degree subjects.

Wolsey Hall, Oxford. Accountancy; Banking; Bookselling; College of Preceptors; General Certificate of Education; Hospital Administration; Insurance; Law; Local Government; Royal Society of Arts; Secretaryship; Statistics; Theology; University Degrees.

All these colleges are privately owned and do not, as yet, come under any form of supervision as do, for example, most private schools.

A Note on Practical Training

Practical training can be difficult to obtain in all technical and commercial subjects, as it depends on the willingness of individual firms to accept trainees. Students already in this country, taking the university or technical college part of a course needing a period of practical training for its proper completion, are normally helped by their universities or colleges to obtain places in firms. Some, especially scholars of their own governments, will be helped by the student officers of their own Embassies or High Commissions in London which have an arrangement with the British Ministry of Overseas Development and the British Ministry of Labour to help them find places in firms. British Government scholars will be placed by the British Ministries.

Students and trainees coming to Britain simply for practical training, without any formal education course, will normally do so under the auspices of their university or government or employer, and will normally have had arrangements made for them with a particular firm – sometimes the British parent or associate company of their own firm; students coming here for practical training only should not in any event come here without prior arrangements.

In the case of the sandwich course, e.g. C.N.A.A. degree courses (page 134) where practical training is an integral and essential part of the courses, a written assurance of a place should be obtained before a student leaves his own country. In these courses, practical training alternates with theoretical work, and the main benefit is lost unless these are taken in proper succession. The students' advisory bureau in the students' home Department of Education, or the British Council representative, should be able to help.

It is particularly difficult at present to obtain practical training in the specialized technologies and techniques of the textile, paper, chemical, aircraft and electronic industries; less so in the general fields of mechanical engineering and building; variably so in civil, electrical and chemical engineering. In civil engineering and building, there are often opportunities in the students' own country. If the student is in search of practical training or experience to help qualify him for membership of one of the British professional bodies, e.g. the Engineering Institutions, the training or experience must be approved by that body.

In the commercial field, there are, again, not many firms both able and willing to take trainees from abroad, e.g. for articles in the case of a professional firm of accountants, or 'on the job' training in a commercial firm. The main reason is that overseas trainees will not be able to stay in their employment when fully trained, and the British employer therefore gets no benefit from training them.

In addition to Embassies and High Commissions in London, the C.B.I. (an association of British employers), the British Council, the Ministry of Labour's regional offices, the Overseas Student Advisory Bureau (an independent body) and the employment registers run for their members by certain professional bodies (not the engineering institutions) may be able to help; also the Professional and Executive Register of the Ministry of Labour (which often makes a point of helping in those cases where a student drops behind schedule by failing examinations and has to have employment or practical training postponed). Wherever possible, it is best that the approach should be made through the students' own national representative, at his Embassy or High Commission office. Names and details of firms can be obtained from:

> *Opportunities for School-Leavers; Opportunities for Graduates; Opportunities for Qualified Men* (published by the Cornmarket Press).
> *Year Book of Technical Education and Careers in Industry* (published by A. & C. Black, available at most public libraries).

Lists of approved firms are supplied by the engineering institutions.

Section IV

The Principal Professions and Vocations

See also the following publications for more details:
Careers Guide, from H.M.S.O. by Ministry of Labour and
National Service; *Careers Encyclopaedia* (published by
Macmillan & Cleaver); *Year Book of Technical Education
and Careers in Industry* (published by A. & C. Black). Also
Careers for Boys and *Careers for Girls,* both by Gavin
Brown (published by Pan Books in the Pan Piper series).
For information on H.M.S.O. publications: See Section
I, page 83.

N.B. – This Section describes the organization of the
principal professions and vocations and is not meant to
suggest that there are openings in them for the permanent
employment of overseas nationals. For information on
employment, see Section I, page 46, and on practical
training, see Section III, page 150.

Section IV

The Principal Professions and Vocations

Engineering

There are many branches of engineering and many different forms of specialization, as can be seen from the list of professional institutions set out below. Industrial firms, government organizations and nationalized industries employ engineers as part of their permanent staffs. There are firms of contracting engineers who undertake the work of particular projects, and there are also consulting engineers whose business it is to advise and supervise. The term 'engineer' has, in Britain, no legal significance, but applies properly to the professionally qualified engineer.

Education and training in engineering is at three main levels:

(i) The technologist or professional level;
(ii) The technician level;
(iii) The craft level.

There is craft training in every country and young men do not often need to come to Britain to be trained as craftsmen; therefore craft training will not be further dealt with in this Section.

(i) At *technologist or professional level*, there is also considerable provision in overseas countries, where some of the universities and technical colleges run courses recognized by British professional institutions. Students should first find out whether suitable courses of study are available in their own countries. Progressively less students are coming to Britain for first degree courses and more for second degree or post-graduate courses.

However, for those students who must come to Britain for the academic qualifications necessary for membership of its professional institutions, the following are the main types of full-time or sandwich courses:

(i) Full-time university degree courses normally lasting three years in England and Wales and four years in Scotland;

(ii) Four-year sandwich courses for Diplomas in Technology;
(iii) Four-year full-time courses leading to the Associateship of a Scottish Central Institution;
(iv) College diploma courses offered by individual technical colleges and recognized for purposes of exemption by the appropriate professional institution, lasting at least three years on a full-time basis or four years on a sandwich basis;
(v) Higher National Diploma courses normally lasting three years on a sandwich basis followed by further study in additional subjects specified by the particular professional institution.

The Higher National Certificate, which is obtained through part-time study, is primarily a higher technician qualification (see (ii) below) but it may carry partial exemption from the examinations of certain of the professional institutions. Normally at least two years' study is necessary to reach the academic standard required by these institutions.

The standard of general education required for entry to the courses described in (i) to (v) is that of G.C.E. at 'A' Level or recognized equivalents (e.g. the Cambridge Higher School Certificate) together with the required 'O' Level passes. For Associateship and Diploma courses, some candidates from overseas may possess Ordinary Certificates or Diplomas (see (ii) below) that will be accepted for entry. Higher technological education in Britain is at present (1965) in a state of change; the Colleges of Advanced Technology are in process of achieving university status and the Dip. Tech. of becoming a degree award. It is therefore particularly important that, before making their plans for further study, students should find out the precise and up-to-date requirements not only for the course of study that they intend to take but also for the professional qualification at which they are aiming.

(ii) *Technician Level*. There is a rapidly growing need in modern industry for well qualified technicians. For many years the City and Guilds of London Institute and other examining bodies have held examinations and awarded a large number of qualifications for technicians. The Ordinary National Certificate is still primarily a technician qualification, as to an increasing extent is the Higher National Certificate. Because of the way they are organized, these National Certificates cannot be studied for overseas, so the C.G.L.I. has for some years offered distinctive technician qualifications for students in overseas countries, namely their Ordinary and Higher Certificates in Mechanical and Electrical Engineering and in Building and Civil Engineering. Following the experience gained it has now been decided that the courses leading to overseas certificates should be run on a full-time or sandwich basis, and be known as Technician Diploma courses. In certain circumstances, students of exceptional ability who have progressed some way with their technician courses, whether at home or in Britain, may have opportunities to transfer to professional courses in Britain; those at home should first inquire about such opportunities in the universities and technical colleges in their own countries.

For notes on practical training in industry, without which all these courses are incomplete, see Section III, page 150.

PRINCIPAL VOCATIONS

The following shows the professional institutions which hold qualifying examinations in the principal branches of engineering. The student should apply to them for more detailed information:

Civil

The Institution of Civil Engineers, Great George Street, London, S.W.1 (railways, roads, waterways, dams, tunnels, harbours, and municipal services and large buildings of all types).

Publications: *Civil Engineering*, K. W. Nash, Target Books, Hale; *Civil Engineering*, from H.M.S.O. Choice of Careers Series, No. 100.

Electrical

The Institution of Electrical Engineers, Savoy Place, London, W.C.2 (power stations, complex electronic devices, sales research).

Mechanical

The Institution of Mechanical Engineers, 1 Birdcage Walk, London, S.W.1 (design, manufacture, operation, etc., and maintenance of machinery of all kinds).

Publications: *Mechanical Engineering*, R. W. Steed, Target Books, Hale; *The Practical Training of Professional Mechanical Engineers*, Institution of Mechanical Engineers; *Engineering Work for Boys*, from H.M.S.O. Choice of Careers Series, No. 78; *Professional Engineers*, from H.M.S.O. Choice of Careers Series, No. 92.

Municipal

The Institution of Municipal Engineers, 84 Eccleston Square, London, S.W.1, *and* The Institution of Civil Engineers, Great George Street, London, S.W.1 (roads, bridges, sewage-disposal systems, water-supply systems, town planning, architecture and engineering and surveying work).

Publications: *The Municipal Engineer*, L. B. Escritt, Allen & Unwin.

Structural

The Institution of Structural Engineers, 11 Upper Belgrave Street, London, S.W.1 (building, bridges, dams, docks, etc.).

Publication: *Structural Engineering – A Career for Ambitious Young Men*, Institution of Structural Engineers.

Mining

The Institution of Mining Engineers, 3 Grosvenor Crescent, London, S.W.1, *and* Institution of Mining and Metallurgy, 44 Portland Place, London, W.1, *and* British Overseas Mining Association, Norfolk House, 7 Laurence Pountney Hill, London, E.C.4 (mineral deposits, extraction of minerals, processing of ore).

Publication: *Careers in Metal Mining Overseas*, obtainable from the British Overseas Mining Association.

Production

Institution of Production Engineers, 10 Chesterfield Street, London, W.1 (manufacture of commodities).

Publications: *Mechanical Engineering*, from H.M.S.O. Careers for Men and Women Series, No. 18; *Production Engineering as a Career*, issued by Institution of Production Engineers.

Marine

The Institute of Marine Engineers, The Memorial Building, 76 Mark Lane, London, E.C.3 (machinery in ships including propelling unit, auxiliary engines, etc.).

Radio and Electronics

The Institution of Electronic and Radio Engineers, 9 Bedford Square, London, W.C.1.

Publications: *Radio and Electronics as a Career*, issued by the Institution of Radio Engineers; *Radio and Television Servicing*, from H.M.S.O. Choice of Careers, New Series, No. 66.

Aeronautical

The Royal Aeronautical Society, 4 Hamilton Place, London, W.1 (aero-engines, air-frames and guided weapons, radar, hydraulic and electrical systems).

Chemical

The Institution of Chemical Engineers, 16 Belgrave Square, London, S.W.1 (design and operation of equipment and plant, in industries such as petroleum, food processing, pharmaceutical, plastics, and nuclear energy).

Publication: *Education and Training in Chemical Engineering*, The Institution of Chemical Engineers.

Gas

The Institution of Gas Engineers, 17 Grosvenor Crescent, London, S.W.1 (plant, gas-burning equipment).

Publication: *Chemical and Mining Engineering and Fuel Technology*, from H.M.S.O. Careers for Men and Women Series, No. 19.

Heating and Ventilating: Refrigeration

The Institution of Heating and Ventilating Engineers, 49 Cadogan Square, London, S.W.1, *and* Institute of Refrigeration, 30 New Bridge Street, London, E.C.4.

Engineering Design

The Institution of Engineering Designers, 38 Portland Place, London, W.1 (draughtsmanship).

Publication: *Engineering Draughtsman*, from H.M.S.O. Choice of Careers, New Series, No. 60.

Illuminating

The Illuminating Engineering Society, 32 Victoria Street, London, S.W.1.

Welding

Institute of Welding, 54 Princes Gate, London, S.W.7 (general mechanical, electrical, metallurgy, chemistry and production engineering).

Automobile

The Institution of Mechanical Engineers, 1 Birdcage Walk, Westminster, London, S.W.1 (chassis and body engineering).

Agricultural

The Institution of Agricultural Engineers, 6 Queen Square, London, W.C.1.

Water

The Institution of Water Engineers, Parliament Mansions, Abbey Orchard Street, London, S.W.1 (water supply – conservation in lakes, rivers, reservoirs and wells).

Public Health

The Institution of Public Health Engineers, 179–81 Vauxhall Bridge Road, London, S.W.1 (sewers, waste disposal, heating, lighting, ventilation, etc.).

Highway

The Institution of Highway Engineers, 47 Victoria Street, London, S.W.1 (roads and road bridges).

General

City and Guilds of London Institute, 76 Portland Place, London, W.1.

Publications: *Industry and Careers*, Iliffe; *The Year Book of Technical Education* and *Careers in Industry*, A. & C. Black; *Professional Engineers*, from H.M.S.O. Choice of Careers Series, No. 92.

Journals

Each of the professional institutions publishes its own journal. Besides these there are *Engineering* (published by Engineering Ltd.), weekly, and other more general publications which cover the whole field of engineering.

Technologies

There are schools and facilities for training in certain technologies, principally metallurgy, textiles, fuel, glass, concrete, paper and plastics.

The overseas student must be sponsored and he should beware of 'training for unemployment' in these skills. He should make sure before embarking on a course that the knowledge he may acquire will be really useful to him on return home. He should also be prepared for the fact that, while the academic side of such training may be relatively easy to arrange, the practical side, involving employment in a firm, may be very difficult. As might be expected, firms are not anxious to part with knowledge of certain techniques which may be their secret, nor to encourage competitors. Textiles, ceramics, glass and paper are particularly difficult. With many chemical processes, there may be agreement to share knowledge, but only with certain companies in other countries. The petroleum companies such as Shell provide a great deal of training for overseas students, but mainly to their own employees.

However, the situation among firms is not uniform. The C.B.I. is prepared to give advice, and application can be made to the Education Offices, The Confederation of British Industry, 21 Tothill Street, London, S.W.1. A list of firms giving training is provided in the *Education Committee Year Book*, and in *Opportunities for Graduates* (published by the Cornmarket Press).

In many cases, you may apply to the relevant professional body or to the leading training or educational establishment for information on courses, etc., e.g.:

In *Textiles:* The Textile Institute, 10 Blackfriars Street, Manchester 3.

In *Plastics:* The Plastics Institute, 6 Mandeville Place, London, W.1.

In *Rubber:* The Institution of The Rubber Industry, 4 Kensington Palace Gardens, London, W.8, *or to* The National College of Rubber Technology, Holloway Road, London, N.7.

In *Technical Chemistry:* The Royal Institute of Chemistry, 30 Russell Square, London, W.C.1.

In *Food Technology:* The National College of Food Technology, St. George's Avenue, Weybridge, Surrey.

T—F

In *Cement:* The Cement and Concrete Association, 52 Grosvenor Gardens, London, S.W.1.

In *Ceramics:* The College of Ceramics, North Staffordshire Technical College, College Road, Stoke-on-Trent, North Staffordshire.

   Publication: *Pottery*, from H.M.S.O. Choice of Careers Series, No. 6.

In *Glass:* Sheffield University.

   Publication: *Glass Manufacture*, from H.M.S.O. Choice of Careers Series, No. 113.

In *Nuclear Technology:* The Atomic Energy Authority, Research Group A.E.R.E., Harwell, Didcot, Berkshire.

In *Paper Science:* The Manchester College of Science and Technology.

In *Leather Science:* Leeds University, *or to* National Leathersellers College, Tower Bridge Road, London, S.E.1.

In *Fuel Science:* Leeds University.

In *Fuel Technology:* Newcastle University and Nottingham University.

In *Fuel Technology and Chemical Engineering:* Sheffield University, *or to* National College for Heating, Ventilating, Refrigeration and Fan Engineering, Borough Polytechnic, Borough Road, London, S.E.1.

Architecture

The work of an architect is to design buildings and to supervise their construction on behalf of the owner. Training as an architect is not usually undertaken by a student who wishes to engage in the building industry (see under 'Building'). Structural Engineering is also a special branch of engineering with a separate professional qualification. The majority of Town Planners are, however, first trained as architects (see under 'Town Planning'). Architects collaborate closely with engineers, builders and planners.

   Most entrants start training at about eighteen. The best method is to take a full-time course of study at one of the thirty-one schools of architecture in the U.K. which give courses recognized by the Royal Institute of British Architects, ten of them attached to universities. They run their own courses and set their own examinations. A full-time student can qualify in six and a half to seven years of which four and a half to five years are spent in the school of architecture. For the other two years the student must do practical training during which he can earn a salary. Arrangements for practical training are flexible: part of the time can be spent with builders, engineers, building manufacturers and others, providing at least a year is spent in an architect's office. If all goes well a student can sit the Intermediate Examination or the equivalent after three years. Usually he then goes to a year's practical training and then returns to his school for a further two years after which he sits the Final Examination. After his second year of practical experience he sits the Professional Practice and Practical Experience Examination. This completes his training and he is then eligible to be elected an Associate of the Royal Institute of British Architects (A.R.I.B.A.). He would also, by that time, normally have his College or University qualification in architecture such as the degree of B.Arch. or a Diploma.

This is the quickest and best method of training and the R.I.B.A. encourages all students to train in this way. If, however, full-time study is not possible, there are part-time courses, but it would be unwise for a student to come from overseas for a part-time course unless already experienced or trained and assured of work in an architect's office with time off for study. Students who attend courses not recognized by the R.I.B.A. sit the external examinations set and marked by the R.I.B.A., but since the failure rate in these examinations is much higher than in the recognized schools the student necessarily takes much longer to qualify and has a reduced chance of success.

Post-graduate Courses in some special aspect of architectural work or education are held at some universities including a course in Tropical Architecture of nine months at the Architectural Association School, 34 Bedford Square, London, W.C.1.

For further information apply to the Royal Institute of British Architects, 66 Portland Place, London, W.1.

Publications
  The Architect, H.M.S.O. Choice of Careers Series, No. 16.
  List of Schools of Architecture, obtainable R.I.B.A., free.
  A Future in Architecture, obtainable R.I.B.A, free.

Journals
  The Architects' Journal (published by Architectural Press Ltd., weekly).

The Architectural Review (published by Architectural Press Ltd., monthly).

The Architectural Association Journal (published by the Architectural Association, monthly).

The R.I.B.A. Journal (published by the R.I.B.A., monthly); and others.

Town Planning

In almost all countries of the world there is an increasing demand for men and women trained to deal with the many different aspects of Town and Country Planning. These range from major national and regional development schemes to the re-planning of the central areas of cities and towns. In Great Britain the generally recognized qualification for Town Planners is Membership or Associate Membership of the Town Planning Institute (M.T.P.I. or A.M.T.P.I.) and these qualifications are also widely accepted for senior posts in many other countries.

Because Town Planning now requires a variety of backgrounds and skills, many enter the profession after previously obtaining a qualification as an architect, surveyor or engineer – or a degree in geography, economics or sociology. In all these cases candidates are exempt from the Intermediate Examination of the Town Planning Institute and may either take the Final Examination direct or proceed to post-graduate courses at a University or College which awards a degree or diploma in Town Planning recognized as giving exemption from the Institute's Final Examination. These courses normally extend over two years full-time or three years part-time study.

The demand for entry to planning schools greatly exceeds the number of available places and candidates are strongly advised to make inquiries at least a year ahead.

Others who do not possess an accepted professional qualification or degree may sit the Institute's Intermediate and Final Examinations. Alternatively, they may take a four-year undergraduate course leading to a degree or diploma in Town Planning, giving exemption from the Intermediate and Final Examination. In all cases applicants must have had two years' practical experience in Town Planning before being accepted for Associate Membership of the Town Planning Institute. It is usual for those taking part-time courses to be employed in a planning office while attending evening classes or taking a correspondence course.

Those entering for the Intermediate Examination are required to become Students of the Town Planning Institute and for this purpose they must be at least 18 years of age, be engaged in the profession and have at least five passes in approved subjects in the General Certificate of Education, including English Language, Mathematics, and either History or Geography or a language other than English. At least two of the five subjects must be at Advanced Level. The Institute also accepts passes at the appropriate level in examinations equivalent to the G.C.E., including the Cambridge Overseas Certificate. Details of the standard required in these equivalent examinations may be obtained on application to the Institute.

Further information and details of where to study and publications may be obtained from The Town Planning Institute, 26 Portland Place, London, W.1.

Building

The building industry in Britain comprises some 70,000 firms varying greatly in size and the type of work undertaken. The industry's output is enormous (over £3,000 million per annum). Its labour force is over one million. By far the largest elements of this are skilled craftsmen and operatives, with whom this publication does not deal at length because facilities are available in the overseas countries where craft examinations such as those of the City and Guilds of London Institute can be taken.

The C.G.L.I. also offers courses and examinations abroad at technician level, equivalent in standard to Ordinary and Higher National Certificates or Diplomas. Preparation for the membership examinations of professional bodies can be undertaken abroad, by correspondence, but for these, and for courses at higher technician level, preparation may sometimes best be made in Britain.

The organization of a building firm in most overseas countries, as in Britain, requires men in more senior positions to carry out some or all of the following functions, which are not exhaustive:

General Management
   Proprietor, partner, director, manager.

Commercial
   Sales – estimator, technical representative.
   Purchasing – buyer.

Construction (including maintenance, alterations and repairs)
   Project /site /department /construction manager; general foreman, foreman, supervisor.
      Supporting Staff (technical): engineers (work study, method
   study, setting out, etc.); surveyors (cost, planning, bonus,
   measuring, quantity, etc.). (Titles may include the prefixes:
   'Assistant', 'Senior' and 'Chief' in several of the above.)
   There may also be draughtsmen and other technical personnel
and there will be purely administrative staff.
   It will be appreciated that the duties and responsibilities and
therefore the requirements in terms of educational level and
personal qualities will vary between a firm with ten employees (in
which one man will carry out several functions) and the very large
firm, handling big contracts, which may well be organized in
large departments, each carrying out one function. A broad
knowledge of building technology and management techniques is
essential for most and desirable for all management and technical
personnel. The basic technical education is provided in general
building courses, divided broadly according to the entrant's
general educational background and using the now accepted terms
(see also under 'Engineering'): 'technician' and 'technologist':

Classification	*General Education*	*General Building Course*
(a) 'Technician'	School-leaving	Construction Technician's Certificate (City and Guilds) (4 years part-time)
(b) 'Higher Techni-cian'	Minimum G.C.E. 4 'O' Level	Higher National Certificate or Diploma (2 years' minimum) Ordinary National Diploma (2 years)

(c) 'Technologist'   Minimum G.C.E.   Degree Level Course
    (or   profes-   2 'A' Level and
    sional)   4 'O' Level

Practical experience is usually necessary to complete a qualification (see Section III). This is sometimes obtainable after passing the examination. There are also a number of schemes run by employers, generally taking not less than four years, which require the student to work for a recognized qualification while at the same time providing him with practical experience both in the office and on building sites.

The Institute of Builders, 48 Bedford Square, London, W.C.1, is the professional institution for building and its membership classes broadly correspond to the above table.

(a) Technician Member   (Tn.I.O.B.)
(b) Licentiate Member   (L.I.O.B.)
(c) Associate or Fellow   (A.I.O.B.) (F.I.O.B.)

In addition there are a number of other institutions which cater for particular functions in the field of building, e.g. The Institute of Clerks of Works of Great Britain, Inc., 5 Broughton Road, Thornton Heath, Surrey, *and* The Institute of Municipal Engineers, 84 Eccleston Square, London, S.W.1.

Further information, including particulars of membership examinations, may be obtained from the professional bodies.

Publications
Building and Civil Engineering Contracting from H.M.S.O. Choice of Careers Series, No. 110.

Journal
The Builder (published by The Builder Ltd.), weekly; and others.

Surveying

Surveying covers a wide field of professional activity and only one professional society examines in all of its branches, i.e. the Royal Institution of Chartered Surveyors, which is the premier professional society for surveyors in the United Kingdom and indeed throughout the world. The Institution has five sections as follows which together form the whole profession:

General Section (including Valuation, Estate Management, Town and Country Planning and Building Surveying).
Quantity Surveying.
Agriculture and Land Agency.
Mining Surveying.
Land Surveying.

In addition, there exist the Institute of Quantity Surveyors not all of whose members are professionally engaged and, in other branches of the profession, the Chartered Auctioneers and Estate Agents Institute and the Chartered Land Agents Society. All of these bodies conduct their own qualifying examinations as do several smaller societies concerned with one or other aspect of the profession.

Opportunities are good in the General and Quantity Surveying Sections of the R.I.C.S. and there still remains a need for young men to practise land surveying in their own countries. There are prospects for the Agricultural Surveyor in many countries outside the United Kingdom and, where appropriate, good opportunities for the Mining Surveyor.

It is stressed overleaf that practical training is necessary before election to corporate membership and students must be sure that they can obtain in their own country suitable practical training after completing a full-time course in the United Kingdom. There are occasionally difficulties in finding posts in Britain for overseas students and, although professional societies will assist in every way, students should not travel to Britain without securing employment beforehand.

There are first degree 3-year courses at the following Universities:

London – B.Sc. (Estate Management);
Cambridge – Land Economy Tripos;
Newcastle – Land Use Studies.

Many technical colleges, in all parts of the country, run both full-time and part-time courses leading to either internal diplomas or external professional examinations, and many more such courses are proposed.

The entry standards of each of the organizations vary and

details should be obtained from them individually. The standards are mostly based on a required number of G.C.E. passes. For example: R.I.C.S. – until 1st October, 1966 – a minimum of five subjects at Ordinary Level to be obtained at one sitting. If English Language and/or Mathematics are not included they must be passed at additional sittings.

After 1st October, 1966 – a minimum of five subjects (two at Advanced Level) including English Language or English Literature and either a mathematical subject or a science subject.

I.Q.S. – five subjects at Ordinary Level at one sitting including English and Mathematics. Entry standards of the various Universities are formulated by the Universities themselves and applications for details should be made direct.

Minimum qualifications for entry into a Technical College are usually those of the professional examining body but due to demand for places individual colleges may impose higher standards. Colleges teaching for internal London University degrees and diplomas will also set their own standards of entry, normally equivalent to university entrance.

There are three main methods of training:

(1) By way of a degree or diploma in a cognate subject followed by practical training in a professional office. The degree or diploma will give certain exemptions from the professional examinations depending on the particular course chosen.

(2) By way of full-time study for the professional examinations. This full-time study is followed normally by a period of practical training after which the candidate is elected to corporate membership.

(3) By way of concurrent practical training in a professional office and part-time study either through day release or evening classes or by way of correspondence course.

All of the professional bodies place great emphasis on the need for practical training in a suitable office and it is not possible to become a corporate member of any of the three Chartered societies without an approved period of practical training.

Candidates are generally required to sit three stages of examination. There is a practical examination at Final Level for those taking the Agriculture and Land Agency examinations of the R.I.C.S.

Considerable exemption from their own examinations is given by most of the societies to holders of degrees cognate to surveying. For example, the B.Sc. (Estate Management) degree of London University exempts holders from the written examinations of the appropriate sections of the R.I.C.S., C.A.E.A.I., and C.L.A.S. examinations.

For further information apply to The Secretary of the individual Societies:

R.I.C.S., 12 Great George Street, London, S.W.1, *or* 7 Manor Place, Edinburgh.

C.A.E.A.I., 29 Lincoln's Inn Fields, London, W.C.2.

C.L.A.S., 21 Lincoln's Inn Fields, London, W.C.2.

I.Q.S., 98 Gloucester Place, London, W.1.

Publication
Surveyor, Land Agent, Auctioneer and Estate Agent from H.M.S.O. Choice of Careers Series, No. 87.

Journals
The Chartered Surveyor (R.I.C.S.) monthly.
The Surveyor and Municipal and County Engineer (published by St. Bride's Press Ltd.), weekly.

Agriculture

Agriculture means the science and practice of farming crops and livestock. In the U.K. mixed farms are most usual; poultry and dairy farming, however, are specialized industries which require separate training.

There are three methods of training:
(1) National Apprenticeship Schemes:

    (*a*) in England and Wales;
    (*b*) in Scotland, of three years' duration leading to the National Certificate.

The City and Guilds Institute also gives a diploma. Classes for these are given by the local authorities at technical colleges and evening institutes.

For further information on the above, apply to National Youth Employment Offices and/or to the City and Guilds of London Institute, Portland Place, or to the addresses given overleaf:

(2) Farm Institutes: one-year courses leading to the Institute Certificate in Agriculture and the National Certificate in Agriculture. Some Institutes give courses for Farm Secretaries.

(3) Agricultural Colleges: two-year courses leading to the college Diplomas or National Diplomas in Agriculture, Dairying, Horticulture, Poultry Husbandry and Agricultural Engineering.

There are also three- to four-year courses in Agriculture at some Universities with the usual entrance requirements.

All these methods require at least a year's practical experience of farming first. Methods (2) and (3) require also 4–5 passes at 'O' Level in G.C.E. including English; and sometimes one or two 'A' Levels. For young people in towns without the opportunity of gaining practical experience easily, the Y.M.C.A. (see page 37) gives introductory courses under 'The British Boys for British Farming Scheme'.

Advice regarding research facilities at Universities and Research Organizations can be obtained from the Ministry of Agriculture, the Agricultural Research Council, the Department of Technical Co-operation or the British Council.

With overseas applicants, it is generally thought better to study for a first degree in a student's own country or, failing facilities there, in a neighbouring country with similar natural conditions and climate.

However, there is everything to be gained from going elsewhere for post-graduate study, or indeed from making a study tour of methods and of social conditions in more than one country. In the U.K., the Second World War greatly advanced mechanization and intensivation of agriculture. Britain today offers a wide field for post-graduate studies in subjects such as agricultural science, agricultural economics, and in the applied sciences and technology relevant to agriculture and horticulture.

For a list of post-graduate full-time courses, see the Department of Education of Science (formerly Ministry of Education) booklet *Full-time Agricultural Education in England and Wales*.

For all further information, apply to:

The Royal Agricultural Society of England, 35 Belgrave Square, London, S.W.1.

The Royal Highland and Agricultural Society of Scotland, 8 Eglinton Crescent, Edinburgh 12.

The National Poultry Diploma Board Ltd., The Bungalow, Chilworth, Nr. Guildford, Surrey.

The National Certificate in Agriculture Examination Boards, 76 Portland Place, London, W.1.

The Royal Association of British Dairy Farmers, 17 Devonshire Street, London, W.1.

The Agricultural Research Council, Cunard Building, 15 Regent Street, London, S.W.1.

Publications

Agriculture and Horticulture (Managerial and Technical Posts) from H.M.S.O. Choice of Careers Series, No. 85.

Farm and Horticultural Workers from H.M.S.O. Choice of Careers Series, No. 86.

List 185: *Full-Time Agricultural Education in England and Wales*, issued annually by the Ministry of Education and the Ministry of Agriculture, Fisheries and Food.

Journals

The Farmer and Stockbreeder (published by Farmer and Stockbreeder Publications Ltd.), weekly.

Farmer's Weekly (published by Longmore Press Ltd.), weekly.

Commonwealth Producer (published by Commonwealth Producers' Organization); and others.

Horticulture

The horticultural industry in the United Kingdom is concerned not only with the commercial production of flowers, fruit, vegetables, bulbs, nursery stock, watercress and mushrooms, but also with private gardens, public gardens and parks. Both the scope of the work and the consequent training required are varied. Entry to any sector can be through one of the specialized apprenticeship courses such as those run by the Y.M.C.A. and the Agricultural Apprenticeship Council. Opportunities occur in both commercial practical work and in organizations associated with horticulture, such as teaching, advice and research and equipment manufacturers. Practical training may be provided, through one of the apprenticeship schemes or, for overseas students, through the United Kingdom Sponsoring Authority for Young Agriculturists (see Section I, page 57).

The training of the new entrant may be effected through one of the apprenticeship schemes. On completion of a year's practical training, entry can be made to one of the nine Horticultural Institutes to obtain the Institute's Diploma of the City and Guilds of London Institute's Stage One, Stage Two and Stage Three Horticultural Examinations. Further training in Commercial Horticulture can be obtained at the Universities of Reading, Wye and Nottingham on three-year courses, with post-graduate courses at Bristol, Wye, Durham, Nottingham and Reading. A four year sandwich course for an honours degree in horticulture started in 1965 at the University of Technology, Bath.

Training in Commercial Horticulture is also available through the Royal Horticultural Society's N.D.H. Examinations for potential gardeners and parks staff are the Diplomas of the Institute of Park Administration, and student training is provided by the Royal Botanic Gardens at Kew and Edinburgh, the Royal Horticultural Society at Wisley and the Botanical Gardens at Cambridge.

For further information apply to:

The Royal Horticultural Society, Vincent Square, London, S.W.1.

The Institute of Park Administration, Lower Basildon, Reading, Berkshire.

The Women's Farm and Garden Association, Courtauld House, Byng Place, London, W.C.1.

National Trust for Scotland, 5 Charlotte Square, Edinburgh 2.

National Farmers' Union of England and Wales, Agriculture House, Knightsbridge, London, S.W.1.

Publications

Farm and Horticultural Workers, from H.M.S.O. Choice of Careers Series, No. 86.

Agriculture and Horticulture (Managerial and Technical Posts), from H.M.S.O. Choice of Careers Series, No. 85.

National Farmers' Union – 'Just the Job for You'.

Horticultural Education Association booklet – 'The Present Pattern of Training and Qualification in Horticulture'.

Department of Education and Science – Ministry of Agriculture, Fisheries and Food booklet – 'Full-time Agricultural Education in England and Wales'.

Journals
   The Grower (published by Grower Publications Ltd.), weekly.
   The Commercial Grower (published by Benn Bros.), weekly.
   Fruit Trades Journal (published by Lockwood Press Ltd.); and others.

Forestry

In Britain, as in many countries, forestry is mainly a government job. A Degree in Forestry at one of the following universities:

   Oxford, Edinburgh, Aberdeen, and the University College of North Wales, Bangor

is required for employment as Forestry Officer with the Forestry Commission or, for U.K. citizens, with the forestry services of overseas governments. At Oxford, the Commonwealth Forestry Institute is merged with the University Department of Forestry and provides undergraduate and post-graduate training, undertakes research, and maintains one of the most complete forestry libraries in the world. Its activities are financed jointly by the University and by contributions from member governments of the Commonwealth. Associated with it is the Commonwealth Forestry Bureau which provides documentation and abstracting services for international forestry.
   Professional Bodies in Forestry are the:

   Commonwealth Forestry Association, Royal Commonwealth Association, Northumberland Avenue, London, W.C.2.
   The Society of Foresters of Great Britain, 3 Belsize Crescent, London, N.W.3.
   Royal Forestry Society of England and Wales, 49 Russell Square, London, W.C.1.
   Royal Scottish Forestry Society, 7 Albyn Place, Edinburgh 2.

Publication
   Forestry, from H.M.S.O. Choice of Careers Series, No. 81.

Journals
   Commonwealth Forestry Review (published by the Commonwealth Forestry Association); and others.

Veterinary Medicine

In general practice the Veterinary Profession is responsible for the maintenance of health and production of farm animals, for the prevention of disease and for the medical and surgical treatment of all animals, including household pets and zoo animals. Veterinary research and teaching in the veterinary schools is constantly expanding. Research is undertaken in the Ministry of Agriculture's laboratories, the veterinary schools and research institutes, financed by the government or by private enterprise. There are opportunities for British nationals for service in countries overseas and for overseas candidates to study in the U.K.

There are six universities in the United Kingdom, namely Bristol, Cambridge, Edinburgh, Glasgow, Liverpool and London, which provide courses of instruction leading to a registrable veterinary degree. The length of the course of instruction varies from four to five and a half years.

Candidates for entry must fulfil minimum matriculation requirements of the university of their choice and may also be required to satisfy course requirements. Applications should be made to the Registrars of the universities for particulars of entry requirements and to the Deans of the veterinary schools for course requirements. Generally speaking, the standard is similar to that for medicine and dentistry.

Applicants who satisfy entry and course requirements are not, however, guaranteed a place; there is intense competition for places.

The Royal College of Veterinary Surgeons is a statutory body with responsibilities concerning discipline and education and for maintaining the Register of Veterinary Surgeons. Membership of the Royal College and registration in the Register of Veterinary Surgeons must be obtained before a veterinarian can practise in the U.K.

Publications

Leaflet, 'The Veterinary Profession' (no charge).

Booklet, *Veterinary Education* (price 1s. 4d., post free, cash with order); both available from The Royal College of Veterinary Surgeons, 32 Belgrave Square, London, S.W.1.

Veterinary Scientist from H.M.S.O. Choice of Careers Series, No. 111.

Journal
    The British Veterinary Journal (published by Baillière, Tindall & Cox, Ltd.), monthly; and others.

Medicine

A student must join a medical school of one of the universities in order to train to become a doctor. Each school can take a limited number of applicants only and places are therefore highly competitive. This means that it is particularly difficult for the student from abroad to be admitted. Universities, however, reserve some places for overseas students and these are usually filled by students recommended by their own Government agencies. Information can be obtained from the local British Council representative. There are a number of post-graduate fellowships in medicine awarded annually by the Ministry of Overseas Development to overseas students sponsored by their governments.

The usual course of training extends over a period of six years but the first-year subjects are usually taken at school before entry to the university. The requirements for admission vary a little at the different universities but are usually two to three passes in the 'A' (Advanced) Level of the examination for the General Certificate of Education, together with certain 'O' (Ordinary) Level passes. Applications should be made about 18 months in advance. The first 2–3 years at the university are spent in the study of the basic sciences and during the last three years of his training the student does clinical work in the university teaching hospitals. On completion of his course, and after passing the final medical examination, the newly-qualified doctor is still required to spend a further year as a junior member of the staff of a hospital to gain further experience before being permitted to undertake independent practice in the United Kingdom.

Before engaging in any kind of work as a medical practitioner a doctor must be registered by the General Medical Council, 44 Hallam Street, London, W.1. The Council may grant, if it thinks fit, temporary registration to foreign medical graduates to allow them work in approved hospital appointments.

The total cost of the training is roughly £2,500 spread over a period of five years. Further information can be obtained from the following publications:

Medicine and Surgery from H.M.S.O. Choice of Careers Series, No. 108.
Becoming a Doctor (published by The British Medical Association).

There are good opportunities for doctors from abroad to undertake post-graduate medical study including such subjects as Anaesthetics, General Medicine and Surgery, in the United Kingdom and it may be possible for them to gain experience by working in British hospitals. It is important that inquiries about these should be made beforehand and further information can be obtained from:

The British Council – local office.
British Post-graduate Medical Federation, 18 Guilford Street, London, W.C.1.
Scottish Post-graduate Medical Association, St. Andrews University, Dundee, Angus.
Commonwealth and International Medical Advisory Bureaux, British Medical Association, Tavistock Square, London, W.C.1 (or from its publication, *Summary of Regulations for Post-graduate Diplomas and of Courses of Instruction in Post-graduate Medicine*).

Journal
The British Medical Journal (published by The B.M.A.), weekly; and others.

Further Note on Post-graduate Medicine
Post-graduate education is available at the Post-graduate Medical School of London (Hammersmith Hospital), where there are departments of general medicine, general surgery, anaesthetics, radiology and pathology, and in the principal clinical branches of medicine and surgery at the following Institutes which are associated with the special hospitals: Institute of Basic Medical Sciences (Royal College of Surgeons of England); Institute of Cancer Research, including the Chester Beatty Research Institute (Royal Marsden Hospital); Institute of Cardiology (National Heart Hospital); Institute of Child

Health (The Hospital for Sick Children, Great Ormond Street, Hammersmith Hospital and the Queen Elizabeth Hospital for Children); Institute of Dental Surgery (Eastman Dental Hospital); Institute of Dermatology (St. John's Hospital for Diseases of the Skin); Institute of Diseases of the Chest (the Brompton Hospital and the London Chest Hospital); Institute of Laryngology and Otology (Royal National Throat, Nose and Ear Hospital); Institute of Neurology (National Hospital for Nervous Diseases, Queen Square, and the Hospital for Nervous Diseases, Maida Vale); Institute of Obstetrics and Gynaecology (Queen Charlotte's Maternity Hospital, The Chelsea Hospital for Women, and the Department of Obstetrics and Gynaecology at the Hammersmith Hospital); Institute of Ophthalmology (Moorfields Eye Hospital); Institute of Orthopaedics (Royal National Orthopaedic Hospital); Institute of Psychiatry (Bethlem Royal and Maudsley Hospitals); Institute of Urology (St. Peter's, St. Paul's and St. Philip's Hospitals).

The British Post-graduate Medical Federation has a Central Office at 18 Guilford Street, London, W.C.1, where inquiries on any aspect of post-graduate medical education are welcomed, and the Director and other members of the medical staff are always glad to see and help graduates requiring advice. The Central Office makes arrangements for post-graduates, including those from the Commonwealth and foreign countries, who require assistance in arranging suitable programmes of study; in doing so, priority is given to those sponsored by their Governments or other official bodies.

It is essential for post-graduate students from overseas to make their arrangements well in advance and prospective students who desire the assistance of the Central Office are advised to get in touch with the Director at least six months before they come to this country.

The Scottish Post-graduate Medical Association has been formed in order to plan and to correlate more effectively the courses given at the four main centres of medical teaching in Scotland, namely, Dundee (University of St. Andrews), Glasgow, Aberdeen and Edinburgh. Inquiries can be sent to the Directors of Post-graduate Medical Studies at these places or to the Secretary of the Association, University of St. Andrews, Queen's College, Dundee, Angus, Scotland.

There are other important schools and faculties of medicine at

Aberdeen, Belfast, Birmingham, Bristol, Cambridge, Edinburgh, Exeter, Glasgow, Leeds, Liverpool, Manchester, Newcastle-upon-Tyne, Oxford, St. Andrews, Sheffield and in Wales. Outside the U.K., there is Dublin (see under Section III, Universities p. 130) with Trinity College and the National University of Ireland. For information on these, write to the university concerned or to the British Medical Association for preliminary advice.

Dentistry

Training for a qualification in dentistry in the United Kingdom, that is, a degree (B.D.S.) or a licence (L.D.S.) in dental surgery, must be undertaken at one of the seventeen university dental schools. The course is five or six years in duration but exemption from the first year may be obtained by passing in appropriate subjects (chemistry, physics and biology or zoology) at the advanced level in the General Certificate of Education. The course covers a wide range of subjects, including anatomy, physiology and biochemistry, medicine and surgery and clinical subjects – conservative dentistry, periodontology, orthodontics, oral surgery, local and general anaesthesia and prosthetics, and includes practical and clinical work in the dental hospital associated with the dental school.

There are a number of post-graduate qualifications including university degrees (Master of Dental Surgery, Doctor of Dental Surgery, Doctor of Philosophy in a dental subject) and Fellowships in Dental Surgery of the Royal Colleges of Surgeons of England and Edinburgh. There are five bursaries awarded annually by the Ministry of Overseas Development for post-graduate studies in dentistry to overseas students sponsored by their governments.

A dentist who wishes to practise in the United Kingdom must be registered with the General Dental Council or the General Medical Council. A dentist from overseas who wishes to hold an appointment at an approved hospital in the United Kingdom for the purposes of post-graduate study may be given temporary registration.

For further information apply to:

The General Dental Council, 37 Wimpole Street, London, W.1.

The International Dental Federation, 35 Devonshire Place, London, W.1.

The British Dental Students Association, c/o The British Dental Association, 13 Hill Street, London, W.1.

Publications

Dentistry, from H.M.S.O. Choice of Careers Series, No. 96.

Dentistry – a Career with a Future (published by the General Dental Council).

Facilities for Post-graduate Study in the United Kingdom and *Higher Dental Qualifications* (published by the General Dental Council).

Journals

The British Dental Journal (published by the British Dental Association), two per month.

Under the heading 'Dentistry' are included, besides dentistry itself, workers such as dental technicians, dental hygienists and dental surgery assistants.

For information on ancillary workers apply to:

Dental Technicians: National Joint Council for Dental Technicians, 13 Hill Street, London, W.1.

Dental Hygienists: General Dental Council, 37 Wimpole Street, London, W.1.

Dental Surgery Assistants: British Dental Nurses and Assistants Society, Bank Chambers, 3 Market Place, Poulton-le-Fylde, nr. Blackpool, Lancs.

Pharmacy

It is important to realize that Pharmacy in Great Britain is highly controlled and that there is a fixed national standard. This means that qualification is by taking either a degree in Pharmacy or the Diploma of the Pharmaceutical Society which is equivalent in standard to a degree. No qualifications other than these are recognized. Moreover, reciprocal recognition of qualification between Britain and overseas is declining and students from abroad should therefore make sure of the position before attempting to embark upon a British course. A qualification in pharmacy cannot be obtained by part-time study or by following a correspondence course; full-time attendance as a student at a School of Pharmacy in Great Britain is essential.

There are post-graduate and research courses at certain Universities and at Colleges of Advanced Technology, for which the ordinary entrance requirements must be fulfilled, and every application is considered individually.

For further details, apply to:

The Pharmaceutical Society of Great Britain, 17 Bloomsbury Square, London, W.C.1.

Publication
Pharmacist, from H.M.S.O. Choice of Careers Series, No. 62.

Journals
The Pharmaceutical Journal (published by The Pharmaceutical Society), weekly.
West African Pharmacist (published by J.M.P. Publishing Services), alternate months.

Nursing

Nurses will always be wanted; and in Britain, as in many other countries, there is a shortage of staff in hospitals. Nevertheless, the nursing authorities are rightly concerned to maintain the highest standards in their profession; and the would-be recruit is well-advised to inquire into all the conditions before embarking on a course of training.

For example, a British nursing registration (S.R.N.) is not always recognized in a foreign country, and vice-versa. In some countries there may even be over-employment in this particular field and the nurse, though registered and recognized both in Britain and in her own country, may not find a job awaiting her on return home. There may not be a job available in Britain, either, for an overseas national who asks for one of the higher nursing posts, for which there may be an over-supply of candidates in relation to demand. For these and other reasons, it is in the student's own interest to apply first to the National Nursing Organization of her own country (or it may be, in some countries, the Ministry of Health or other authority) and having discovered the circumstances, if she wants to take a British Training and Registration, to arrange to be properly sponsored.

It may also be of interest to note here that there is well-organized service by the authorities in all countries of international nursing exchange and nurses are able, if they wish, to work in countries other than their own to gain particular skills, within the proviso of registration.

Training in nursing is given in nearly all large hospitals in the United Kingdom. The General Nursing Councils (see addresses below) can supply names of training hospitals and addresses. A registration in nursing may also nowadays be combined with a degree course. In England and Wales minimum age of entry is 18. A General Certificate of Education or equivalent with at least two passes, one of them English, is required, together with a statement from a headmaster or headmistress that a satisfactory level has been attained in five other subjects; *or* the candidate is subjected to a special entrance test. A science subject may also be a help. Some hospitals may like four subjects at 'O' Level, as well as a statement that a satisfactory standard has been reached in Arithmetic.

The basic qualification is State Registered Nurse (following a course of three years in the nursing school of a hospital) with further courses of one or two years available for additional training.

No fees are charged, and in fact a Training Allowance is paid of £365 in the first year rising to £420 in the third year. Residential accommodation including full board is provided at many hospitals, for a set charge of £143 a year, which is deducted from the Training Allowance.

Another source of information on actual jobs in hospitals are the Ministry of Labour offices anywhere in the U.K. These will help in the case of the overseas candidate (e.g. an 'au pair' girl) who is already in the United Kingdom and wishes to obtain employment or training in nursing.

For all further information, write to:

Nursing Recruitment Service, 6 Cavendish Square, London, W.1.

General Nursing Council for England and Wales, 23 Portland Place, London, W.1.

General Nursing Council for Scotland, 5 Darnaway Street, Edinburgh 3.

Royal College of Nursing and National Council of Nurses of the United Kingdom, 1A Henrietta Place, Cavendish Square, London, W.1.

Central Midwives Board for England and Wales, 73 Great Peter Street, London, S.W.1.

Publications
Nursing as a Career, Peggy Nuttall (published by Batsford).
Nursing, Lilian Darnell (published by Hale).
Nursing for Men, from H.M.S.O. Choice of Careers Series, No. 89.
Nursing and Midwifery from H.M.S.O. Choice of Careers Series, No. 82.

Journals
The Nursing Mirror (published by Iliffe), weekly; also advertises appointments.
The Nursing Times (published by Macmillan & Co.), weekly; also advertises appointments.

Further Professions and Vocations Allied to Medicine

For information on training for professions allied to medicine, the following addresses may help:

Audiology
Department of Audiology, Faculty of Medicine, Manchester University.

For Technicians
The Society of Audiology Technicians, c/o St. Helier Hospital, Wrythe Lane, Carshalton, Surrey.

*Chiropody
The Society of Chiropodists, 8 Wimpole Street, London, W.1.

Publication: *Chiropodist* from H.M.S.O. Choice of Careers Series, No. 61.

*Dietetics
The British Dietetic Association, 351 Brompton Road, London, S.W.1. (See 'Home Economics', page 193.)

Medical Laboratory Technology
The Institute of Medical Laboratory Technology, 74 Cavendish Street, London, W.1.

Publication: *Medical Laboratory Technician* from H.M.S.O. Choice of Careers Series, No. 57.

Medical Social Work (*Almoners*)
The Institute of Medical Social Work, 42 Bedford Square, London, W.C.1.

Occupational Therapy
The Association of Occupational Therapists, 251 Brompton Road, London, S.W.3.

Publication: *Occupational Therapist*, from H.M.S.O. Choice of Careers Series, No. 53.

Optical
The British Optical Association, 65 Brook Street, London, W.1.

Dispensing
The Association of Dispensing Opticians, 50 Northumberland Place, London, W.1.

Ophthalmic
The Association of Optical Practitioners, 65 Brook Street, London, W.1.

Publication: *Ophthalmic Optician and Dispensing Optician* from H.M.S.O. Choice of Careers Series, No. 74.

Orthoptic
British Orthoptic Board, Tavistock House (North), Tavistock Square, London, W.C.1.

Publication: *Orthoptist*, from H.M.S.O. Choice of Careers Series, No. 69.

Photography
Medical
Secretary of any large hospital, *or* Institute of British Photographers, 36 Bedford Square, London, W.C.1.

Physics
Hospital Physicists Association, Hammersmith Hospital,

Du Cane Road, Shepherds Bush, London, W.12, or Institute of Physics, Belgrave Square, London, S.W.1.

Physics Technician
National and Local Government Officers Association, 1 York Gate, Regent's Park, London, N.W.1.

Psychiatric Social Work
Association of Psychiatric Social Workers, 1 Park Crescent, London, W.1.

Physiotherapy
The Chartered Society of Physiotherapy, Tavistock Square, London, W.C.1, and The Faculty of Physiotherapists, 29 Waterloo Street, Glasgow, C.2.
Publication: *Physiotherapist and Remedial Gymnast*, from H.M.S.O. Choice of Careers Series, No. 52.

Psychology
British Psychological Society, Tavistock House (south), Tavistock Square, London, W.C.1.

Radiography and Radio Therapy
The Society of Radiography, 32 Welbeck Street, London, W.1.
Publication: *Radiographer*, from H.M.S.O. Choice of Careers Series, No. 41.

Remedial Gymnastics
The Society of Remedial Gynmasts, Physical Medical Department, Northampton General Hospital, Northampton.

Speech Therapy
The College of Speech Therapists, 68 Queen's Gardens, London, W.2,
Publication: *Speech Therapist*, from H.M.S.O. Choice of Careers Series, No. 51.

Health Inspection (for Health Inspection Overseas)
Royal Society of Health, 90 Buckingham Palace Road, London, S.W.1.

Nursery Nursing
The National Nursery Examinations Board, 90 Buckingham Palace Road, London, S.W.1.

For other medical organizations in Britain, see the *Hospitals Year Book* (published by the Institute of Hospital Administration) and the *Medical Directory* (published by J. & A. Churchill Ltd.).

*These professions are now State-registered under the general supervision of the Council for Professions Supplementary to Medicine, York House, Westminster Bridge Road, London, S.E.1.

The Law

The legal profession in England and Wales consists of two quite different branches – solicitors and barristers (and the same division exists in Scotland and in the Republic of Ireland and Northern Ireland). For both branches there are separate systems of training and examination controlled by distinct and autonomous professional bodies.

It is only by completing the prescribed course of professional education and passing the required professional examinations that anyone can become qualified to practice either as a solicitor or as a barrister. A degree in law from a university, whilst of great advantage to a law student, does not entitle anyone to practice law. Neither, with a few exceptions, does a legal qualification obtained overseas.

Moreover, only British subjects may be admitted as solicitors and while this does not preclude one who is not a British subject from following the prescribed courses of professional training, it should be clearly understood that the demand for places in these courses is very heavy – particularly so in the solicitors' branch of the profession. First place therefore is given to those who will be entitled to use their professional qualification, as a practising member of the profession, when they obtain it.

Solicitors

The training of future solicitors falls into two parts: first, a period of practical training as an articled clerk in a solicitor's office, and, secondly, a period of theoretical instruction at a law school in preparation for the Qualifying Examination of The Law Society (The Law Society's Hall, Chancery Lane, London, W.C.2.)

The Qualifying Examination is in two parts and both parts of the Examination are held twice a year. Candidates are required to have a General Certificate of Education in five subjects (including English) with two passes at Advanced Level. Those over the age of 28 may take, instead of the General Certificate of Education Examination, the Law Society's preliminary examination. Students who have a university degree may obtain partial exemption from Part I of the Qualifying Examination and, in the case of law graduates, from the whole of Part I.

Compulsory courses in preparation for the Qualifying Examinations may be taken at the College of Law (in London and Guildford) and at Birmingham, Bristol, Leeds, Liverpool, Manchester and Newcastle-upon-Tyne Colleges of Commerce and at the Nottingham District Technical College. Inquiries should be made to The College of Law, 38 Portsmouth Road, Guildford, Surrey.

Law school training and examination fees amount to about £185 (or in the case of those exempted from Part I of the Examination about £120). Articled clerks may be required to pay a premium to the solicitor to whom they are articled, although, as against that, they will normally be paid a salary during part at least of their period of articled clerkship.

There are various scholarships and bursaries available and particulars of these, as well as information relating to all aspects of training, may be obtained from:

> The Secretary, The Law Society, The Law Society's Hall, Chancery Lane, London, W.C.2.

The details given above apply, at least in general terms, to training for the solicitor's branch of the legal profession in Scotland and the Republic of Ireland and Northern Ireland. Detailed information may, however, be obtained from:

> The Secretary, The Law Society of Scotland, Law Society's Hall, North Bank Street, Edinburgh.
> The Secretary, The Incorporated Law Society of Ireland, Solicitors Buildings, Four Courts, Dublin 7.
> The Secretary, The Incorporated Law Society of Northern Ireland, Royal Courts of Justice, (Ulster), Belfast.

Barristers

Anyone who wishes to read for the Bar has first to be enrolled as a student of one of the four Inns of Court – the governing bodies of the barristers' branch of the profession. All four of the Inns of Court are in London.

The minimum qualification for enrolment as a student is the General Certificate of Education in five subjects (including English) – two of them at Advanced Level. A student of an Inn of Court is required to 'keep terms' at his Inn – eight terms in all. This means, since there are four terms in the legal year, that two years must elapse after a candidate is admitted as a student by his Inn before he can be called to the Bar.

Before call he must also pass the Bar examination which is in two parts: Part 1 may be taken in countries of the Commonwealth. A student who has a university degree in Law and has reached the appropriate standard may claim exemption from certain subjects in the first part of the Bar examination. A student may 'keep terms' at his Inn at the same time as he is reading for a university degree at any university in the U.K.

Courses of lectures and tutorials for students taking the Bar examination are held each year in London only, at the Inns of Court School of Law, at some of the larger technical colleges and colleges of commerce and at The College of Law Ltd., 27 Chancery Lane, London, W.C.1. The body officially responsible for the Bar examination is the Council for Legal Education, Gray's Inn Place, London, W.C.1.

After he has kept the required number of terms at his Inn and passed the Bar examination, a student is eligible for call to the Bar, but before he can practise as a barrister in his home country he may be required to undergo a period of practical training.

Studentship fees payable to the Inn of Court to which a student is attached, tuition and examination fees, and fees associated with call to the Bar amount to approximately £130. In addition a student may be required on registration as such to deposit two sums of money – one of £100 which is returned to the student when he is called to the Bar or if he withdraws before doing so, and another of £50 for call fees.

Information relating to all aspects of training, examination and student membership of an Inn may be obtained from any of the four Inns of Court at the following addresses:

Under-Treasurer and Steward, Lincoln's Inn, London, W.C.2.
Sub-Treasurer, Inner Temple, London, E.C.4.

Under-Treasurer, Middle Temple, 2 Plowden Buildings, Temple, London, E.C.4.

Under-Treasurer, Gray's Inn, 8 South Square, Gray's Inn, London, W.C.1.

Council for Legal Education, Gray's Inn Place, London, W.C.1.

Publication

Law, from H.M.S.O. Choice of Careers Series, No. 26.

Journals

The Law Journal (published by Butterworth), weekly.

The Law Society's Gazette (published by The Law Society), monthly.

Public Administration

Public Administration in Britain includes the Central Government, Local Government, Nationalized Industries and the State-run social services. These public bodies employ a very wide variety of staff, many of whom receive their training in the course of their employment. Such persons do not usually have a formal professional qualification. Those who are professionally qualified cover a very wide range of professions, some of which are not peculiar to the public services, e.g. architects, engineers, doctors. Some professions are, however, exclusive to the public services, e.g. weights and measures inspectors and tax officers, and special institutions exist for them.

For overseas students, administrative training is generally available only for those specifically sponsored by their governments. For professional training, it is necessary to make direct arrangements with the professional body concerned, which may – or may not – cater for overseas students.

It must be emphasized, however, that any course undertaken in Britain should be checked against recognition and suitability for the purposes of qualification overseas.

For further information, apply to the following addresses:

The National and Local Government Officers Association, Nalgo House, 8 Harewood Row, London, N.W.1.

The Local Government Examinations Board, 41 Belgrave Square, London, S.W.1.

The Joint University Council for Social and Public Administration, 218 Sussex Gardens, London, W.2.

N.B. – The Royal Institute of Public Administration, 24 Park Crescent, London, W.1, runs courses for overseas administrators at higher levels, but only by arrangement with governments, and not with individuals.

There are various journals, etc. Inquire from the addresses given above.

Social Service

There are several types of social work. These comprise family case work (helping families in difficulty); child care, including care of the invalid and handicapped; old people's welfare; care of the blind, the deaf; care of people in hospital who are in personal difficulty, i.e. medical social work; moral welfare work; probation officers' work to look after those who have been brought before the courts of law; group work and community organization; youth work; advisory services such as the Citizens' Advice Bureau and Marriage Counsellors, housing management and industrial and personnel welfare.

There are degree and diploma courses in sociology and social studies at the universities and some courses are arranged specially for students from overseas. The most well-known of the latter is at Swansea. For further details on courses apply to:

The Joint University Council for Social and Public Administration, 218 Sussex Gardens, London, W.2.

or to:

The Council for Training in Social Work, Clifton House, Euston Road, London, N.W.1.

Practical short courses in the various branches of social service are organized for overseas students by many of the voluntary bodies. For names and addresses with a brief description of the work they do, see Section 1, National and Voluntary Organizations and Societies, pages 34 to 36.

Publications
Training and Employment in Social Work (published by the National Council of Social Service, 26 Bedford Square, London, W.C.1), price 5s.
Social Workers, from H.M.S.O. Choice of Careers Series, No. 102.

Journal
Social Service Quarterly (published by The National Council of Social Service).

Teaching

Training for teaching in the U.K. is conceived in two halves:

(1) The academic side, in which the student may develop his study of the subject or subjects in which he expects ultimately to teach, i.e. history, mathematics, languages, etc.; (2) The theoretical and practical study of education over the whole period of childhood, including psychology, teaching methods, with some attention to the philosophy and history of education.

With this conception as the basis of the British system, there are then three methods of training open to the student:

(1) He may take a university degree, followed by a one-year post-graduate course at a University Department of Education or at a college of education in order to gain a Diploma in Education or a Post-graduate Teachers' Certificate.
(2) He may take a four-year concurrent course at a College of Education in which he studies for both a Teacher's Certificate and a degree examination at the same time.
(3) He may take a three-year course at a College of Education for a Teacher's Certificate, or if he is an older student and has academic qualifications well above the minimum, he may be considered for a 'shortened' course.

Minimum requirements for entry to courses mentioned under (3) are at least five passes at G.C.E. 'O' Level, but in the case of older and overseas students, other qualifications may be accepted. Candidates wishing to take the four-year concurrent course must make sure they possess the necessary entry and faculty requirements laid down by the university.

In teaching, special arrangements have been made for overseas candidates, principally for Commonwealth students. Under the Commonwealth Bursaries scheme, 400 or more students are accepted each year. To meet their needs, both post-graduate and shortened initial teacher-training courses of approximately one year are provided, chiefly in constituent colleges of Institutes of Education.

Commonwealth students should apply at least one year in advance to the Ministry or Department of Education in their own country, unless they are already in the United Kingdom, in which case they should first apply to their own country's Student Officer or Cultural Officer in London (see pages 28–32).

Foreign students should apply direct to the Central Register and Clearing House, 151 Gower Street, London, W.C.1, for information.

Young British graduates wishing to teach in the Commonwealth for a year or two should apply to The Ministry of Overseas Development, Eland House, Stag Place, Victoria, London, S.W.1., *or* to The Committee on Overseas Service, 26 Bedford Square, London, W.C.1 (see also page 40).

There are certain difficulties in the way of teacher exchange between foreign countries at present, owing to differences of language, salary, etc., but those who are interested should apply to The Department of Education and Science as above *or* The Central Bureau for Visits and Exchange (see page 54).

Publication
 Handbook on Training for Teaching (published by Methuen), Association of Teachers in Colleges and Department of Education. (4th edition, published June 1964.)

Journals
 Education for Teaching (published by Association of Teachers in Colleges and Departments of Education), three per annum.
 Oversea Quarterly (published by Department of Education in Tropical Areas, Institute of Education, University of London).
 Times Educational Supplement (published by Times Publishing Co., Ltd.), weekly; and others.

Home Economics and Domestic Science

Home Economics, which includes teaching, demonstrating and catering for institutions, can be studied both by women and by men. It may lead also to work in dietetics. A good general education, preferably with one or two science subjects in G.C.E., is necessary before making professional studies in cooking, catering and domestic management.

There are three types of training in the U.K. for which requirements vary from a minimum of three 'O' Level subjects for an I.M.A. (Institution of Management Association) Certificate to at least five subjects with two 'A' Levels, for a university degree:

(1) A three-year degree course at a university – for women and men. (See under universities, pages 130–133, Section III)

(2) A three-year course for a Teacher's Diploma at a College of Education (see under Teaching, page 191) – for women only.

(3) One- to four-year courses leading to one of the City and Guilds of London Institute examinations in Domestic Science, which may be taken at a technical college or at a private school teaching Domestic Science – women only.

There are also Post-graduate Courses at London University for the Post-graduate Diplomas in Nutrition and Dietetics, and in Home Economics related to Community Development.

For information on private schools, which give short cookery courses and craft training, apply to the:

Gabbitas-Thring Educational Trust, Sackville Street, Piccadilly, London, W.1, *or to* Truman & Knightley Educational Trust Ltd., 93 Baker Street, London, W.1.

For part-time courses and cookery classes under local authority, apply to the local town hall or institute; in London the Inner London Education Authority booklet, *Floodlight* (obtainable from County Hall, Westminster), sets out part-time courses, but is not available for students overseas.

T—G

For further inquiries, the following addresses may be useful:

The Institutional Management Association, Swinton House, 324 Gray's Inn Road, London, W.C.1.

The Hotel and Catering Institute, 24 Portman Square, London, W.1.

The City and Guilds of London Institute, 76 Portland Place, London, W.1.

The National Council for Domestic Studies, 75 Ferme Park Road, Crouch End, London, N.8.

Ministry of Education, Curzon Street, London, W.1.

British Dietetic Association, 251 Brompton Road, London, S.W.3.

Association of Teachers of Domestic Subjects, Hamilton House, Mabledon Place, London, W.C.1.

Royal Society of Health, 90 Buckingham Palace Road, London, S.W.1.

Publications

Domestic Science and Dietetics, from H.M.S.O. Choice of Careers, New Series, No. 13.

Teaching Housecraft, H.M.S.O. (free from Ministry of Education).

Management in the Hotel and Catering Industry, from H.M.S.O. Choice of Careers Series, No. 15.

Hotel and Catering Occupations from H.M.S.O. Choice of Careers Series No. 33.

Training for Home Management by M. Weddell (published by Routledge).

Journals

Journal of the Institutional Management Association (which advertises appointments, part-time jobs, etc.).

British Nutrition and Dietetics Association Journal – members only.

Home Economics (published for the Association of Home Economists), monthly.

Good Housekeeping Journal (published by National Magazine Co.); and others.

Librarianship

Qualification in Librarianship is obtained by membership and the examinations of the Library Association. Professional examinations are held by this body in two parts. University graduates take a special post-graduate course. In addition, the candidate, to be fully qualified, must have been a member of the Association for three years and have completed a minimum of three years' full-time paid library service under the supervision of a Chartered Librarian. He may then apply to be entered on The Register of Chartered Librarians as an Associate (A.L.A.).

Requirements for entry to Part I of the examinations are G.C.E. or equivalent (see Section III, page 128) with at least five passes, one of which is in English and two of which are at 'A' Level.

Most candidates attend schools of librarianship but it is sometimes possible to get part-time classes in large population centres. There is considerable pressure for places in schools of librarianship, so application should be made not later than January for the following October.

There are also post-graduate diplomas and qualifications in librarianship offered at certain universities, and these exempt from the examinations of the Library Association.

Short introductory courses of about a week in specialized librarianship are run by Aslib, 3 Belgrave Square, London, W.1, for its members. Special courses for overseas students are run by the North-West Polytechnic, Prince of Wales Road, London, N.W.5.

For all further information, apply to:

The Library Association, 7 Ridgemount Street, Store Street, London, W.C.1.

Publications
The Student's Handbook (published by the Library Association).
Librarianship, from H.M.S.O. Choice of Careers Series, No. 4.

Journals
Library Association Record, monthly.

Education Libraries Bulletin (published by University of London Institute of Education), three per annum; and others.

See also Section I, Libraries, page 80.

Theology

The normal method of training for an intending minister in the U.K. is either to take a university degree in a suitable subject followed by a course of training at a theological college of one of the denominations (i.e. a Church College) or to go to a Church College for his full training. There are honours degree courses and general degree courses containing theology at many universities. Universities do not provide professional training. This is given by the Churches in their own colleges.

For details on these and on all courses in religious ministry and in missionary work, candidates should apply to the central educational offices of the Churches: These are:

For the *Church of England*, which is Anglican and is the national Church of England: The Central Advisory Council for the Ministry, Church House, Westminster, London, S.W.1.

For the (*Roman*) *Catholic Church*: The Catholic Educational Council for England and Wales, 41 Cromwell Road, London, S.W.7.

For the *Baptist Union:* The General Secretary, Baptist Church House, 4 Southampton Row, London.

For the *Congregational Union:* The Secretary, Congregational Union of England and Wales, Memorial Hall, Farringdon Street, London, E.C.4.

For the *Methodist Church:* The Ministerial Training Department, 1 Central Buildings, Central Hall, Westminster, London, S.W.1.

For the *Church of Scotland*, which is Presbyterian, and the *National Church of Scotland*: The Secretary, Committee on Education for the Ministry, Church of Scotland Offices, 121 George Street, Edinburgh.

The *Presbyterian Church of England* has offices at: 86 Tavistock Square, London, W.C.1.

Publications

For books, journals, etc., inquire from individual Church Educational Offices.

Seafaring

There are four branches of employment in the British Merchant Navy: (1) 'Deck' or Navigation; (2) Engine Room; (3) Catering; (4) Radio.

This applies equally to officers and ratings. Physical fitness for all branches must be high, and sight tests are required before candidates are accepted for training in navigation. In general, the opportunities for foreigners to serve in the British Merchant Navy are extremely rare and tied to trade union regulations. On the other hand, the facilities for training in navigation, engineering and radio which exist for British seafarers are often available to foreign and Commonwealth students, who may use the certificate of competency gained in Britain for advancement in the Merchant Navies of their own respective countries. In this case, when making the necessary arrangements, for example, for apprenticeship with a shipping company, or in aiming at a post-experience certificate, government sponsorship is an important factor and will help. Aliens are not examined for certificates other than the Second Mate's (foreign-going) in navigation and the Second Class certificate in marine engineering.

For (1) Navigation, the Board of Trade's first certificate of competency, the Second Mate's (foreign-going) Certificate, is issued on examination. The normal British qualification is a four-year apprenticeship at sea, starting at 16 to $17\frac{3}{4}$ years of age. There are a number of nautical schools in the U.K. which provide pre-sea training courses for boys between the ages of 13–17, in whose case the period of apprenticeship at sea may be less.

For (2) Engineering Officers, the Board of Trade's first certificate of competency, the Second Class Engineer's Certificate, is issued on examination to candidates who have taken an Ordinary National Certificate or Diploma in engineering (O.N.C. or O.N.D.) or who have served a full apprenticeship in heavy engineering ashore, combined with practical work and 15 months' experience at sea. There are a number of nautical colleges and engineering or technical colleges with a marine department.

For (3) Catering, training as a cook or chef in a hotel is sometimes required with several years' seagoing experience (for catering, see also page 193). Schools of Nautical Cookery offer short courses leading up to the Board of Trade Ship's Cook's Certificate. Candidates must have worked for at least one year in a ship's galley.

For (4) Radio, qualification is by the Postmaster General's Certificate of Competency in Radio. Instruction is offered in a number of radio colleges, some run by local authorities, some independent, but all authorized by the Postmaster General and recognized by the Department of Education and Science. Only British-born subjects may be employed as Radio Officers in British merchant ships.

Correspondence courses are an important method of studying in seafaring and for information on these, for library services to help with study at sea, and for information generally on training facilities, apply to The Seafarers' Education Service, 207 Balham High Road, London, S.W.17.

Other addresses are:

The Board of Trade, St. Christopher House, Southwark Street, London, S.E.1.

The Shipping Federation, 146–50 Minories, London, E.C.3.

G.P.O. Radio Services Department, Union House, St. Martins le Grand, London, E.C.1.

The Marine Society, Clarks Place, Bishopsgate, London, E.C.2.

Publications

Careers Pamphlets, from H.M.S.O. Choice of Careers Series, Nos. 72 and 73.

The Merchant Navy as a Career by Peter Padfield (published by Batsford, 21s.).

Introduction to the Merchant Navy (published by Seafarers' Education Service, 3s. 6d.)

Board of Trade Leaflets, Nos. M.117 and M.112.

List of Shipowners in the U.K. who engage Navigation Apprentices: Departmental Paper No. 505; and others.

Various journals; inquire from addresses given above.

Civil Aviation

Civil aviation is still a growing profession but there is generally no shortage of staff in Britain. In common with certain other technically advanced countries, Britain assists with the training of personnel for countries where there is still a shortage, as it is the aim of most countries to replace expatriate staff with their own nationals.

Aviation is governed by international standards maintained throughout the world. These are laid down by the International Civil Aviation Organization, 1080 University Street, Montreal 3, Province of Quebec, Canada, whose aims are the development of the principles and techniques of International Air Navigation and fostering the planning and development of International Air Transport.

There are three international aviation languages, English, French and Spanish. The most widely used of these is English and a knowledge of this language is an essential prerequisite for aviation training in the U.K.

Civil aviation personnel can be divided into two main groups, consisting of flying staff – pilots, flight engineers, air stewards and stewardesses – and ground staff. The latter cover a wide range of specialized trades, such as aircraft maintenance engineers, metalworkers, air traffic control officers and assistants, radio maintenance engineers, firemen, airport staff, etc. All of these staff need intensive specialized training.

To become an airline pilot one of three professional licences must be obtained. The basic licence is the Commercial Pilot's licence, followed by the Senior Commercial Pilot's licence and the Airline Transport Pilot's licence. The following training establishments are the only ones approved by the Ministry of Aviation for the training of professional pilots and therefore the only schools where candidates, on successful completion of their Commercial Pilot's licence course, can obtain their first licence. (The other licences can be obtained by taking further tests and by obtaining the necessary additional flying experience.)

Airwork Services Training, Perth Aerodrome, Perth, Scotland.
Oxford Air Training School, Oxford Airport, Kidlington, Oxford.

The London School of Flying, Elstree Aerodrome, Elstree, Herts.

The College of Air Training, Hamble, Southampton, Hants, runs an approved Commercial Pilot's licence course; this school, however, is primarily intended for U.K. students, with a few vacancies for Commonwealth and Colonial students. Applicants for a Commercial Pilot's licence course are usually required to have passed the General Certificate of Education or equivalent in five subjects which include English, Mathematics and a Science subject and preferably including two at Advanced Level. The fees for a Commercial Pilot's licence course in the U.K. at the present time amount to £3,000 or more for a one-year residential course.

For private flying, a Private Pilot's licence must be obtained. This requires fewer hours of flying experience, and the cost of training is about £300 to £400. Many flying clubs in Britain give private training.

For further information, the following addresses may be useful:

The Ministry of Aviation, Shell Mex House, The Strand, London, W.C.2.

The Chief Personnel Officer, British Overseas Airways Corporation, London Airport, Hounslow, London.

The Personnel Officer, British European Airways Corporation, Bealine House, Ruislip, Middlesex.

The Secretary, The British Independent Air Transport Association, 8 Waterloo Place, London, S.W.1.

And addresses already mentioned above and overleaf.

Publications

The Aeroplane Directory of British Aviation (obtainable at most public libraries). From H.M.S.O. Civil Aviation. Choice of Careers Series, No. 116.

And among pamphlets issued by the Ministry of Aviation, 'The Student Pilot's and Private Pilot's Licences'.

Journals

Flight, Aeroplane and others.

Transport

The usual method of achieving qualification is to get a job by applying to one of the transport undertakings and then to study for the Institute of Transport or other examinations. In allocating places to students, the colleges give preference to those with working experience.

Transport is divided into the following principal branches:

Air Transport
  See under 'Civil Aviation', page 199.

British Railways
  For graduate training schemes apply to:

   Director of Training and Education, British Railways, 222 Marylebone Road, London, N.W.1.

For employment and other training schemes: Chief Establishment and Staff Officers of any one of the six Regions of British Railways:

  Eastern Region: Liverpool Street Station, London, E.C.2; *London Midland Region:* Euston Station, London, N.W.1; *North Eastern Region:* Headquarters Offices, York; *Scottish Region:* 302 Buchanan Street, Glasgow, C.2; *Southern Region:* Waterloo Station, London, S.E.1; *Western Region:* Paddington Station, London, W.2.

Industrial Transport
  For large firms, operating their own vehicles, i.e. lorries, ships, barges, even railways, inquiries should be addressed to Company's Personnel or Transport Manager.

Inland Water Transport
  Inquiries to Principal Staff and Establishment Officer, British Waterways, Melbury House, Melbury Terrace, London, N.W.1.

London Transport
  For apprenticeships and garage posts apply to Staff or Welfare Officer, 280 Marylebone Road, London, N.W.1.

For clerical, technical and scientific posts apply to Staff or Welfare Officer, 55 Broadway, London, S.W.1.

Port Administration

Apply for names of independent dock undertakings to Dock and Harbour Authorities Association, 18 Queen Anne's Gate, London, S.W.1; *or to Shipping World Year Book.*

Also the National Dock Labour Board, 22–6 Albert Embankment, London, S.E.11, *or* to Chief Staff and Establishment Officer, British Transport Docks Board, Melbury House, Melbury Terrace, London, N.W.1.

Road Haulage

Names and addresses of hauliers and contractors from *Goods Vehicle Year Book* or *ABC Goods Transport Guide*. For British Road Services, apply to British Road Services Federation Ltd., Melbury House, Melbury Terrace, London, N.W.1.

Road Passenger Transport

A list of bus undertakings can be seen in the *Passenger Transport Year Book*, obtainable through local libraries. Two large firms which operate trainee apprenticeship schemes are the British Electric Traction Company Ltd., Stratton House, Piccadilly, London, W.1; and the Tilling and Scottish Groups: Tilling Group, 215 Great Portland Street, London, W.1; Scottish Omnibuses Group, New Street, Edinburgh.

The Royal Society of Arts, 18 Adam Street, London, W.C.2, also holds examinations for a group certificate in Road Transport.

Shipping

See under 'Seafaring'. For all further details of careers, courses and examinations apply to The Institute of Transport, 80 Portland Place, London, N.W.1.

Publications, including journals: inquire from addresses given above.

Banking

On the east side of London is the small area commonly known as 'the City'. Although it covers only a square mile or so, there can be found here offices or representatives of many of the world's major financial institutions. There is a high degree of specialization, and the outsider may sometimes be surprised to find companies whose sole activity is one which elsewhere would be carried out by, say, a bank department.

The banking system itself contains five main types of institution, whose size varies greatly and whose main functions are quite different.

(1) The Bank of England is the state-owned central bank of the United Kingdom, and acts as banker to the Government and to the other banks. It is the Government's adviser on financial policy and its agent in important financial operations. It undertakes the management of the National Debt and the administration of exchange control.

(2) The 'joint stock banks', or commercial banks, are all public companies with a large number of shareholders. Their main function is the receipt, transfer and encashment of deposits (over 50 per cent of deposits are in the form of credit balances on current account, repayable on demand). This function entails the clearing of vast numbers of cheques and the administration of accounts.

Much of the banks' profit comes from advances to customers, by means of overdrafts or loans, for a wide variety of purposes. They deal in foreign currency for their customers, and their expanding executor and trustee departments offer a wide range of services in connection with the management of estates and investments.

There are eleven clearing banks in all, the biggest of them, with branches throughout the U.K., being known as the 'Big Five': Barclays, Lloyds, Midland, National Provincial and Westminster.

(3) The twelve discount houses, which constitute London's Money Market, are unique in the financial world. Their main business consists quite simply in borrowing the banks' surplus funds on a short-term basis – 'call-money' – and lending it at a profit, chiefly by the purchase of Treasury bills and short-dated government stocks.

(4) The functions of the 'merchant banks' are far-reaching and diverse. One of their main concerns is the financing of

imports and exports to and from Britain by the 'acceptance' of bills of exchange. Some of them specialize in the provision of medium- and long-term finance for overseas governments and institutions, in foreign exchange dealings, insurance and investment management.

Another group of merchant banks – the issuing houses – are experts in transactions connected with the capital structure of companies.

(5) The last group is formed by the Post Office Savings Bank and the Trustee Savings Banks. The former is one of the largest organizations of its type in the world, with over 22 million active accounts. The trustee savings banks are local banks, about eighty in number, which also cater mainly for the small investor and have some 9 million active accounts.

All banks in this group deal on behalf of their customers in government securities and all forms of national savings.

Education and Training

Terms of service and recruitment into banking vary widely from one bank to the next, and details should be obtained direct from the institution in question.

New entrants into the joint stock banks usually undergo a formal period of training in their early days, with frequent transfers between departments and courses at the banks' own training centres, designed to equip them with the basic techniques as early as possible.

They are encouraged at the same time to study for the Diploma of The Institute of Bankers, mainly in their own time, through classes at the technical colleges or through correspondence courses. (Anyone interested may obtain further details from the Institute at 10 Lombard Street, London, E.C.3.)

Occasionally some of the banks run short courses for overseas bankers and students, by arrangement with banks in the countries concerned.

Publications

The British Banking System, H.M.S.O. (published by Central Office of Information).

Banking and the Stock Exchange, from H.M.S.O. Choice of Careers Series, No. 67.

Journals
   Institute of Bankers Journal, alternative months; and others.

Accountancy

An accountant may work in public practice as a member of a professional firm which specializes in auditing, accounting and all kinds of financial advising, or he may be employed in an office as accountant or secretary to a commercial company or public department.

Training takes about five years (less in the case of university graduates). It combines theoretical study with practical experience of office work (frequently under 'articles of clerkship', i.e. apprenticeship, in a firm of practising accountants). Salaries are paid during training. A premium is rarely asked.

The examination and other regulations of the various professional bodies differ. They should be consulted (see names and addresses below). The professional bodies may also be able to advise on a firm which will offer practical experience, but they do not guarantee to place candidates.

Minimum entry requirements are a good pass in G.C.E. in five subjects including English and Mathematics. Some of the bodies require a higher minimum standard. Training is usually started on leaving school or after graduation.

Some universities provide degree courses in which accountancy is a main subject of study, but graduates still have to acquire practical experience and take at least the Final Professional Examination. Preparation for the professional examinations is by correspondence course or in some cases by attendance at technical colleges. For further details of conditions of entry, experience and examinations, and on methods of study, apply to:

The Institute of Chartered Accountants in England and Wales, City House, 56–66 Goswell Road, London, E.C.1.

The Institute of Chartered Accountants of Scotland, 27 Queen Street, Edinburgh 2; *and* 218 Vincent Street, Glasgow C.2.

The Institute of Chartered Accountants of Ireland, 7 Fitzwilliam Place, Dublin 2.

The Association of Certified and Corporate Accountants, 22 Bedford Square, London, W.C.1.

The Institute of Cost and Works Accountants, 63 Portland Place, London, W.1.

The Institute of Municipal Treasurers and Accountants, Buckingham Place, London, S.W.1.

N.B. – The first four bodies provide a general qualification in all branches of accountancy.

The other two give particular emphasis to cost accounting and accounting in local government respectively.

Apprenticeship to a chartered accountant in practice is essential in the first three cases.

The other bodies will accept approved employment in industry, commerce or local government.

For the overseas student, the nature of accountancy and of the conditions of training raise the following problems:

(1) The demand for apprenticeship or approved employment exceeds the supply of places, so it is difficult to get a place.

(2) Arrangements for a place cannot usually be made unless the candidate is available for interviews.

(3) Although study is concurrent with employment, the training is long and the salary too small for a student away from home to live on. Therefore, the student must make sure that he will have sufficient other funds to maintain himself for the full training period of five years.

Publications

Monthly journals produced by each of the professional bodies named above. Also a weekly journal, *The Accountant* (published by Gee & Co. Ltd.)

The Accountant, from H.M.S.O., Choice of Careers Series, No. 59.

Insurance

Insurance in the U.K. consists mainly of insurance companies, Lloyd's underwriters and insurance brokers, and it is divided into four main classes: Accident, Fire, Life, and Marine. State social insurance, covering health, pensions and unemployment, is administered through government departments. 'Lloyd's' is a society, the only one of its kind, which undertakes insurance risks from all over the world. A number of overseas nationals from Europe and America as well as from the developing countries undergo training for periods from six months to two years with employers in Britain. Employers give preference to their own overseas staffs or to those who are officially sponsored by foreign insurers or governments.

The normal insurance qualifications are the Diplomas of the Chartered Insurance Institute, the examinations for which can be studied in many parts of the world. Details of overseas tuition courses and examination centres, may be obtained from The Secretary, Chartered Insurance Institute, 20 Aldermanbury, London, E.C.2.

The minimum age of entry is 16 and a General Certificate of Education (or accepted equivalent) in five subjects is required. The Institute's Associateship Diploma may be taken in any of the various branches of insurance and is designed to take three years. A further two years' study would normally be required to obtain the Fellowship Diploma.

For those who have worked in insurance abroad, have passed Part A of the qualifying examination and have the recommendation of their insurance employers, the C.I.I. operates a training scheme for overseas students. Places are limited and preference is given to students who apply from abroad.

In 1965 four five-week advanced insurance courses (two in life assurance and two in general insurance) were offered at the C.I.I. College of Insurance for overseas students who were sponsored by their employers. It is anticipated that these courses will be held again in 1966.

In addition to the C.I.I.'s tuition courses, correspondence courses are available in the U.K. from the Metropolitan College, St. Albans. Insurance classes are also held in many commercial colleges throughout the country. The costs in each case are small.

For all further information, write to The Chartered Insurance Institute, address as above, or to The Corporation of Insurance Brokers, 3 St. Helens Place, London, E.C.3.

Publications
   Insurance from H.M.S.O., Choice of Careers Series, No. 94.
   From the C.I.I.: *The Journal* (published annually); *Overseas Tuition Prospectus, Examination Handbook.*

Management Studies

A 'management course' does not, as with Engineering or Medicine, set out to produce a professionally qualified man, a 'manager'. However, the modern problem of working in increasingly large organizations has produced a demand for studies in this field. To meet the pressure, there are many courses in the U.K., dealing with background subjects such as economics, sociology and law, as well as with relevant and specialized techniques such as computor and quantitative analysis, preparing for automation, trade union negotiation, etc.

Courses may be divided into three groups:

Undergraduate: Business studies incorporated into or forming part of a degree course.

Post-graduate: One-year courses of introduction to Industry.

Post-experience: Short courses for practising managers.

Some universities and technical colleges and, for senior executives only, independent colleges such as the Administrative Staff College, Henley-on-Thames, Ashridge, and certain consultancy firms provide one or other of these courses.

For all further information apply to: The British Institute of Management, Management House, 80 Fetter Lane, London, E.C.4.

The British Institute of Management is not an examining body.

Publications

A Conspectus of Management Courses (published by B.I.M.).

Advanced examinations of a specialized kind and intended for candidates preparing for management, are held by a number of professional bodies. A particular note is, however, required of the following:

Purchasing

This demands a knowledge of business organization, statistics, control and storage of stock, transport, accounting and law. Highly advanced examinations on these subjects are set by: The Purchasing Officers' Association, York House, Westminster Bridge Road, London, S.E.1.

It must be emphasized that a good knowledge of English is

essential and some previous commercial experience before attempting one of these courses. The Purchasing Officers' Association will shortly also require that overseas students shall be sponsored by their firms before registering for examination courses.

Marketing and Export

Involves a wide familiarity with market research, evaluation techniques, distribution and the principles underlying advertising and promotion activities, for which a knowledge of economics, statistics, law and accounting is considered essential.

The qualifying examinations are set by: The Institute of Marketing, Richbell Place, Lamb's Conduit Street, London, W.C.1.

The examiners stress the importance of a good standard of written English and a previous qualification, including this subject, is required for candidates proceeding to the final papers.

Approved courses of instruction for both of the above qualifications are provided by most local authority Technical Colleges and postal tuition of a high standard is also available.

The Institute of Export, 14 Hallam Street, London, W.1, examines in export practice, marketing overseas, international trade and payments, commercial geography, insurance of export cargoes, the law of carriage of goods, etc. Requirements for registration are G.C.E. in at least three subjects and a bona-fide intention of making a career in export. Examinations are held once a year at centres throughout the United Kingdom and, where necessary, throughout the world. Preparation is normally available at local Colleges of Commerce or Technology or by correspondence.

Three further important institutes in management holding advanced examinations for which considerable practical experience and a good knowledge of English is required, are:

(1) The Institution of Works Managers, 34 Bloomsbury Way, London, W.C.1.

The courses deal with production management, its planning, organization control, and with the use of modern techniques. They also include economics, law, human relations and communications.

(2) The Institute of Personnel Management, 80 Fetter Lane, London, E.C.4.

This body does not itself run courses of training for a career in Personnel Management, but it co-operates with many universities and technical colleges who offer courses. The Institute has an Overseas Company Service Scheme which offers to overseas companies an information service and short courses of training for practising Personnel Officers.

(3) The Institute of Office Management, 167 Victoria Street, London, S.W.1.

This body awards diplomas either by examination or exemption for students at an advanced level who already hold a suitable qualification, e.g. in clerical work or in business studies. It awards certificates for Associate Membership at a less advanced level in office supervision and in 'O' and 'M'. Its other services include information, research and the organization of residential courses.

For further details and publications, journals, etc., apply to the institutions as above.

N.B. – Public Administration does not, for the purposes of this book, come into the same category as Business and Industrial Management and is dealt with on page 189. To complete the sphere of Management, the professional bodies in Accountancy and Company Secretaryship (see below) should also be noted.

Company Secretaryship

Every commercial or industrial company is required by law to have a secretary. He has special duties and responsibilities to the company, to the investor and to the Government. He must know something about accountancy, economic theory, and the law relating not only to the Companies Act of his own national government, but to local government, the nationalized industries, co-operative societies, etc.

There are two professional bodies which examine in company secretaryship:

The Chartered Institute of Secretaries, 14 New Bridge Street, London, E.C.4.

The Corporation of Secretaries, Devonshire House, Devonshire Street, London, W.1.

The Chartered Institute of Secretaries is primarily a Commonwealth body and one half of its members and students are overseas. Arrangements for study and examinations are made in many overseas countries.

The Corporation of Secretaries also has special arrangements and conditions for overseas candidates. It has a number of overseas registrars, including one in Western Europe.

Full details of the services and facilities, examinations and syllabus, etc., may be obtained from the two bodies at the addresses given above.

Part-time and a few full-time courses are available at technical and commercial colleges throughout the country: details from the colleges themselves or from the local authority (see list, page 136). For preparation by correspondence course, see page 147.

Publication

Company Secretary, from H.M.S.O., Choice of Careers Series, No. 29.

Journals from the professional bodies as named overleaf.

Advertising and Public Relations

Advertising can provide a good career for those who are prepared to work hard. Opportunities can be found in agencies which place their clients' advertising in what are called 'media' (press, posters, television, etc.), and in the advertising departments of large companies and advertisement departments of media owners.

Although the advertising industry handles about £500 million of business anually, the number of people employed is not very large. Consequently vacancies for trainees are limited.

There are two examining professional bodies:

The Advertising Association, 1 Bell Yard, London, W.C.2.

Institute of Practitioners in Advertising, 44 Belgrave Square, London S.W,.1.

These, at present, combine in examinations at the Intermediate Level. To some extent studies overlap with marketing, but some branches of advertising work, such as 'media' planning, copywriting and research, are highly specialized and need special training.

Full-time and part-time courses are run at some Technical

and Commercial Colleges and correspondence courses by International Correspondence Schools. There are no University courses at present, but Chairs of Marketing are now being established at London and Lancaster Universities.

Courses and Examinations in Public Relations, i.e. in the establishment and maintenance of all relations between an organization and its public, are arranged by The Institute of Public Relations, Templar House, 81–7 High Holborn, London, W.C.1.

Publications
Advertising from H.M.S.O., Choice of Careers Series, No. 44.
Journals from the professional bodies as named here.

General Commercial and Secretarial Training for Girls

General Commercial and Secretarial work involves business correspondence, English, typing, shorthand, book-keeping and accounts, arithmetic, office techniques and practice generally – sometimes also language interpreting. All these subjects can be studied separately or in comprehensive courses, part-time or full-time by men or women. For women, however, a secretarial training is generally necessary to get a start in a career in commerce or industry. The Technical Colleges and local Evening Institutes provide established courses and there are many private schools which specialize in commercial and secretarial training. There should be no difficulty for the average student, providing his English and general standard of education is adequate, either from home or overseas, in finding a course suited to his or her needs or in preparing for a qualification which will be widely recognized. For employment either during or after training, overseas students should study the Home Office regulations (Section I, pages 46–52).

Application should be made to school or college direct. Age and entry requirements depend upon the particular establishment which the student chooses. There are no fixed rules. For advanced courses, a good G.C.E., including English, is usually essential. In the case of the student whose native tongue is not English, it is usual to have a pass in one of the Cambridge Examinations or equivalent (see Section II, page 115).

The length of a very intensive course for a native English speaker can be as little as 15 weeks; for a general course for an overseas student, poor in English, one year or more.

Costs at a Technical College may be very small, about £30 a year for tuition; at a privately-owned school anything from £75 a year (average £90) depending on the course and whether day-time or residential. These costs do not include books which may cost as much as £6 for a full secretarial course.

The advantages of a Technical College are the low fees with good tuition; the disadvantages are that entry is usually at the beginning of September only each year, that there is no adjustment of classes, which are larger, sometimes with 30 students or more; by comparison the private schools have regular and irregular intakes and can give more individual attention.

The following institutions award certificates to successful students from the elementary stage upwards in commercial arithmetic, book-keeping, geography, commercial English, etc., as well as in typing and shorthand:

> Pitman Examinations Institute, Pitman House, nr. Godalming, Surrey (with centres in all countries abroad).

> The London Chamber of Commerce, 69 Cannon Street, London, E.C.4 (with centres in many countries abroad, mainly Commonwealth).

> The Royal Society of Arts, 18 Adam Street, Adelphi, W.C.2 (with centres in some countries abroad, mainly Commonwealth).

There are a number of other examining boards in general commercial and secretarial training, local to parts of Britain. It will also be included as a subject in the Certificate of Secondary Education, but shorthand and typewriting are not included in G.C.E.

Most private schools award their own diplomas and these also are often widely accepted.

There are also National Certificate or Diploma courses in Business Studies, arranged by the Technical or Commercial Colleges in conjunction with the Department of Education and Science.

Among the best known non-residential private training schools are:

> Pitman's College, 154 Southampton Row, London, W.C.1.

Clark's College, 126 Chancery Lane, London, W.C.2.
Skerry's College, 13 Bath Street, Glasgow, C.2.

These schools have a number of branches, and will provide all details and addresses on request.

For all private schools, a few of which are residential, lists and information can be obtained free of charge from such private agencies, or consultants as:

Gabbitas-Thring Educational Trust Ltd., 6–8 Sackville Street, Piccadilly, London, W.1.
Truman & Knightley Educational Trust Ltd., 93 Baker Street, London W.1.

For information on Technical and Commercial Colleges under local authority, and on Evening Institutes, see Section III, pages 134–135, and under Section V, Central Areas, for some of the local addresses, also for the London area, the Inner London Education Authority publication *Floodlight* for part-time courses.

Publication
Office Work from H.M.S.O., Choice of Careers Series, No. 65.

Journals
Business Education; Overseas Commercial Teachers' Review; Office Practice; Shorthand Teachers Supplement (Pitman publications).

Journalism

Most countries have a system of journalistic training based on Schools of Journalism or University Faculties of Journalism, but since 1945 the British newspaper industry has organized its own Training Scheme – The National Scheme. The main difference between the two methods is that the 'Schools of Journalism' system accentuates the theory and the general educational background, whereas the British method, based on apprenticeship in a newspaper office or news agency, puts the emphasis on training 'on the job'. The former is a training for journalists in the sense that the students hope to become journalists after their training, whereas the National Scheme is for training journalists already employed as such. It is important to remember, therefore, that under the British system the trainee must already be earning his living as a working apprentice journalist before he can be registered as a trainee at all. The scheme is operated by the National Council for the Training of Journalists and since 1961 the training scheme has been compulsory for all new entrants to provincial newspapers in England and Wales. Neither the National Council nor any other organizations can help to find anyone employment in the profession and the only way to become a journalist is by persuading an editor or free-lance employer to offer employment as a trainee journalist. The present minimum educational requirements are three 'O' Level passes in G.C.E. (shortly to be raised to five 'O' Levels) and as most newspapers have more applicants than there are vacancies they can, therefore, give priority to local candidates. About 400 new entrants – a fifth of them girls – join provincial and London suburban newspapers each year and over a thousand young journalists are undergoing training in the National Scheme at any one time.

Full particulars of the Scheme can be obtained from The Director of the National Council for the Training of Journalists, 6 Carmelite Street, London, E.C.4.

The Thomson Foundation has established a training centre for overseas journalists at Cardiff where three courses are held annually and to which the Foundation offers twelve scholarships. The aims of the course are to cover all journalist techniques – reporting, feature writing, sub-editing, typography and layout – supplemented by lectures in ancillary subjects. Candidates must be over 21 years of age with a minimum of three years' employment as a staff journalist on a newspaper, magazine, or news agency. They must be fluent English-speaking journalists, of either sex, and the employees of Government-owned journals are not excluded provided they otherwise satisfy the qualifications prescribed. Applications must be sponsored by the newspaper or periodical for whom the candidates work and must be made to the Director of The Thomson Foundation, 9 John Street, London, W.C.1. The Foundation also offers a limited number of fellowships for senior overseas journalists to enable them to pursue specialist studies in the United Kingdom.

Pre-entry Training

The Polytechnic, 307–11 Regent Street, London, W.1, offers a pre-entry course of a year's duration. The course includes:

Practical Journalism, British Life and Institutions, a modern language, and Shorthand and Typing. In addition to lectures, the course includes practical work, visits to newspaper offices and lectures by specialists engaged in the different branches of newspaper production. A Diploma is awarded to successful students. The number of students is limited to 25 a year and about a third of the places is reserved for Commonwealth students.

It should be emphasized that there is no pre-entry training in Journalism which would exempt candidates from the Proficiency Test or from the examination required for the National Diploma referred to above.

Publications

  Handbook of Training, National Council for the Training of Journalists.

  Journalism from H.M.S.O. Choice of Careers Series, No. 83.

Journal

  World's Press News and Advertising Review (published by World's Press News Publishing Co. Ltd.), weekly.

Printing

Printing is a very big industry in Britain employing a great number of people. Letterpress, Lithography and Photogravure are the names of the three principal methods. Within the industry there is a great variety of skilled occupations, each requiring special training. Since most of the processes include colour printing, it can be a serious disadvantage if you are colour-blind.

If you are an overseas student, you should have a good knowledge of English, for it is almost impossible to do any printing by British methods without it.

You should also apply to a college before coming to Britain. Printing is taught in three types of school: (1) Large Printing Colleges such as the London College of Printing; (2) Technical Colleges with Printing departments; (3) Colleges of Art with Printing departments. Most of them are prepared to take overseas students, but applications for admission should be made in advance to ensure that candidates are qualified for entry and that a place is available.

Where apprenticeship is concerned, a British firm will not normally agree to accept an overseas student unless he has cleared his position with the appropriate trade union(s) first. For this purpose he must become a member of a printing union in his own country. It is then possible that he will be accepted on a temporary basis in Britain.

Special academic qualifications are not always required, though special aptitudes and abilities are essential. Courses in printing schools in art and technical colleges usually lead to examinations of the City and Guilds of London Institute. The British Federation of Master Printers (which is the printing employers' association) conducts correspondence courses in printing administration and the colleges offer courses in printing crafts and management. There is also the Institute of Printing which sets examinations leading to full professional status.

For further information, apply to: The Institute of Printing, 44 Bedford Row, London, W.C.1, *or to* The British Federation of Master Printers, 11 Bedford Row, London, W.C.1.

Publications
   Craftsmanship in the Printing Industry (price 9d., post paid, from Joint Industrial Council of the Printing and Allied Trades, 11 Bedford Row, London, W.C.1).
   Choice of Careers Series: from H.M.S.O.
       Printing, No. 43.
       Composing Room Crafts, No. 46.
       Machine Room Workers, No. 47.
       Graphic Reproduction Processes, No. 48.
       Bookbinding and Printers' Warehouse Work, No. 49.

Journal
   British Printer (published by Maclean-Hunter, Ltd.), monthly.
   For further information on Select Bibliography in Printing, apply to the B.F.M.P. as above.

Art and Design

The world of art has two main divisions, Fine Art and Design.
   The Fine Arts, chiefly painting and sculpture, are taught in specialized form by the Slade School of Art of London University, by the Royal Academy School, by the Royal College of Art, and by many centres elsewhere. Full-time courses for the Diploma in Art and Design are offered and there are also part-time courses, sometimes only for recreational purposes, at the Technical Colleges and evening institutes.

Design covers the industrial and commercial application of art in such spheres as textiles, furniture, ceramics, jewellery, engineering, graphic design, fashion, etc., also typography, print-making and film and television. At the centre of Design is the independent Royal College of Art, but all over the country there are local authority art schools preparing candidates for the Dip.A.D., which is equivalent to a first degree.

There are also teacher-training colleges and small private schools specializing in Art. Several of the Universities now have courses in Fine Art, both practical and historical, leading to a degree or diploma.

On the Design side, employment may be found for the really gifted, British or foreign. Employers may even recruit for their design offices and workrooms among students who have not yet completed their studies. On the Fine Art side, students must be sure that they can have sufficient means to support themselves properly before they undertake a full-time course which is often quite exacting, with teaching at the end as possibly the only certain means of livelihood.

For the principal colleges, students should apply nearly a year in advance. Requirements are G.C.E. or equivalent, including English, the submission of work, some previous art school training, personal recommendations if possible and competitive entrance examinations in some cases.

At some colleges there are arrangements for international exchange, short courses and for special entrants from abroad.

The following addresses may be useful:

Council of Industrial Design, 28 Haymarket, London, S.W.1.

Council of Industrial Design, Scottish Committee, 46 West George Street, Glasgow C.2.

The National Council for Diplomas in Art and Design, 24 Park Crescent, London, W.1.

Royal Academy of Art, Burlington House, Piccadilly, London, W.1.

Slade School of Fine Art, University College, Gower Street, London, W.C.1.

Royal College of Art, Kensington Gore, London, S.W.7.

St. Martin's School of Art, Charing Cross Road, London, W.C.2.

Central School of Arts and Crafts, Southampton Row, London, W.C.1.

Chelsea School of Art, Manresa Road, London, S.W.3.

Hornsey School of Art, Crouch End Hill, London, N.5.

Publication
Art and Design, from H.M.S.O. Choice of Careers Series, No. 103.

Journal
Design Magazine (published by Council of Industrial Design), monthly; and others.

Music

Training in Music is given mainly by a number of specialist Colleges of Music. In London, the Royal Academy of Music, the Royal College of Music, Trinity College of Music and the Guildhall School of Music and Drama. University Degrees in Music, D.Mus., and B.Mus. are granted by many universities. Training for Degrees and recognized diplomas may also be had at some Colleges of Technology.

Entrance requirements may vary with different colleges and depend to a large extent and in the first place on personal recommendation from a suitable specialist authority. Normally the principal colleges take advanced students only and require candidates to pass a high selective audition test. In the case of candidates applying from abroad, this would mean first, recommendation and examination by a representative of the British Council or other authority acting as agent, and all applications should be made through the Government Education Department. Courses last from three years full-time to any length, also part-time training may be had at some colleges.

Graduate qualifications, G.R.S.M. (Graduate of the Royal Schools of Music) at the Royal Academy of Music and the Royal College of Music, G.T.C.L. (Graduate of Trinity College of Music), G.G.S.M. (Graduate of Guildhall School of Music) may be awarded following a three-year continuous course. Successful graduate students may enter for a further training as teachers for one year at the University of London Institute of Education, Malet Street, London, W.C.1, or a similar institution in other universities and, if successful, will be awarded the Teacher's Certificate of the University.

Students may enter the Royal Schools and Trinity College of Music as undergraduates of the University of London to read for a Degree in Music. Special arrangements are made for post-graduate students, depending on their field of study. Faculties of Music in many universities provide facilities for reading music. In London the University of Music is based on King's College, Strand, London, W.C.2. Courses are also provided by some Ministry of Education and Science Teacher-Training Colleges.

Publications
   Music, from H.M.S.O. Choice of Careers Series, No. 101.
   Various journals and magazines.

Cinema

There is no national school for training in the British Cinema Industry. There are two private schools which give courses of six months to a year, but as their resources are limited, not all branches of film-making can be taught at advanced levels. They are:

   The London School of Film Technique, 24 Shelton Street, London, W.C.2.
   The Overseas Film and Television Centre, 109–123 Clifton Street, London, E.C.2.

Many technical schools give courses in photography, some even in 16 mm. cinematography.

The Polytechnic, Regent Street, London, W.1, gives a year's instruction in cinematography and also part-time and evening classes.

The Royal College of Art (see under Specialist Colleges, page 143) has a three-year course in design, which includes instruction in film-making but does not cover branches of the industry such as camera work, sound engineering or script-writing. The Slade School of Art, London University, has a department in research and theoretical studies. Other schools and colleges are developing studies in film-making, and a national school may emerge some day.

None of the above schools can guarantee entry into the industry and at the moment apprenticeship to a studio is still the method of training for many. However, this is difficult for two reasons: (*a*) it requires membership of the cinema trade union,

The Association of Cinema and Television Technicians. This is not easy to obtain, since there is a good deal of under-employment in the film world. (b) Film companies make films in separate units. They do not offer continuous employment and only occasionally contracts. There is a certain amount of recruitment to the cinema from television where apprenticeship and employment are easier, and from the top of other professions such as the theatre, writing, etc.

For further information, write to one of the addresses above or to: The British Film Institute, 81 Dean Street, London, W.1.

This latter is not a school but a cultural body which runs the National Film Theatre, holds The National Film Archive and can offer library and research facilities and information for theoretical studies.

Owing to the divided nature of training facilities for the cinema in Britain, all students, but particularly those from overseas, are strongly advised to make the fullest inquiries before taking any steps.

Publications

The Film Maker and His World (A Young Person's Guide), by R. J. Minney (published by Victor Gollancz).

Photography and Cinematography, from H.M.S.O. Choice of Careers Series, No. 115.

Journal

British Kinematography, British Kinematography Society; monthly.

Television

Entry into Television

Television in the U.K., as it is indeed in many other countries, is at once an open field and a closed shop.

It is an open field because in rare cases one can gain entry into it with little or no television qualifications at all, and it is a closed shop because apart from those rare cases, entry into the world of television is almost as difficult as it is into the film world.

The field can, in any case, be divided into two broad sections:

(a) Engineering (including transmission) and all allied aspects.
(b) Production and all allied aspects.

Engineering

Entry into the field of television engineering can be gained through:

(1) University qualifications in physics, electronics, electrical engineering, etc., supplemented by some practical training.

(2) Polytechnic courses leading to diplomas or degrees in the subjects mentioned in (1) followed by practical training.

(3) The City and Guilds of London Institute qualifications in telecommunications and electronics, etc.

(4) B.B.C. engineering courses (mainly designed for B.B.C. staff).

(5) The General Post Office ('G.P.O.') courses for its own staff.

(6) In certain cases, limited and specialized training can be obtained at the training centres of Marconi and Pye.

Production

(1) From time to time the B.B.C. or one of the commercial television companies invite applications for trainee directors and a number of those accepted for training are young men or women of obvious abilities with no television background at all. This number, which does not exceed a dozen in any one year, represents the rare cases to which reference has been made above. Normally trainee director/producers are recruited from among those working on the floor, as it were – floor managers, cameramen, production assistants, etc.

(2) In the early stages of television in the U.K., before the television industry was well enough established to provide its own way to the top, just about the only sources from which television director/producers could be recruited were radio, the cinema and theatre. Nowadays there is much less call for outside talent, and it is only the eminent among stage or film director/producers who are likely to be invited by the B.B.C. or the commercial television companies to produce on television.

(3) A number of private organizations offer courses in television production, but it would be difficult to assess the chances of gaining entry into television after attending any of these courses.

Television Training for Overseas Students

Training for overseas candidates who intend to work on television in their own countries is provided by:

(1) The Thomson Foundation Television College, where two courses are held every year and to each of which the Foundation offers eighteen scholarships: Kirkhill House, Newton Mearns, Glasgow, Scotland.

Training at the Thomson College falls into three main categories:

(a) Station technical maintenance;
(b) Studio operations (switching, camera, microphone and telecine operation, simple 'sound on film' shooting, editing and processing, simple design and captions, lighting, vision and sound mixing, etc.);
(c) Production, direction, programme planning, administration advertising.

(2) The B.B.C., Broadcasting House, Regent Street, London, W.1.

(3) Centre for Educational Television Overseas (C.E.T.O.), which confines its training to Educational Television: The Studio, Nuffield Lodge, Regent's Park, London, N.W.1.

(4) Television courses are now offered by a number of British universities. The most established courses are offered by Bristol University.

(5) Limited courses in certain aspects of television are offered by The Royal Academy of Dramatic Art, 62 Gower Street, London, W.C.1.

Conditions for joining any of the above-mentioned courses, whether in engineering or production, vary considerably from course to course.

Journal

Film and TV Technician, Association of Cinematograph, Television and Allied Technicians Trade Union Journal, monthly.

Drama

Training in all branches of theatre work is given at drama schools, most of which are independent. Entry is competitive and by audition. There are no fixed educational requirements, except for courses for teachers of drama, although a good knowledge of English is essential and, in the case of overseas students, personal recommendation from a suitable authority, also. For teaching in drama, a degree course at a university or a course in teacher-training is available.

The following addresses may be useful:

Royal Academy of Dramatic Art, 62–4 Gower Street, London, W.C.1.

The Guildhall School of Music and Drama, John Carpenter Street, Victoria Embankment, London, E.C.4.

Central School of Speech and Drama, Embassy Theatre, Swiss Cottage, London, N.W.3.

The Rose Bruford Training College of Speech and Drama, Lamorbey Park, Sidcup, Kent.

The Webber-Douglas School of Singing and Dramatic Art, 34 Clareville Street, London, S.W.7.

Italia Conti Stage School, Avondale Hall, Landor Road, Stockwell, London, S.W.9.

Corona Stage School, 26 Wellesley Road, Chiswick, London, W.4.

British Drama League, 9 Fitzroy Square, London, W.1.

Royal Scottish Academy of Music, College of Dramatic Art, St. George's Place, Glasgow.

Publications

Drama by Eric Capon (published by Batsford).

Dramatic Art, from H.M.S.O. Choice of Careers Series, No. 98.

See also *Dancing*, from H.M.S.O. Choice of Careers Series, No. 99.

Journal

Stage and Television To-day (published by Carson & Comerford Ltd.), weekly.

Section V

Main Centres of Study

T—H

Main Centres of Study

Bath, Somerset

Bath (population 80,865), Britain's oldest and most famous Spa. Roman Baths, Hot Springs, Pump Room, Assembly Rooms, Museums of Costume, Abbey. The most perfect example of an eighteenth-century city in existence. Most of the squares and crescents have remained unaltered with the original interior decoration.

EDUCATION

Bristol College of Science and Technology (to be given university status in 1966. Shortly moving to Bath).

Technical Colleges, etc.
Bath Academy of Art, Corsham Court, Corsham, Wilts.
Bath College of Education (Home Economics) Sion Hill Place, Bath.
Newton Park College of Education, Newton St. Loe, nr. Bath.
City of Bath Technical College, Lower Borough Walls, Bath.
City of Bath Technical School, Brougham Hayes, Bath.

Private School of English for Foreign Students.
Bath Language Centre, 13 Russell Street, Bath.

ACCOMMODATION, HOSPITALITY, SOCIAL CLUBS AND SOCIETIES

Full details of all clubs and societies are obtainable from:

✣ Information Bureau, Abbey Churchyard, Bath.

For information on historical monuments and museums, sport and entertainment, and also for publications, apply to the Information Bureau.

Birmingham, Warwickshire

Second largest city in Britain after London (population 1,106,040); road and railway centre with many factories mostly connected with the metal trade. Its chief products are motor-cars and accessories, hardware, jewellery, electrical equipment, brass foundry and tools.

It is situated near the beautiful Cotswold countryside, not far from Shakespeare's birthplace, Stratford-upon-Avon, with its Royal Shakespeare Theatre.

EDUCATION

University of Birmingham. Founded 1900. Students 5,300 (1964), approximately 8 per cent overseas.

Faculties: Arts, Commerce, and Social Science, Law, Medicine, Science and Engineering.

Technical Colleges, etc.

College of Advanced Technology (University of Aston in Birmingham, designate), Gosta Green, Birmingham 4.

Birmingham College of Food and Domestic Arts, Brasshouse Passage, Birmingham 1.

Birmingham College of Art and Crafts, Gosta Green, Birmingham 4 and Margaret Street, Birmingham 3.

College of Commerce, Gosta Green, Birmingham 4.

Aston Technical College, Whitehead Road, Birmingham 6.

Hall Green Technical College, Stratford Road, Birmingham 28.

Handsworth Technical College, Goldshill Road, Birmingham 21.

Brooklyn Technical College, Aldridge Road, Birmingham 22A.

Garretts Green Technical College, Garretts Green Lane, Birmingham 33.

Matthew Boulton Technical College, Suffolk Street, Birmingham 1.

Erdington Technical College, Edward Road, Birmingham 24.

City of Birmingham College of Commerce, Birmingham 4.

Selly Oak College, 998 Bristol Road, Birmingham 29.

South Birmingham Technical College, Bristol Road South, Birmingham 31.

For other information about these and other places of education, apply either to the Principal of the College, or to:

The Overseas Students' Office, The British Council, 120 Colmore Row, Birmingham 3; *or to:*

The Chief Education Officer, Council House, Margaret Street, Birmingham 3.

ACCOMMODATION

Hotels

For a list of hotels and boarding-houses see booklet *Birmingham Accommodation and General Information*, obtainable from:

✠ The Information Department, Council House, Victoria Square, Birmingham 1.

Boarding-houses

Prices range from £4 10s. per week with all meals except lunch on weekdays. Names and addresses may be found through Accommodation Bureaux and Clubs.

Hostels and Residential Clubs

Central Y.M.C.A., Snow Hill, Birmingham 4; with two branches.

Central Y.W.C.A., Stone Road, Birmingham 15; with seven branches.

Christian Alliance of Women and Girls Residential Club, 29 Portland Road, Edgbaston, Birmingham 16.

HOSPITALITY, SOCIAL CLUBS AND SOCIETIES: apply to:—

British Council, 120 Colmore Row, Birmingham 3.

Central Y.M.C.A., Snow Hill, Birmingham 4.

Erdington Y.M.C.A., Reservoir Road, Birmingham 23.

Northfield Y.M.C.A., Bunbury Road, Northfield, Birmingham 31.

Birmingham Y.W.C.A. House, 1 Stone Road, Birmingham 15.

Y.W.C.A. Area Office, 3 Stone Road, Birmingham 15.

Hagley Grove Y.W.C.A., 50–6 Hagley Road, Birmingham 16.

Edencroft Y.W.C.A., 64 Wheeley's Road, Edgbaston, Birmingham 15.

Y.W.C.A., 74–6 Alcester Road, Birmingham 13.

Fallowfield Y.W.C.A., 29 Norfolk Road, Birmingham 15.

Five Ways Y.W.C.A., Ladywood Road, Edgbaston, Birmingham 16.

Moncrieff Y.W.C.A., 65–6 Wheeley's Road, Edgbaston, Birmingham 15.

Birmingham Council of Social Service, 161 Corporation Street, Birmingham 3.

The East and West Friendship Council, 37 College Road, Birmingham 32.

International Friendship League, 163 Buryfield Road, Solihull.

Erdington Branch, I.F.L., 108 Wyrley Road, Witton, Birmingham 6.

Methodist International House, 52 Oakfield Road, Selly Park, Birmingham 29.

Rotary Clubs – British Council.

Toc H is a fellowship of men: 6 Wake Green Road, Moseley, Birmingham 13.

Townsend Club, 65 Church Street, Birmingham 3.

Central Council of Physical Recreation, 256 Moseley Road, Birmingham 12; for information about sporting activities.

CENTRAL POLICE STATION

Steelhouse Lane, Birmingham 4.

ALIENS REGISTRATION OFFICE

Birmingham City Police, Council House Extension, Edmund Street.

LOST PROPERTY

Steelhouse Lane, Birmingham 4.

Losses on Corporation buses: Miller Street Garage, Aston, Birmingham 6.

EMPLOYMENT

Ministry of Labour, 281 Corporation Street.

See also Employment, Section I, pages 46–52.

PUBLIC LIBRARIES

Central Library and Reference Library, Ratcliff Place; and branches throughout the City.

Technical Library, Ratcliff Place.

Commercial Library, Council House Extension, Great Charles Street, Birmingham 3.

The Birmingham Collection, Ratcliff Place.

MUSEUMS

City Museum and Art Gallery, Congreve Street, Birmingham 3.

Museum of Science and Industry, Newhall Street, Birmingham 3.

The Barber Institute (Art Gallery and Recitals of Music).

The University, Edgbaston, Birmingham 15.

Shakespeare Memorial Library: Central Reference Library, Ratcliff Place.

Aston Hall, Blakesley Hall, Yardley.

The Birmingham Corporation Information Department, The Council House, Birmingham, publishes guides, pamphlets and sketch maps, including a Plan of the City Centre; *What's On In Birmingham* (published weekly) and *Accommodation and General Information*.

For information on sport of all kinds, music and concerts, theatres, cultural activities, and entertainments, and for publications, apply to: The Information Department, Council House.

Bournemouth, Hampshire

Bournemouth (population 154,296) is a favourite resort both in summer and winter on account of its mild climate. It has recently become a centre for English Language schools.

EDUCATION

Technical Colleges, etc.

The Bournemouth Municipal College of Technology and Commerce, Lansdowne, Bournemouth.

The Bournemouth Municipal College of Art, Lansdowne, Bournemouth.

Private Schools of English for Foreign Students

Anglo-Continental School of English, 33 Wimborne Road, Bournemouth.

A.V.E.A. Summer School, 278A Holdenhurst Road, Bournemouth.

English Language Summer Schools, Ellerslie Chambers, 2 Hinton Road, Bournemouth.

European Education Centre, 26 Dean Park Road, Bournemouth.

Gresham School of English, 489 Charminster Road, Bournemouth.

King's School of English, 58 Braidley Road, Bournemouth.

Kingsnorth Academy, 53 Old Christchurch Road, Bournemouth.

Scanbrit School, 20 Church Road, Southbourne, Bournemouth.

ACCOMMODATION

Boarding-houses
  Names and addresses may be found from:
✠ The Official Information Bureau, Westover Road.

Hostels and Residential Clubs
  The Ladies' Residential Club, 24 and 26 Poole Road.
  Y.M.C.A., Westover Road.

POLICE STATION AND ALIENS REGISTRATION OFFICE, ALSO LOST PROPERTY

  Bournemouth Borough Police (Headquarters), Madeira Road.

EMPLOYMENT

  Ministry of Labour, Yelverton Chambers, Yelverton Road.
  Youth Employment Office, Punshon Memorial Office, Exeter Road.
  See also Employment, Section I, pages 46–52.

PUBLIC LIBRARY

  The Central Public Library, Lansdowne, Meyrick Road; and branches.

MUSEUMS AND MONUMENTS

  The Russell-Cotes Art Gallery and Museum, Russell-Cotes Road.

Rothesay Museum, 11 Bath Road.

For information on sport of all kinds, hospitality, theatres and entertainment, and for publications, apply to: The Official Information Bureau, address as given overleaf.

Brighton, Sussex

The largest and most popular seaside resort within easy reach of London (population 162,910) on the edge of the Sussex Downs; sea views, good air and many facilities for residents' entertainment and comfort. The most important sight is the astonishing Pavilion, built by King George IV in an eccentric oriental style. Brighton also possesses some beautiful eighteenth-century houses.

EDUCATION

University of Sussex.

Faculties: Social Studies, European Studies, English and American Studies, African and Asian Studies, Mathematical and Physical Sciences, Arts, etc.

Technical Colleges, etc.

Brighton College of Technology, Lewes Road, Moulscoomb, Brighton 7.

Brighton Technical College, Richmond Terrace, Brighton.

Brighton College of Art, Grand Parade, Brighton.

Brighton College of Education, Eastern Terrace, Brighton.

Private

Educational Arts School, 37 Millers Road, Brighton.

Gregg School, 69 Montpelier Road, Brighton.

Hove Secretarial College, 61 Portland Road, Hove 3; and others.

ACCOMMODATION

Boarding-houses

Names and addresses may be found from Y.W.C.A. or Y.H.A., or The International Friendship House, 46–8 Marine Parade, Brighton.

Hostels and Residential Clubs
> Y.W.C.A., Regency House, Oriental Place, Brighton 1.
> Y.H.A., Patcham Place, Brighton 6.
> Y.M.C.A., 55 Old Steine, Brighton 1.

HOSPITALITY, SOCIAL CLUBS AND SOCIETIES

Names and addresses from:
✠ The Brighton Information Office, Royal York Building, Old Steine, *and* King's Road (summer only), *and* Central Library, Church Street.

POLICE STATION AND ALIENS REGISTRATION OFFICE, ALSO LOST PROPERTY

Police Station, Market Street.

EMPLOYMENT

Ministry of Labour Employment Exchange, Crown House, 21 Upper North Street, Brighton.
See also Employment, Section I, pages 46–52.

PUBLIC LIBRARY

Central Library, Church Street, consists of lending, reference and children's library.

MUSEUMS AND MONUMENTS

The Royal Pavilion Estate.
The Willett Collection of English Pottery.
Early and Modern English Water-colours.
The A. C. Spencer Collection of early Musical Instruments – all in Church Street.
The Booth Bird Museum, Dyke Road.
The Rudyard Kipling and Toy Museum, The Grange, Rottingdean.
The Motor Museum, Aquarium.

For information on sport, theatres and entertainments of all kinds, and for publications, apply to The Brighton Information Office, address as given above.

Bristol, Somerset

A handsome old city, a manufacturing town, and seaport (population 433,920). It is situated on the River Avon, about 7 miles from the Bristol Channel. It does a large Atlantic trade, importing grain, provisions, mineral oils, tobacco leaf, timber and wood pulp; most important industries: tobacco, chocolate, aircraft, engineering, printing, boots and shoes. Many beautiful churches, particularly St. Mary Redcliffe.

EDUCATION

University of Bristol (approximately 4,650 students, including 318 from abroad).

Faculties: Arts, Engineering, Medicine, Law, Science.

Institutes of Education, Agriculture, Domestic Science and Theology. School of Management Studies.

Technical Colleges, etc.

Bristol College of Science and Technology, Ashley Down, Bristol 7. (To become University of Bath, 1966.)

Bristol Technical College, Ashley Down, Bristol 7.

Bristol Theological College, Stoke Hill, Bristol 9.

Bristol College of Commerce, Unity Street, Bristol 1.

West of England College of Art, Queens Road, Bristol 8.

Redland College, Redland Hill, Bristol 6.

Private

Bristol Modern Office Training College, Linden Road, Bristol 6; and other secretarial schools.

ACCOMMODATION

Boarding-houses

A list can be obtained from: The City Public Relations Office, Council House, College Green, Bristol 1; *or at:*

✠ The City Information Bureau, City Centre, Bristol 1.

Hostels and Residential Clubs

Y.M.C.A., Colston Street, Bristol 1.

Y.W.C.A., 102 Pembroke Road, Clifton, Bristol 8.

Y.W.C.A., 15 Berkeley Square, Clifton, Bristol 8.

G.F.S. Hostel, 2–3 Arlington Villas, Clifton, Bristol 8.

Youth Hostels Association, Thorpe Lodge, Cotham Side, Bristol 6 (open to members only).

Methodist International House, Rodney House, Clifton Down Road, Bristol 8.

HOSPITALITY, SOCIAL CLUBS AND SOCIETIES

Apply to: The British Council, 7 Priory Road, Tyndall's Park, Bristol 8; *or to:* The City Information and Advice Bureau, The City Centre, Bristol 1.

POLICE STATION AND ALIENS REGISTRATION OFFICE, ALSO LOST PROPERTY

Bridewell, Bristol 1.

EMPLOYMENT

Ministry of Labour, Regional Office, Bridge House, Bristol 8.

Employment Exchange, 20 Nelson Street, Bristol 1.

Youth Employment Service, Old Library, King Street, Bristol 1.

See also Employment, Section I, pages 46–52.

PUBLIC LIBRARY

The Central Library, College Green, Bristol 1; and branches.

MUSEUMS AND MONUMENTS

The City Museum and The City Art Gallery, Queen's Road, Bristol 8.

Bristol Cathedral.

The Cabot Tower on Brandon Hill.

The Suspension Bridge.

St. Mary Redcliffe Church.

St. John's Church and Gateway.

The Red Lodge in Park Row, and the Georgian House.

(See Town Guide for surrounding area.)

For information on sport of all kinds, cultural activities, theatres and entertainment, and for publications, apply to The City Information Bureau, address as given above.

Cambridge, Cambridgeshire

A city dominated by its University although, like its twin, Oxford, it has industries too, such as Pye Radio and Electrical Works. Its ancient colleges are famous for the beauty of their setting on the River Cam. King's College Chapel, the Great Court of Trinity and the Senate House are particularly worth seeing; also the Fitzwilliam Museum, one of the largest and richest museums outside London. At Ely, 16 miles from Cambridge, there is a beautiful medieval cathedral. The population of Cambridge is approximately 98,390. As at Oxford, there are several English Language schools outside the University.

EDUCATION

In 1318 Cambridge received from Pope John XXII formal recognition as a *Studium Generale* or *Universitas.*

Faculties: Classics, Divinity, English, Fine Arts, Modern and Medieval Languages, Music, Oriental Studies, Economics and Politics, History, Law, Moral Sciences, Engineering, Geography and Geology, Physics and Chemistry, Agriculture, Archaeology and Anthropology, Biology A and B, Medicine.

Technical Colleges, etc.
Cambridge College of Arts and Technology, Students' Guild, Collier Road, Cambridge.

Private
Bell School of Languages, 1 Red Cross Lane, Cambridge.
Davies' School of English, 69 Bateman Street, Cambridge.
Fereday School of English, 4 Trumpington Street, Cambridge; and others.

ACCOMMODATION

Boarding-houses
Names and addresses may be found from: The Information Bureau at the City Reference Library, Y.M.C.A., *or* Y.H.A.

Hostels and Residential Clubs
Y.H.A., 97 Tenison Road, Cambridge.

HOSPITALITY, SOCIAL CLUBS AND SOCIETIES: apply to:

British Council, 1 Portugal Place, Cambridge.

✠ Information Bureau, City Reference Library (behind Guildhall), Market Hill, Cambridge.

Youth Hostels Association, 97 Tenison Road, Cambridge.

Cambridge Association for Social Welfare, 9 Petersfield, Cambridge.

Cambridge International Club, 2 Falcon Yard, Cambridge.

International Centre, 14 Trinity Street, Cambridge.

POLICE STATION AND ALIENS REGISTRATION OFFICE, ALSO LOST PROPERTY

Police Station (Headquarters), St. Andrew's Street, Cambridge.

EMPLOYMENT

Ministry of Labour, Employment Exchange, Brookland's Avenue, Cambridge.

See also Employment, Section I, pages 46–52.

PUBLIC LIBRARY

Central Library, Wheeler Street, Cambridge; *also:*

Central Lending Library, Reference Library and Information Bureau.

County Library, Shire Hall, Cambridge.

MUSEUMS AND MONUMENTS

Archaeology and Ethnology Museum, Downing Street, Cambridge.

Sedgwick Museum of Geology, Downing Street, Cambridge.

Scott Polar Research Institute, Lensfield Road, Cambridge.

Folk Museum, Castle Street, Cambridge.

Cambridge and County Folk Museum, 2–3 Castle Street, Cambridge.

The Fitzwilliam Museum, Trumpington Street, Cambridge.

Museum of Classical Archaeology, Little St. Mary's Lane, Cambridge.

For information on sport, cultural activities of all kinds, theatres, concerts, etc., apply to The Information Bureau, City Reference Library.

Canterbury, Kent

Canterbury (population 31,030) is the seat of the Archbishop of Canterbury, and the centre of the Anglican Church. Its magnificent Cathedral is one of the largest Gothic structures in Christendom and has perfect medieval glass. On account of the murder here of St. Thomas à Becket, it was for hundreds of years a great pilgrim shrine. It has also Roman remains, a garden-like countryside, corn, cattle and vegetable markets, and general market.

EDUCATION

University of Kent at Canterbury. Charter granted 1964. Collegiate system proposed.

Christchurch Teachers' Training College, North Holmes Road, Canterbury.

Technical Colleges, etc.

Canterbury Technical College, New Dover Road, Canterbury.
Canterbury College of Art, St. Peter's Street, Canterbury.

Private

St. Giles School of Languages, St. Alphage Lane, Canterbury.

ACCOMMODATION

Boarding-houses

Names and addresses may be obtained from:

✠ Entertainments Publicity Department, 2 Marlowe Avenue, Canterbury; *or:*

National Assistance Board Area Office, 71 New Dover Road.
Y.H.A., New Dover Road, Canterbury.

Hostels and Residential Clubs

Oddfellows Canterbury District Office, Club and Institute, 15 Orange Street, Canterbury.

East Kent Federation of Women's Institutes, 24 St. Margaret Street, Canterbury.

HOSPITALITY, SOCIAL CLUBS AND SOCIETIES: apply to:

British Red Cross Society, Lower Chantry Lane, Canterbury.
Rotary Club, County Hotel, Canterbury.
Canterbury Corporation, Municipal Building, Canterbury.
Boy Scouts Association, Sturry Road, Canterbury.
International Hebrew Christian Alliance, Doreden, 18 Nelson Crescent, Ramsgate.
East Kent Federation of Women's Institutes, 24 St. Margaret Street, Canterbury.
W.V.S., 2 Castle Street, Canterbury.

POLICE STATION AND ALIENS REGISTRATION OFFICE, ALSO LOST PROPERTY

Rhodus Town, Canterbury.

EMPLOYMENT

Ministry of Labour, Employment Exchange, St. John's Lane, Canterbury.
Youth Employment Bureau, 78–9 London Road, Canterbury.
See also Employment, Section I, pages 46–52.

PUBLIC LIBRARY

Royal Museum and Public Library, High Street, Canterbury.

MUSEUMS AND MONUMENTS

Royal Museum and Public Library, High Street, Canterbury.
The Slater Art Gallery.
Canterbury Cathedral.
Tower House and Westgate Gardens.
St. Augustine's Abbey and Ruins.
Buffs Museum, 21A Stour Street, Canterbury.
Westgate Tower Museum, Westgate, Canterbury.
Roman Pavement, Burgate Lane, Canterbury.
Norman Castle, Castle Street, Canterbury.

For information on sport, cultural activities and entertainments, apply to The Entertainments Publicity Department, address as given above.

Colchester, Essex

Colchester is the oldest city in Britain, originating in Centic times. It is a historic Roman site and garrison town as well as an agricultural centre (population 65,072). The oyster fisheries on the River Colne are famous.

EDUCATION

University of Essex, Wivenhoe Park, Colchester. Opened 1964. *Faculties:* Social Studies, Physical Sciences.

Technical Colleges, etc.
North-East Essex Technical College and School of Art, Sheepen Road, Colchester.

ACCOMMODATION

Boarding-houses
Names and addresses may be obtained from:
✤ The Town Clerk's Office, Colchester.

Hostels and Residential Clubs
Y.H.A., East Bay House, Colchester.

HOSPITALITY, SOCIAL CLUBS AND SOCIETIES: apply to:

Colchester Club, D'Arcy House, Culver Street.
Colchester Co-operative Society Ltd. (Education Department), 6 Newtown Road, Colchester.
British Red Cross Society, 30 East Stockwell Street, Colchester.

POLICE STATION AND ALIENS REGISTRATION OFFICE

Police Headquarters, Queen Street, Colchester.

PUBLIC LIBRARY

Shewell Road, Colchester.
For information on employment, historical monuments, museums, sport and entertainment, apply to The Town Clerk's Office, address as given above.

Coventry, Warwickshire

Coventry is an ancient city, important both in history and in industry (population 330,000). Largely rebuilt in contemporary style, owing to war damage, it has a famous modern Cathedral with stained glass and sculpture. Centre of motor-car and other industries.

EDUCATION

University of Warwick. Incorporated 1964, is under construction on a site three miles from the centre of Coventry.

First-degree subjects will be arranged in Schools of Art, Science (including Engineering) and Social Science.

Technical Colleges, etc.
Lanchester College of Technology, Priory Street, Coventry.
Coventry College of Art, Cope Street, Coventry.
Coventry Technical College, The Butts, Coventry.
Henley College of Further Education, Bell Green, Coventry.

ACCOMMODATION

Details from:
✛ Public Relations Officer, Council House, Coventry.

Boarding-houses
Names and addresses from Public Relations Officer, Council House, Coventry, *or* Citizens' Advice Bureau.

Hostels and Residential Clubs
Y.W.C.A., New Oxford House, Corporation Street, Coventry; *also:* Sherbourne House, The Butts, Coventry.
Y.M.C.A., 10 Quadrant, Warwick Road, Coventry.

PUBLIC LIBRARY

Gulson Central Library, Trinity Churchyard, Coventry.

HOSPITALITY, SOCIAL CLUBS AND SOCIETIES

Details from:

Municipal Information Bureau, Council House, Coventry.

Citizens' Advice Bureau, St. Mary Street, Coventry.

British Legion, Warwick County Committee, 1 Dalton Road, Coventry.

General Charities Office, Old Bablake, Hill Street, Coventry.

United Nations Association, 3 Grosvenor House, Grosvenor Road, Coventry.

POLICE STATION AND ALIENS REGISTRATION OFFICE, ALSO LOST PROPERTY

Police Headquarters, Little Park Street, Coventry.

EMPLOYMENT

Ministry of Labour, Cheylesmore, Coventry.

See also Employment, Section I, pages 46–52.

MUSEUMS AND MONUMENTS

The Coventry Cathedral.

The Chapel of Unity.

The Herbert Art Gallery and Museum, Jordan Well, Coventry.

For information on sport of all kinds, theatres including repertory, cultural activities and entertainment, apply to The Public Relations Office, address as given overleaf.

City of Durham

On a peninsula almost surrounded by the River Wear (population 22,740), with a Norman Cathedral and Castle. The cathedral is one of the most impressive in England.

EDUCATION

University of Durham. Founded 1832, approximately 5,000 students, 7 per cent from abroad.

Faculties: Arts, Education, Music, Science, Theology.

Technical Colleges, etc.
    Durham Technical College, Framwellgate Moor, Durham.
    School of Agriculture, Houghall, Durham.

ACCOMMODATION

Boarding-houses
    Names and addresses may be obtained from: The Town Clerk,
32 Claypath, Durham.

Hostels and Residential Clubs
    . None.

INFORMATION

    The Town Clerk's Office, 32 Claypath, Durham.
    National Assistance Board, 2 Ravensworth Terrace, Durham.

POLICE STATION AND ALIENS REGISTRATION OFFICE, ALSO LOST PROPERTY

    Police Office, Old Elvet, Durham.

EMPLOYMENT

    Ministry of Labour, Local Office, Saddler Street, Durham.
    See also Employment, Section I, pages 46–52.

LIBRARIES

    South Street, Durham.
    Cathedral Library.
    St. Chad's College Library.

MUSEUMS AND MONUMENTS

    Durham Castle.
    Durham Cathedral.
    Gulbenkian Museum of Oriental Art, Elvet Hill Road, Durham.
    For information on hospitality, sport and entertainment apply
to The Town Clerk's Office, address as given above.

Exeter, Devonshire

Exeter, the county town of Devon (population 80,321). Interesting and historic city, with an old Cathedral and a market.

EDUCATION

University of Exeter. Established 1955, University precinct covering 250 acres. Approximately 2,450 students, 10 per cent from abroad.

Faculties: Arts, Law, Science and Social Studies, Institute and Department of Education.

St. Luke's College. A residential training college for schoolmasters. Approximately 750 students.

Technical Colleges, etc.
Exeter Technical College, Hele Road, Exeter.
Exeter College of Art, Gandy Street, Exeter.

Private
International School of English, 1 Mount Radford Crescent, Exeter; and others.

ACCOMMODATION

Boarding-houses
Names and addresses from:
✠   The Information Bureau, 18 Queen Street, Exeter.
The Warden, Y.W.C.A., Grendon Road, Exeter.

Hostels and Residential Clubs
Y.W.C.A., Grendon Road, Exeter.
Y.H.A., Mount Wear House, Countess Wear Road, Exeter.

HOSPITALITY, SOCIAL CLUBS AND SOCIETIES: apply to:

British Council, Brookfield, New North Road, Exeter.
Official Publicity and Information Bureau, 18 Queen Street, Exeter.

British Red Cross Society, 60 St. Leonard's Road, Exeter.
Devon and Exeter Institution, 7 Cathedral Close, Exeter.
Exeter Council of Social Service, 2 Waterbeer Street, Exeter.
International Friendship League, 'Kendon', Oakfield Avenue, Crediton, Exeter.
Y.M.C.A., 41 St. David's Hill, Exeter.

POLICE STATION AND ALIENS REGISTRATION OFFICE, ALSO
LOST PROPERTY

Central Police Station, Heavitree Road, Exeter.

EMPLOYMENT

Ministry of Labour, 74 Queen Street, Exeter.
See also Employment, Section I, pages 46–52.

LIBRARIES

Public Library, Castle Street, Exeter.
County Library, Barley House, St. Thomas, Exeter.
Law Library, Cathedral Close, Exeter.

MUSEUMS AND MONUMENTS

The Cathedral and Old Buildings in Cathedral Close.
Northernhay Gardens under the site of the old Castle with City War Memorial and other monuments.
Guildhall.
Museum and Art Gallery in Royal Albert Memorial Museum, Queen Street, Exeter.
Historic Underground Passages, off High Street.
St. Nicholas Priory.
City Walls, partly from Roman times.
For information on sport and entertainment and for publications, apply to The Official Publicity and Information Bureau, address as given overleaf.

N.B. – Also at Plymouth (see map):

The Plymouth College of Technology, Students' Union, Tavistock Road, Plymouth.
For information apply to:
⚜ Municipal Offices, Civic Centre, Plymouth.

Hull (Kingston-upon-Hull), Yorkshire

The City and County of Kingston-upon-Hull has a population of over 300,000 and is pleasantly situated in a predominantly rural area.

Hull is Britain's third largest port and first fishing centre. It has the largest cod-liver oil installation in the world. Other principal industries are chemicals, paint manufacturing, engineering, ship repairing, timber (second only to London for importation of soft-woods), and pharmaceuticals.

EDUCATION

University of Hull. Number of students 1965–66: 3,100. Notable for its admission of overseas students.
Faculties: Arts, Sciences, Social Sciences and Law.
Centre for South-East Asian studies.

Technical Colleges, etc.

Chief Education Officer, Education Department, Guildhall, Hull; for all information concerning Local Education Authority Courses.
College of Technology, Queen's Gardens, Hull.
College of Commerce, Brunswick Avenue, Beverley Road, Hull.
Regional College of Art and Crafts, Anlaby Road, Hull.
College of Education, Cottingham Road (next to University), Hull.
Endsleigh Training College (R.C.), Beverley High Road, Hull.

Private

Gregg School (Hull) Ltd., 80 Beverley Road, Hull.
(Commercial and general courses.)

ACCOMMODATION
Boarding-houses

Can be found in the Classified Section of the Telephone Directory under 'Hotels' and 'Hotels – Private Boarding Establishments', or from:

✛ City Information Service, Central Library, Albion Street, Hull, which provides an up-to-date list free of charge.

Hostels
   Y.W.C.A. House, Princes Avenue, Hull.
   International House, 96–8 Westbourne Avenue, Hull.

HOSPITALITY, SOCIAL CLUBS AND SOCIETIES: apply to:
   British Council, 7 Newland Park (near University).
   Hull Incorporated Law Society, Bowlalley Lane, Hull.
   Hull Literary and Philosophical Society, c/o 10 Parliament Street, Hull.
   Young People's Christian and Literary Institute ('Y.P.I.'), 83–93 George Street, Hull (sports, games, etc.).
   Hull and East Riding Amateur Athletic Ground, Chanterlands Avenue North, Hull (rugby, squash, badminton, etc.).
   Hull Junior Chamber of Commerce, Samman House, Bowlalley Lane, Lowgate, Hull.

POLICE STATION AND ALIENS REGISTRATION OFFICE
   Central Police Station, Queen's Gardens, Hull.

LOST PROPERTY
   General: Central Police Station.
   Transport: Paragon Station, *or* Central Bus Station, Ferensway.

EMPLOYMENT
   Ministry of Labour, Employment Exchange, Market Place, Hull.
   Youth Employment Services, Union Street, Albion Street, Hull.
   See also Employment, Section I, pages 46–52.

PUBLIC LIBRARY
   Central Library, Albion Street, Hull.
   Lending, record, technical and commercial, reference, and local history libraries. News reading-room.
   Branch libraries in various parts of the city.

MUSEUMS AND MONUMENTS

Wilberforce House, High Street, Hull.

Georgian Houses, High Street.

Transport Museum and Mortimer Collection, High Street, Hull.

Maritime Museum, Pickering Park, Hull.

St. Mary the Virgin, Lowgate; Holy Trinity, Market Place; both built in the fourteenth century.

Art Gallery, City Centre, Queen Victoria Square, Hull.

General Post Office (site of Suffolk Palace).

Wilberforce Monument, Queen's Gardens (site of Queen's Dock).

Ye Olde White Harte, Silver Street, Hull (approximately 400 years old).

High Street, Old Hull (previously home of merchants, etc.).

Trinity House, Trinity House Lane, Hull.

For surrounding area apply to:

City Information Service, Central Library, Albion Street, Hull.

For information on sport, concerts, and cultural activities and for publications apply to The City Information Service, address as given overleaf.

Keele and North Staffordshire

The area of the County of Stafford north of the town of Stafford forms a centre in itself, comprising Stoke-on-Trent, the Boroughs of Burton-upon-Trent and Newcastle-under-Lyme, and the neighbouring rural districts.

Stoke is in the centre of the area known as 'The Potteries', long famous for its ceramics industry. Keele is a village two miles west of Newcastle-under-Lyme.

EDUCATION

University of Keele. Charter 1962. Originally founded as University College of North Staffordshire 1949. Unique features include residence for all students and staff; four-year course for B.A. includes some science, some non-science for all (Studies in Humanities, Science, Social Science; first (foundation), year course of background to the modern world is common to all students).

Numbers 1965–66: 1,150 undergraduates, 100 post-graduate students.

Enquiries to the Registrar, The University, Keele, Staffs.

Technical Colleges, etc.

Stafford College of Technology, Beaconside, Stafford.

North Staffordshire College of Technology, Stoke-on-Trent.

Burton-upon-Trent Technical College, Burton-upon-Trent.

Newcastle-under-Lyme School of Art and Crafts, 7 Sidmouth Avenue, Newcastle.

Stafford College of Further Education, Stafford.

School of Art and Crafts, Waterloo Street, Burton-upon-Trent.

College of Art, Queen Street, Burslem.

College of Commerce, Stoke Road, Shelton, Stoke-on-Trent.

College of Building, College Road, Shelton, Stoke-on-Trent.

The Elms Technical College (for women), Cauldon Place, Shelton, Stoke-on-Trent.

For further general information on the area, apply to:

The Town Clerk's Office, Derwent House, The Brampton, Newcastle-under-Lyme; *or to:*

Civic Information Service, Public Library, Union Street, Burton-upon-Trent; *or to:*

Town Clerk's Office, Borough Hall, Stafford.

Lancaster, Lancashire

Lancaster (population 47,860) is the ancient county town of Lancashire; historical associations; Castle and Cathedral and museum; a new university opened 1964. It is well situated between the Yorkshire Dales, Lake District and with seaside towns near by.

EDUCATION

University of Lancaster. Charter granted 1964. Collegiate system.

St. Martin's College of Education, Bowerham, Lancaster. (Church of England Teacher Training College.)

Technical Colleges, etc.

The Lancaster and Morecambe College of Further Education, Torrisholme Road, Lancaster.

College of Arts and Crafts, Storey Institute, Lancaster.

Private

Lancaster Commercial College, China Street, Lancaster; and others.

ACCOMMODATION

Boarding-houses

Names and addresses may be obtained from:

The Lancaster League of Help and Citizens' Advice Bureau; *or*

The Lancaster Corporation (Town Hall).

HOSPITALITY, SOCIAL CLUBS AND SOCIETIES: apply to:

Lancaster Charities, 16 Castle Park, Lancaster.

Lancaster League of Help and Citizens' Advice Bureau, Church Street, Lancaster.

Lancaster and Morecambe Students' Association, Torrisholme Road, Lancaster.

Lancaster and District Congregational Council, 38 Derwent Road, Lancaster.

Rotary Club, c/o The Cross Keys Hotel, Market Street, Lancaster.

Youth Advisory Committee, High Street, Lancaster.

Boy Scouts Association, 55 Arnside Crescent, Morecambe.

Women's Evening Institutes, Queen Street, Lancaster.

Red Cross Society, 16 Hala Grove, Lancaster.

POLICE STATION AND ALIENS REGISTRATION OFFICE, ALSO LOST PROPERTY

Lancaster Police Station, at the Centre and Skerton.

EMPLOYMENT

Ministry of Labour, King Street, Lancaster.

The Youth Employment Office, Arndale House, King Street, Lancaster.

See also Employment, Section I, pages 46–52.

PUBLIC LIBRARY

The Central Library, Market Square, Lancaster.

MUSEUMS AND MONUMENTS

The Lancaster Museum and The King's Own Regimental Museum (in old Town Hall).

The Lancaster Castle.

The Priory and Parish Church.

The Cathedral.

For information on sport, cultural activities and entertainments, and for publications, apply to The Town Hall.

Leeds, Yorkshire

Leeds, on the River Aire, is a city of comparatively modern development, but of great industrial importance. Centre of the English making-up trade, woollen cloth factories and engineering works; population approximately 508,790.

EDUCATION

University of Leeds. Originally part of Victoria University, Manchester, established independently in 1904. Apply to Registrar or to Warden of Overseas Students.

Faculties: Arts, Economics, Social Studies, Law, Science, Technology, Institute of Education, Medicine and Dentistry.

Technical Colleges, etc.

Leeds College of Art, Vernon Street, Leeds 2. (Students' Union, University Road, Leeds 2.)

Leeds College of Technology, Calverley Street, Leeds 1. (Students' Union, Calverley Street, Leeds 1.)

Leeds College of Commerce, 43 Woodhouse Lane, Leeds 2. (Students' Union, College of Commerce, 43 Woodhouse Lane, Leeds 2.)

Yorkshire Training College of Housecraft, Vernon Road, Leeds 1.

Leeds City Training College, Becketts Park, Leeds 6.

Private

Pitman's College, 129 Kirkgate, Leeds 1; and others.

ACCOMMODATION

Boarding-houses
   Names and addresses from: Y.M.C.A. *or* Y.W.C.A.
   Leeds Accommodation Agents, 40 Great George Street, Leeds 1.

Hostels and Residential Clubs
   Y.W.C.A., 9 Lovell Street, Leeds 7; 38 Hanover Square, Leeds 3; *and* Cromer Hall, Cromer Terrace, Leeds 2.
   Y.M.C.A., Allerton Hill, Leeds 7: and 35 Albion Place, Leeds 1.
   Girls' Friendly Society, St. Mark's Avenue, Leeds 2.
   Methodist International House, Cliff Road, Park Lane, Leeds.

HOSPITALITY, SOCIAL CLUBS AND SOCIETIES: apply to:
British Council, 1 St. Mark's Avenue, Leeds 2.
   Central Information Bureau, Municipal Buildings, Calverley Street, Leeds 1.
   Leeds Council of Social Service, 6 Church Row, Kirkgate, Leeds.
   Women's Voluntary Service, Bishopgate House, Bishopgate Street, Leeds 1.

POLICE STATION AND ALIENS REGISTRATION OFFICE
   Westgate, Leeds 1.

LOST PROPERTY
   Town Hall, Leeds 1.

EMPLOYMENT
   Employment Exchange (Office), 4 Eastgate, Leeds 2.
   See also Employment, Section I, pages 46–52.

PUBLIC LIBRARY
   Central Library, Municipal Buildings, Calverley Street, Leeds 1.

MUSEUMS AND MONUMENTS

The City Museum, Park Row, Leeds 1.
The Abbey House Museum, Kirkstall, Leeds 5.
Art Gallery, Municipal Buildings, Leeds 1.
Temple Newsam House.

For information on sport, theatres and concerts, and for publications, apply to The Central Information Bureau, address as given overleaf.

Leicester, Leicestershire

Leicester is a busy industrial and historical city (population 267,050). Centre of the hosiery trade and boot and shoe manufacture. Light engineering a major industry. Many local industries are ancillary to the staple trades.

EDUCATION

University of Leicester. Founded as a University College 1918.
Faculties: Arts, Science (including Engineering), Social Sciences; School of Education.

Technical Colleges, etc.
Leicester College of Art and Design, The Newarke, Leicester.
Leicester Regional College of Technology, The Newarke, Leicester.
Charles Keene College of Further Education, Painter Street Leicester.
City of Leicester College of Education (Teacher-Training), Scraptoft, Leicester.
The College of Domestic Science (Women), Knighton Fields, Leicester.

ACCOMMODATION
Boarding-houses
Names and addresses from:
✢   The City Information Bureau, 12 Bishop Street, Leicester.

Hostel and Residential Clubs
  Y.M.C.A., 113 Granby Street, Leicester.
  Y.W.C.A. (Hostel), 5 Granville Road, Leicester.

HOSPITALITY, SOCIAL CLUBS AND SOCIETIES: apply to:

  The British Council, 259 London Road, Leicester.
  Anglo-Overseas Centre, Friends' Meeting House, Queen's Road, Leicester.
  Information from: City Information Bureau, 12 Bishop Street, Leicester.

POLICE STATION AND ALIENS REGISTRATION OFFICE, ALSO LOST PROPERTY

  Police Headquarters, Charles Street, Leicester.

EMPLOYMENT

  Ministry of Labour, Charles Street, Leicester.
  Youth Employment Bureau, Pocklington's Walk, Leicester.
  See also Employment, Section I, pages 46–52.

PUBLIC LIBRARIES

  City Reference Library and Reading Room, Bishop Street, Leicester.
  Commercial and Technical Library, Bishop Street, Leicester.
  Central Lending Library, Belvoir Street, Leicester.
  The Goldsmiths Music and Records Library, Bishop Street, Leicester.

MUSEUMS AND MONUMENTS

  Leicester Castle, Castle Yard, Leicester.
  Jewry Wall Roman Site and St. Nicholas Church, St. Nicholas Square, Leicester.
  The Guildhall, Guildhall Lane, Leicester.
  William Carey's Cottage, Harvey Lane, Leicester.
  City Museum and Art Gallery, New Walk, Leicester.
  The Newarke Houses Museum, The Newarke, Leicester.
  Belgrave Hall Period Museum, Belgrave, Leicester.
  The Clock Tower (city centre).

For information on sport, theatres, concerts, cultural activities and entertainment, and for publications, apply to The City Information Bureau, address as given above.

Liverpool, Lancashire

Situated on the north bank of the Mersey estuary, 30 miles from Manchester, 100 miles from Birmingham, 200 miles from London. The city area is 27,818 acres (about 43½ square miles). Population approximately 747,490. Liverpool is one of the largest ports in the U.K.

EDUCATION

University of Liverpool. Founded 1881, originated 1878. Students: 5,074 (1963), 6 per cent from abroad.

Faculties: Arts and Sciences, Engineering, Law, Medicine, Veterinary Science.

Technical Colleges, etc.

Liverpool College of Art, Hope Street, Liverpool 1.

Liverpool College of Building, Clarence Street, Liverpool 3.

City College of Commerce, Tithebarn Street, Liverpool 2.

City College of Technology, Byrom Street, Liverpool 3.

College of Crafts and Catering, Colquitt Street, Liverpool 1.

Mabel Fletcher Technical College, Sandown Road, Liverpool 15.

Millbank College of Commerce, Bankfield Road, Liverpool 13.

City Institute of Further Education (Institute High School for Boys), *Office:* Myrtle Street, Liverpool 7.

Nautical Catering College, Canning Place, Liverpool 1.

Newsham Drive Women's Centre, 83 Newsham Drive, Liverpool 6.

North-East Liverpool Technical College, Muirhead Avenue East, Liverpool 12.

Old Swan Technical College, Broadgreen Road, Liverpool 13.

Riversdale Technical College, Riversdale Road, Liverpool 19.

Walton Technical College, Walton Road, Liverpool 4.

Private

Gregg Schools Ltd., 36A Rodney Street, Liverpool 1 (Commercial); and others.

ACCOMMODATION

Boarding-houses

Names and addresses can be obtained from:

The Citizens' Advice Bureau, 34 Stanley Street, Liverpool 1.

Y.M.C.A., *or* Y.W.C.A.

✠ The Town Clerk's Public Relations Office, Dale Street, Liverpool 2.

The Students' Welfare Office, Education Department, Sir Thomas Street, Liverpool 1.

Hostels and Residential Clubs

Y.M.C.A., Mount Pleasant, Liverpool 3; *and* 120 Everton Road, Liverpool 6.

Y.W.C.A., 18 Slater Street, Liverpool 1 (Office); *and* 1A Rodney Street, Liverpool 1 (Hostel).

HOSPITALITY: apply to:

The British Council, 80 Lord Street, Liverpool 2.

For list of social clubs, societies, etc., see Liverpool Red Book, etc., at Libraries.

INFORMATION CENTRES

The Citizens' Advice Bureau, 34 Stanley Street, Liverpool 1.

Liverpool Council of Social Service, 14 Castle Street, Liverpool 2.

Town Clerk's Public Relations Office, Municipal Buildings, Dale Street, Liverpool 2.

POLICE STATION AND ALIENS REGISTRATION OFFICE

Headquarters: Hardman Street, Liverpool 1.

EMPLOYMENT

Ministry of Labour and National Service, Employment Exchange, 27 Leece Street, Liverpool 1.

See also Employment, Section I, pages 46–52.

PUBLIC LIBRARIES

Liverpool Central Libraries, William Brown Street, Liverpool 2.

T—I

There are also 29 branch libraries in other parts of the city.

Bluecoat Central Lending Library, Bluecoat Chambers, School Lane, Liverpool 1.

MUSEUMS AND MONUMENTS

The Town Hall, Dale Street, Liverpool 2.

The Liverpool Cathedral, St. James Mount, Liverpool 1.

The Liverpool Metropolitan Cathedral, Mount Pleasant, Liverpool 3.

The Museum, Libraries and Walker Art Gallery, William Brown Street, Liverpool 3.

Sudley Art Gallery, Mossley Hill Road, Liverpool 18.

Speke Hall (Elizabethan House), Liverpool 24.

For information on sport of all kinds, theatres, concerts, cultural activities and entertainment, and for publications, apply to The Public Relations Office, Municipal Buildings, address as given above.

London, capital of England and of the United Kingdom

One of the largest cities in the world in area, with a population of over 8 millions; the historic seat of British government; the second largest port in Europe; the world's biggest money market; centre for the arts and theatre; the United Kingdom's largest University; and with a major proportion of British consumer industries represented at least in part, e.g. motor-cars, furniture, light engineering, chemicals, etc. The visitor can find almost everything somewhere in London, but his difficulty will lie in how and where to find it; and also in the time he must allow, in this widespreading metropolis, for travelling from one part to another.

Central, and therefore more expensive, residential areas are Hampstead, Kensington and Chelsea. Beyond these are vast suburbs, and it takes at least one hour, by any method of transport, to reach the open countryside from a focal point such as Hyde Park Corner. However, both within and outside London, there are many parks and gardens, characteristic of England; and the River Thames flows past many sights of interest.

The principal shopping streets are Oxford Street, Regent

Street, Bond Street, Piccadilly and Knightsbridge; these are included in the area known as the 'West End' where are situated the famous theatres, restaurants and places of entertainment – many of which, however, owing to British licensing laws, are open at restricted times or on the basis of 'clubs'.

The British Travel Association, London Tourist Board, and many other agencies are anxious to help you with information on how you may enjoy your stay in London; and anyone, student or otherwise, is strongly advised to use the guide-books and bureaux such as are listed here. Otherwise you may find yourself at a loss in this very busy and confusing city.

If you find yourself in difficulties when you arrive in London at Victoria or Liverpool Street Station, go to the International Travellers' Aid kiosk. The assistants there will help you to reach your destination. If you would like to be met and escorted across London, write a fortnight in advance to: International Travellers' Aid, 108 Baker Street, London, W.1. A small fee is charged for escorting.

Other Addresses

✛ British Travel Association, 64 St. James's Street, London, S.W.1. Tel. MAYfair 9191.

The London Tourist Board, 29 St. James's Street, London, S.W.1. Tel. MONarch 3030.

British Railways Travel Centre, Lower Regent Street, London, W.1. Tel. TRAfalgar 4343.

London Transport Inquiry Office, 55 Broadway, London, S.W.1. Tel. ABBey 1234. (St. James's Park Underground Station.)

Publications

What's On (published weekly, 1/3, obtainable at all bookstalls).
What's Where in London (published by B.P. Guide).
This Month in London (published by B.T.A.).
N.U.S. Student Guide to London (published by National Union of Students).

In addition, the entertainment columns of the national newspapers (*Evening Standard*, *The Times*, *Daily Telegraph*, etc.) give each day the names, addresses, and 'what's on' of the London cinemas, theatres, art galleries and concert halls.

EDUCATION

London University. Senate House, Malet Street, London, W.C.1.

The only University in the United Kingdom to grant external degrees. It consists of a number of large federated Colleges or Schools, residential and non-residential, which are scattered throughout various parts of London. It includes also a number of post-graduate specialist institutes. There is an Advisory Service for external degree students which gives guidance on syllabuses, reading material for examinations, etc. The adminstrative centre and University Library are off Russell Square, near the British Museum. There are, outside the University, institutions such as certain of the technical colleges, which can take students for London internal degree and post-graduate courses.

Admission of internal students is controlled by the schools and colleges of the University individually.

Almost every known subject is covered by the University, and for further details, the names and addresses of the individual colleges with the faculties they each provide, etc., application should be made to The University of London, Senate House, London, W.C.1. The University issues free on application two information pamphlets: 'General Information for Internal Students', and 'General Information for External Students'.

London University Adviser to Overseas Students: Miss C. M. Prince, B.A., University of London Union, Malet Street, London, W.C.1.

(1) *Colleges of Advanced Technology*

Battersea College of Technology,* Battersea Park Road, London, S.W.11 (expected to move and to become a University after 1964).

Brunel College of Advanced Technology, Woodlands Avenue, London, W.3.

Chelsea College of Science and Technology,* Manresa Road, London, S.W.3.

Northampton College of Advanced Technology,* St. John Street, London, E.C.1.

(2) *Regional Colleges*

Borough Polytechnic, Borough Road, London, S.E.1.

Brixton School of Building, Ferndale Road, London, S.W.4.

Kingston College of Technology, Penryhn Road, Kingston, Surrey.

Northern Polytechnic,* Holloway Road, London, N.7.

The Polytechnic, 309 Regent Street, London, W.1.

Sir John Cass College, Jewry Street, Aldgate, London, E.C.3.

South East Essex College of Technology, Longbridge Road, Dagenham, Essex.

West Ham College of Technology,* Romford Road, London, E.15.

Woolwich Polytechnic,* 31–3 Thomas Street, London, S.E.18.

(3) *Area Technical Colleges*

Balham and Tooting College of Commerce, Tooting Broadway, London, S.W.17.

City of London College, Moorgate, London, E.C.2.

Chiswick Polytechnic, Bath Road, London, W.4.

College for the Distributive Trades, 107 Charing Cross Road, London, W.C.2.

Cordwainers' Technical College, 182 Mare Street, Hackney, London, E.8.

Ealing Technical College, St. Mary's Road, Ealing, London, W.5.

Enfield College of Technology, Queensway, Enfield, Middlesex.

Ewell County Technical College, Reigate Road, Ewell, Surrey.

Faraday House (*Independent:* Engineering), 66 Southampton Row, London, W.C.1.

Hammersmith College of Art and Building, Lime Grove, London, W.12.

Hendon Technical College, The Burroughs, Hendon, London, N.W.4.

(4) *Other Principal Colleges*

Acton Technical College, High Street, Acton, London, W.3.

Holborn College of Law, Languages and Commerce, Red Lion Square, London, W.C.1.

North-Western Polytechnic, Prince of Wales Road, London, N.W.5.

Norwood Technical College, Knight's Hill, Norwood, London, S.E.27.

London College of Printing, Elephant and Castle, London, S.E.1.

South-West Essex Technical College and School of Art, Forest Road, Walthamstow, London, E.17.

Twickenham Technical College, Egerton Road, Twickenham, Middlesex.

Willesden Technical College, Denzil Road, London, N.W.10.

Colleges marked with * give London University internal degree courses. For part-time courses, see Inner London Education Authority booklet *Floodlight*, obtainable at W. H. Smith's branches and at H.M. Stationery Office, available in London, but not for overseas.

Education Officer, Inner London Education Authority and Information Bureau, The County Hall, Westminster Bridge, London, S.E.1.

For information on private education in London and on independent schools of various kinds, see directions given under Section II, English Language.

ACCOMMODATION

The following is a list of non-University hostels in the Central Area:

Owing to the pressure on accommodation, there may be difficulty in getting a place in these and in other hostels.

Alliance Club Hostel, 1–2 Bedford Place, London, W.C.1.

East Africa House, 36 Great Cumberland Place, London, W.1 (primarily for East Africans).

Hong Kong House, 74 Lancaster Gate, London, W.2.

Impala House, 8 Chalcot Square, N.W.1 (flatlets for the married families of post-graduates).

Indian Students' Hostel (Y.M.C.A.), 41 Fitzroy Street, London, W.1.

London House, Guilford Street, London, W.C.1 (for graduates from Commonwealth countries and the U.S.).

Malaysia Hall, 44 Bryanston Square, London, W.1 (primarily for students from Malaysia).

Methodist International House, 4 Inverness Terrace, London, W.2.

Pakistan Students' Hostel, 15–16 Chesham Place, London, S.W.1.

William Temple House, 29 Trebovir Road, London, S.W.5.

Young Men's Christian Association, Great Russell Street, London, W.C.1 (and others in suburbs).

Young Women's Christian Association, Great Russell Street, London, W.C.1 (and others in suburbs).

William Goodenough House, Mecklenburgh Square, London, W.C.1 (women and married families).

International Students' House, 1–6 Park Crescent, London, W.1.

Lee Abbey International Students' Club, 26–7 Courtfield Gardens, London, S.W.7.

N.B. – Students from certain Commonwealth countries who are recommended under a scheme operated with the British Council may find accommodation in one of the four British Council residences.

Dormitory Accommodation

Hyde House (Y.W.C.A.) Youth Hostel, 9 Bulstrode Street, London, W.1. Tel. WELbeck 7887.

Y.W.C.A., Bedford House, 108 Baker Street, London, W.1 (and branches). Tel. WELbeck 1706.

Y.M.C.A., Great Russell Street, London, W.C.1.

International Catholic Girls' Society, 86 Ebury Street, London, S.W.1. Tel. SLOane 7220.

Holiday Fellowship, Starcross School, Gower Street, London, W.1. Tel. EUSton 2474.

Youth Hostels Association, Holland House, London, W.8 (and branches). Tel. WEStern 1748.

Boy Scouts Association, Baden-Powell House, Queen's Gate, London, S.W.7. Tel. KNIghtsbridge 0671.

Church Army, 61 Bryanston Street, London, W.1. Tel. PADdington 4280.

Salvation Army, 66 Buckingham Gate, London, S.W.1. Tel. ABBey 1164.

General

Y.W.C.A., Great Russell Street, London, W.C.1. Tel. MUSeum 4363.

Y.M.C.A., Great Russell Street, London, W.C.1. Tel. MUSeum 4363.

Salvation Army, 37 Hunter Street, London, W.C.1. Tel. TERminus 1654.

Destitute People

Church Army, 61 Bryanston Street, London, W.1 (and branches). Tel. PADdington 4280.

St. Louisa's Hostel, 33 Medway Street, London, S.W.1. Tel. ABBey 6225.

Inner London Authority, 22 Gordon Road, Peckham, London, S.E.15. Tel. NEW Cross 1025.

Salvation Army, Hope Town Hostel, Hope Town Street, Whitechapel, London, E.1 (and branches). Tel. BIShopsgate 2693.

For Permanent Residence try

London Accommodation Bureau, 33 Wardour Street, London, W.1. Tel. GERrard 9050.

There are a number of private agencies and bureaux for accommodation, of which the following in London are among the more well known:

Gabbitas-Thring Educational Trust, Advisory Service, 6 Sackville Street, London, W.1.

Truman & Knightley Educational Trust Ltd., Educational Agents, 93 Baker Street, London, W.1.

En Famille Agency, 1 New Burlington Street, London, W.1.

(All the above specialize in finding accommodation in families for students from Europe both in London and outside.)

Hotel Agencies

Rosenthal Hotel Booking Service, 190 Shaftesbury Avenue, London, W.C.2. Tel. TEMple Bar 5377.

London Hotels' Information Service (overseas visitors only). Tel. MAYfair 5414.

Hotac, 93 Baker Street, London, W.1. Tel. WELbeck 2555.

Hotel Bookings Service, 5 Coventry Street, London, W.1. Tel. GERrard 5052.

Hotel Booking and Information Ltd., 47 Charing Cross Road, London, W.C.2. Tel. REGent 7560.

Other organizations able to help in finding accommodation are:

(a) The Lodgings Bureau at the University or College where you have been placed.

(b) Students accepted at the University of London should apply to:

> University of London Lodgings Bureau, c/o University of London Union, Malet Street, London, W.C.1.

(c) The student office of your Embassy or High Commissioner's Office in London.

(d) Other organizations:

> The British Travel Association, 64–5 St. James's Street, London, S.W.1.
>
> Young Men's Christian Association, Great Russell Street, London, W.C.1.
>
> Church Missionary Society, 6 Salisbury Square, London, E.C.4.
>
> Methodist Missionary Society, 25 Marylebone Road, London, N.W.1.

Students who are studying full-time in Britain and who are recommended by their national authorities (Embassy or High Commission) may make use of the accommodation service provided by The British Council, 11 Portland Place, London, W.1.

TRANSPORT

Most parts of London are served by the Underground Railway system.

The London Bus service (double-deck red buses) covers the whole of the London area; rates may be discovered from the lists attached to bus stops or by inquiring at the London Transport Inquiries Office, 280 St. Marylebone; also at Piccadilly and St. James's Park Underground Stations; Tel. ABBey 1234. Green Line coaches serve the suburbs and surrounding towns near London.

Bus, Underground and Green Line Coach Maps and attractive post-cards, posters and booklets are obtainable at station bookstalls or from London Transport Inquiries Offices, as above.

Transport by coach to all other parts of the United Kingdom runs from Victoria Coach Station, Buckingham Palace Road, London, S.W.1. Tel. SLOane 0202.

Nine main railway stations, under nationalized British Railways, King's Cross (North-east), Euston (for the North-west),

Paddington (for the West), Liverpool Street (East), St. Pancras (Midlands), Victoria (South, and Waterloo (South-west), Charing Cross (South), London Bridge (South and South-East) connect London with all regions of the British Isles.

For information on the railways, telephone 'Inquiries' at the relevant station telephone number.

POLICE

Metropolitan Police Headquarters, New Scotland Yard. Tel. WHItehall 1212.

Aliens Registration Office, Metropolitan Police, S.7. Branch, 10 Lambs Conduit Street, London, W.C.1. Tel. HOLborn 7991.

LOST PROPERTY

Police Lost Property, 109 Lambeth Road, London, S.E.1 (for British Railways trains, taxis and anywhere except below).

200 Baker Street, Marylebone, London, N.W.1 (for articles left in Tube, trains or buses).

GENERAL HOSPITALS

All the Teaching Hospitals run open casualty departments for injuries great or small; and they will also advise:

St. Bartholomew's Hospital, Smithfield, London, E.C.1.
Charing Cross Hospital, Charing Cross, London, W.C.2.
St. George's Hospital, Hyde Park Corner, London, S.W.1.
London Hospital, Whitechapel, London, E.1.
Middlesex Hospital, Mortimer Street, London, W.1.
Royal Free Hospital, Gray's Inn Road, London, W.C.1.
St. Thomas Hospital, London, S.E.1.
Westminster Hospital, London, S.W.1.
For local general hospitals, inquire at the Borough Town Hall.

BANKS

The headquarters of all the big English commercial banks are in the City of London. Nicknamed 'the big five', they are the Midland, Westminster, Barclays, National Provincial, Lloyds, and a sixth sometimes included, Martins.

Most Commonwealth and Foreign banks are also represented in the City. For all addresses, look under their names in the London Telephone directory.

EATING OUT

Prices in London restaurants and snack-bars vary greatly.

There are a large number of foreign restaurants, particularly in Soho – perhaps the most common and least expensive being Indian, Chinese and Greek. Prices for a meal can range from 5s. to £5, for a single dish from 2s. 6d. to 30s.

For English cooking, there is one famous (and not the most expensive) restaurant, 'Simpsons' in the Strand (price around £1 per head for a meal without wine).

But for general everyday eating out, there are the innumerable self-service branches of 'Lyons', with large multiple restaurant 'Corner Houses' at Marble Arch and Tottenham Court Road. The latter serve meals at all prices and are open, at least partially, all twenty-four hours.

Similar to Lyons are the ABC restaurants; like Lyons, they also sell baked and other food of all kinds, and sandwiches to take away. The Kardomahs, and Kenya Coffee Houses and a large number of chain snack-bars, such as Forte's and Wimpey's, all sell quick meals with good, clean food at reasonable prices.

HOSPITALITY, SOCIAL CLUBS AND SOCIETIES

Useful addresses:

British Council Overseas Students' Centre, 21 Portland Place, London, W.1. Tel. GROsvenor 8011. (Hospitality and cultural centre.)

Citizens' Advice Bureaux for all local information and advice (particularly on smaller local social clubs).

Central Office: 296 Vauxhall Bridge Road, London, S.W.1. Tel. VICtoria 7334. Branches in all London Boroughs.

Committees of Friendship for Overseas Students (hospitality among English families).

Central Office: Friendship Clubs Central Committee, 291 Gray's Inn Road, London, W.C.1. Tel. TERminus 4716. Branches in most London Boroughs.

Social Advisory Group, 108 Baker Street, London, W.1. Tel. WELbeck 6591. (Hospitality and introductions, particularly for Europeans.)

The International Friendship League. *Central Office:* Mary Ward Centre, Tavistock Place, London, W.1. Tel. EUSton 1816. (For social evenings and introductions.)

Victoria League (Commonwealth only), 38 Chesham Street, London, S.W.1. Tel. BELgravia 2201. (Club facilities.)

Commonwealth Students' Club, Commonwealth Institute, Kensington High Street, London, W.8. Tel. WEStern 8252. (Club facilities.)

Friends' International Centre, 32 Tavistock Square, London, W.C.1. Tel. EUSton 5648. (Quaker – Talks and discussions.)

Hillel House, Endsleigh Street, London, W.C.1. Tel. EUSton 7845. (Jewish – Club and lectures.)

London Newman Centre, 21A Soho Square, London, W.1. Tel. REGent 5992. (Catholic and graduates only.)

Lutheran Students' House, 21 Pembridge Gardens, London, W.2. Tel. PARk 5924. (Social meetings.)

Student Movement House, 103 Gower Street, London, W.C.1. Tel. EUSton 1640. (Club facilities and S.C.M. meetings.)

Y.M.C.A., Great Russell Street, London, W.C.1. Tel. MUSeum 8954. (Club facilities.)

Y.W.C.A., Central Club, Great Russell Street, London, W.C.1. Tel. MUSeum 7512. (Club facilities.)

East and West Friendship Council, 101 Gower Street, London, W.C.1. Tel. EUSton 8525. (Private hospitality.)

World University Service, 5A Gloucester Place, London, W.1. Tel. WELbeck 3921. (Student exchange.)

International House, 40 Shaftesbury Avenue, London, W.1. Tel. GERrard 9167. (Most facilities.)

There are many other social clubs, including those designed for young English people but which are perfectly ready to welcome overseas students including 'au pair' girls. Most of the churches, too, Methodist, Catholic, Anglican and others, offer or can arrange hospitality. See also Section I, General Information, pages 32–46.

In cases of doubt for the name and address of someone with whom to make contact, apply to one of the Citizens' Advice Bureaux which are, in fact, the local area 'experts'.

EMPLOYMENT BUREAUX

See under Employment, pages 46–52, Section I, General Information.

PUBLIC LIBRARIES

Every London borough has one or more public libraries, usually situated close to the borough or 'Town' hall.

The big Central borough libraries are:

Holborn Central Library, 32 Theobalds Road, London, W.C.1.
Islington Central Library, Holloway Road, London, N.7.
Lambeth Central Library, Brixton Oval, London, S.W.2.
Paddington Central Library, Porchester Road, London, W.2.
Marylebone Public Library, Marylebone Road, London, N.W.1.
Westminster Central Library, 4 Charing Cross Road, London, W.C.2.

N.B. – See also: Westminster Reference Library, St. Martin's Street, London, W.C.2.

Apart from the borough public libraries there are a number of other libraries in London which may be useful, viz.:

The British Museum Library, London, W.C.1.
Royal Commonwealth Institute Library, Kensington High Street, London, W.8.
Royal Institute of International Affairs, 10 St. James's Square, London, S.W.1.
Guildhall Library, London, E.C.2.
The British Council Library, 59 New Oxford Street, London, W.C.1.
The Patent Office Library, Southampton Buildings, Chancery Lane, London, W.C.2 (shortly to be moved to become a National Reference Library for Science and Invention); and, of course, your University, School or College library, e.g. London University Library, Senate House, Malet Street, London, W.C.1.

FOR PLACES OF WORSHIP

See under Churches, page 32, Section I, General Information.

For information on Museums, Travel, Sport, Entertainment and Bookshops in London, see headings in Section I, General Information.

Further Publications
* * *London: Benn Pocket Guide.*
  Guide to London (H.M.S.O.)
  Wonderful London (published by *Evening News*).
* * *Visitors' London* (published by London Transport).
  London (published by Random House, New York).
  London for Everyman (published by Dent).
* * *Muirhead's Guide to London* (published by Benn).
* * *Penguin Guide.*

Books marked with * give specially detailed descriptions of historic monuments, houses, museums, etc.

Maps
For a Street Guide of London and the Suburbs: *The Geographers A to Z* and *The Geographers Map of London* (obtainable most booksellers and newsagents).

Loughborough

Loughborough is an ancient borough with a population of 39,270 (mid-summer 1964) situated in the Soar Valley on the fringe of Charnwood Forest within easy reach of Leicester, Nottingham and Derby. The principal industries include engineering, bell founding, hosiery and knitwear manufacturing.

EDUCATION

Loughborough College of Advanced Technology. Expected shortly to be granted University status.

Loughborough Teacher-Training College.

Loughborough College of Further Education and Art.

The Student Body governing the affairs of all the Colleges jointly is the Union of Loughborough Colleges, Union Office, Edward Herbert Building, Ashby Road, Loughborough.

ACCOMMODATION, HOSPITALITY, SOCIAL CLUBS AND SOCIETIES: apply to:

The Citizens' Advice Bureau, 24 Ashby Road, Loughborough.

The Loughborough Council of Social Service, 'Setoc', Prestwold Lane, Hoton, nr Loughborough.

A list of local organizations and societies is available at:
The Town Clerk's Office, Southfields, Loughborough.
The Central Library, Granby Street, Loughborough.

EMPLOYMENT

Ministry of Labour, Employment Exchange, Craddock Street, Loughborough.

Youth Employment Service, 1 Frederick Street, Loughborough.

See also Employment, Section I, pages 46–52.

MUSEUMS AND MONUMENTS

Loughborough's Carillon Tower, built in 1922 as a War Memorial, stands in Queen's Park and contains a small war museum. The Memorial houses 47 bells and is open to the public at a small charge. Recitals are held each week during the season.

For information on sport and entertainment, apply to The Town Clerk's Office, Southfields, Loughborough.

Manchester, Lancashire

Manchester is the principal city of the North-west of England, with a population in Greater Manchester of $2\frac{1}{2}$ millions and within the City of 644,500. Manchester is the newspaper, television and radio centre of the North; its business, banking, distributing, insurance and shopping centre, and the centre of a large number of industries – engineering, clothing, footwear, paper and printing, foodstuffs, chemicals, electronic equipment and textiles.

EDUCATION

University of Manchester, Oxford Road, Manchester. Founded in 1851. 8,500 students, many from abroad.

Faculties: Arts, Science, Law, Medicine, Music, Economics and Social Studies, Theology, Technology, Education, Biochemistry, Youth Work.

Educational Precinct now approved is an area about $1\frac{1}{2}$ miles by ½ mile, containing the University, the Institute of Science and Technology, the Manchester College of Art and Design, the Royal Manchester College of Music and other institutions.

The Institute of Science and Technology, Sackville Street, Manchester 1, is a faculty of the University, in addition to its other departments. Has 2,261 students and sixteen departments.

John Dalton College of Technology, Chester Street, Manchester 1, is a major technological college.

Hollings College for the Food and Fashion Industries, Old Hall Lane, Rusholme, Manchester 14.

Royal College of Advanced Technology, The Crescent, Salford 5, will shortly become a second University of South-east Lancashire.

College of Building, Hardman Street, Manchester 3.

College of Commerce, 103 Princess Street, Manchester 1.

ACCOMMODATION

Boarding Houses, Flats, Apartments
Current vacancies advertised in: *Manchester Evening News and Chronicle*, 3 Cross Street, Manchester 2.

Hostels and Residential Clubs
Y.W.C.A., 16–18 Queen Street, Manchester (N.W. Area Office).

Y.M.C.A., 56 Peter Street, Manchester (N.W. Area Office).

Y.H.A., 16–18 Queen Street, Manchester.

Ashton House Women's Municipal Hostel, Corporation Street, Manchester 4.

Britannia Hostel, 107 Chester Road, Manchester 15.

Christian Alliance of Women and Girls' Residential Club, 75 Daisy Bank Road, Manchester 14.

Church Army Residential Hostel (for men), 174 Plymouth Grove, Manchester 13.

Methodist Hostel, 37 Mayfield Road, Manchester 16; and others.

INFORMATION

✣ The Publicity and Information Office, The Town Hall, Manchester 2.

HOSPITALITY, SOCIAL CLUBS AND SOCIETIES: apply to:

British Council, Woodstock, 139 Barlow Moor Road, West Didsbury, Manchester 20.

International Centre, 64 George Street, Manchester 1.

POLICE HEADQUARTERS AND NATIONALITY OFFICE

South Street, Albert Square, Manchester 2.

LOST PROPERTY

Lost in buses – apply to The Transport Department Offices, 2 Devonshire Street North, Ardwick, Manchester 12.

Lost in trains – apply to The Lost Property Office at the railway stations.

Lost in taxis – apply to Police Headquarters, South Street 2.

Lost in public conveniences – apply to The Health Department, Room 418, Town Hall, Manchester 2.

EMPLOYMENT

Manchester Employment Exchange, Aytoun Street, Manchester.

Ministry of Labour, Regional Office, Albert House, Bridge Street, Manchester.

See also Employment, Section I, pages 46–52.

PUBLIC LIBRARIES

Central Library, St. Peter's Square, Manchester 2.

The Portico Library, Mosley Street, Manchester 2.

The John Rylands Library, Deansgate, Manchester 3.

Chetham's Library, Hunt's Bank (opposite Manchester Cathedral).

Cotton Board Colour, Design and Style Centre Library, 19 York Street, Manchester 1.

The University Library, Oxford Road, Manchester 13.

MUSEUMS AND ART GALLERIES

The City Art Gallery, Mosley Street, Manchester 2.

Heaton Hall Gallery, Heaton Park, Manchester 8.

The Gallery of English Costume, Platt Hall, Rusholme, Manchester.

Manchester College of Art and Design Museum, Cavendish Street, Manchester.

Whitworth Art Gallery, Whitworth Park, Oxford Road, Manchester.

Queen's Park Gallery, Queen's Park, Manchester.

Wythenshawe Hall Gallery, Wythenshawe Park, Manchester.

For information on sport of all kinds, theatres, concerts, cultural activities and entertainment, and for publications, apply to The Publicity and Information Office, Town Hall.

Newcastle upon Tyne, Northumberland

Newcastle is a city and county in its own right, though within the geographical county of Northumberland. It is the chief city of North-east England with a population of 260,750 (1964).

The industries include coal-mining, shipbuilding, ship-repairing, flour milling, heavy engineering, paint manufacture, detergents, etc.

EDUCATION

University of Newcastle upon Tyne. Founded nineteenth century, reconstituted 1963.

Faculties: Medicine, Dental Surgery (sub-faculty), Arts, Fine Art, Architecture and Town and Country Planning (sub-faculty), Science, Applied Science, Economic and Social Studies, Law, Agriculture, and Education.

Technical Colleges, etc.

College of Art and Industrial Design, Clayton Road, Newcastle upon Tyne 2.

Charles Trevelyan Technical College, Maple Terrace, Newcastle upon Tyne 4.

College of Further Education, Bath Lane, Newcastle upon Tyne 1.

Municipal College of Commerce, College Street, Newcastle upon Tyne 1.

Rutherford College of Technology, Ellison Place, Newcastle upon Tyne 1.

University of Newcastle upon Tyne, Department of Adult Education, St. Thomas's Street, Newcastle upon Tyne 1.

The Workers' Educational Association, 51 Grainger Street, Newcastle upon Tyne 1.

There are also three teacher-training colleges in the area.

Private

Institute of Modern Languages, 3 Lambton Road, Newcastle upon Tyne 2 (and other schools).

ACCOMMODATION

A list of hotels, boarding-houses and details of furnished rooms, board and lodgings and hostel accommodation may be obtained from:

✠ The City Information Service, Central Library, New Bridge Street, Newcastle upon Tyne 1.

HOSPITALITY, SOCIAL CLUBS AND SOCIETIES: apply to:

British Council, 5 Windsor Crescent, Newcastle upon Tyne 2.

Y.W.C.A., 3–4 Saville Place, Northumberland Street, Newcastle upon Tyne 1.

Y.M.C.A., Blackett Street, Newcastle upon Tyne 1.

Methodist International House, 76 Osborne Road, Newcastle upon Tyne 2.

Citizens' Advice Bureau, 17 Ellison Place, Newcastle upon Tyne 1.

POLICE STATION AND ALIENS REGISTRATION OFFICE, ALSO LOST PROPERTY

Police Headquarters: New Market Street, Newcastle upon Tyne 1.

EMPLOYMENT

Employment Exchange: Prudhoe House, Prudhoe Street, Newcastle upon Tyne 1.

See also Employment Section 1, page 46–52.

PUBLIC LIBRARIES

Central Library; Reference Library; Lending Library; Commercial and Technical Library; City Information Service.

MUSEUMS AND MONUMENTS

Black Gate Museum, near The Keep.

The Castle or Keep, Castle Square, Newcastle upon Tyne 1.

Hancock Museum, Barras Bridge, Newcastle upon Tyne 1.

Laing Art Gallery, Higham Place, Newcastle upon Tyne 1.

Museum of Antiquities, The Quadrangle, The University, Newcastle upon Tyne 1.

Museum of Science and Engineering, Exhibition Park, Newcastle upon Tyne 1.

The Grey Monument, Blackett Street, Newcastle upon Tyne, 1.

For information on sport of all kinds, theatres, concerts and entertainment and for publications, apply to: The City Information Service, address as given on page 275.

Norwich, Norfolk

One of the most interesting and beautiful towns in England, Norwich (population 119,150) is the capital of Norfolk; famous for its Norman Cathedral; other churches and buildings of interest, mostly medieval, old mansions; one of the largest cattle-markets in England.

EDUCATION

University of East Anglia. Incorporated 1964.

Faculties: Studies in Arts and Sciences organized in schools, i.e. English Studies, European Studies, Social Studies, Biology Studies, Chemistry Studies, Fine Arts, Mathematics and Physics.

Technical Colleges, etc.

The Norwich City College, Ipswich Road, Norwich.

The Norwich Art School, St. George's, Norwich.

Norfolk School of Agriculture, Easton Hall, Norwich.

Training College for Teachers, Keswick, Norwich.

ACCOMMODATION

Boarding-houses

Names and addresses may be found from: Y.M.C.A., *or* Y.W.C.A., *or* Y.H.A.

Hostels and Residential Clubs

Y.M.C.A., City and County Office, 48 St. Giles's Street, Norwich.

Y.W.C.A., Hostel, Marjorie Hinde House, 61 Bethel Street, Norwich.

Y.W.C.A., Warden, 61 Bethel Street, Norwich.

Y.H.A., 9 Earlham Road, Norwich.

HOSPITALITY, SOCIAL CLUBS AND SOCIETIES: apply to:

Y.M.C.A., City and County Office, 48 St. Giles's Street, Norwich.

Youth Hostel Association, 9 Earlham Road, Norwich.

Caley's Recreation Association, Unthank Road, Norwich.

Civil Service Sports Association, 28 St. Giles's Street, Norwich.

Young Men's Christian Association, 48–50 St. Giles's Street, Norwich.

Christian Alliance of Women and Girls, 38A St. Giles's Street, Norwich.

Norwich International Club, Music House, King Street, Norwich.

✠ City Information, c/o The Town Clerk, City Hall, Norwich.

The Norwich Publicity Association, 24 Exchange Street, Norwich.

POLICE STATION AND ALIENS REGISTRATION OFFICE, ALSO LOST PROPERTY

Norwich City Police Station, City Police Offices, Bethel Street, Norwich.

Sub-Stations: Magdalen Road, Woodcock Road, Kett's Hill and Earlham Road.

EMPLOYMENT

Ministry of Labour, Colegate, Norwich.

Youth Employment Service, 21 Thorpe Road, Norwich.

See also Employment, Section 1, pages 46–52.

PUBLIC LIBRARIES

The Central Public Library, Bethel Street, Norwich; and branches.

Norfolk and Norwich Record Office, Central Library, Bethel Street, Norwich.

American Memorial Library; Colman and Rye Libraries of Local History; Central Library, Bethel Street, Norwich.

Norfolk County Library, Thorpe Road, Norwich.

Norfolk and Norwich Library, Guildhall Hill, Norwich (subscription library).

University of East Anglia, Wilberforce Road, Norwich.

Dean and Chapter's Library, Cathedral Close, Norwich.

Norwich City College, Ipswich Road, Norwich.

MUSEUMS AND MONUMENTS

Castle Museum.

Strangers' Hall, Charing Cross, Norwich.

Bridewell Museum, Bridewell Alley, Norwich.

St. Peter Hungate Church, Princes Street, Norwich.

For information on employment, sport of all kinds, theatres and concerts, entertainment, and for publications, apply to The City Hall, address as given overleaf.

Nottingham, Nottinghamshire

Nottingham (population 315,050) is an industrial city with various manufactures (pharmaceutical products, bicycles, tobacco, furniture, telecommunications equipment, coal-mining). It is also one of the chief centres of the lace and hosiery industry in the world.

EDUCATION

University of Nottingham. Originated in 1798.

Faculties: Agriculture and Horticulture, Applied Science, Law and Social Sciences, Pure Science excluding Pharmacy, Education, Arts.

Institute of Education, University Park, Nottingham.

Technical Colleges, etc.

Nottingham Regional College of Technology, Burton Street, Nottingham.

Nottingham College of Art and Design, Waverley Street, Nottingham.

Nottingham College of Education, Clifton.

Clarendon College of Further Education, Pelham Avenue, Sherwood Rise, Nottingham.

People's College of Further Education, Maid Marian Way, Nottingham.

County (adjacent to Nottingham.)

Arnold and Carlton College of Further Education, Digby Avenue, Mapperley, Nottingham; Beeston College of Further Education, High Road, Chilwell.

Private

Miller's Business College, 15 Wheeler Gate, Nottingham.

Secretarial Training College, Minerva House, Spaniel Row, Nottingham; and others.

ACCOMMODATION

Boarding-houses

Names and addresses may be obtained from the Publicity and Information Department.

Hostels and Residential Clubs

Methodist International House (Overseas Students' Home), 8 Second Avenue, Sherwood Rise, Nottingham.

Girls' Friendly Society, 6 Regent Street, Nottingham.

Y.W.C.A., 42 Shakespeare Street, Nottingham.

Y.M.C.A., Shakespeare Street, Nottingham.

Alexandra Court, Woodborough Road, Nottingham.

HOSPITALITY, SOCIAL CLUBS AND SOCIETIES: apply to:

British Council, 8 Sherwood Rise, Nottingham.

✠ Also, list available from Publicity and Information Department, 54 Milton Street, Nottingham.

POLICE STATION AND ALIENS REGISTRATION OFFICE, ALSO LOST PROPERTY

Police Headquarters, The Guildhall, North Church Street, Nottingham.

EMPLOYMENT

Ministry of Labour Employment Exchanges, Castle Boulevard and Valley Road, Basford, Nottingham.

Youth Employment Bureau (County), 9 Musters Road, West Bridgford, Nottingham.

Youth Employment Bureau (City), St. James's Terrace, Standard Hill, Nottingham.

See also Employment, Section I, pages 46–52.

PUBLIC LIBRARY

Central Public Library, Sherwood Street, Nottingham; and branches.

MUSEUMS

Castle Museum and Art Gallery, Nottingham Castle.

Museum of Natural History, Wollaton Hall, Nottingham.

For information on sport of all kinds, repertory and other theatres, cultural activities, and for publications, apply to The Publicity and Information Department, address as given above.

Oxford, Oxfordshire

Oxford has some of the most beautiful buildings in England, including Magdalen College, the Radcliffe Camera Library, the Bodleian Library, the Sheldonian Theatre, Christ Church, St. John's College and New College. Its Ashmolean Museum is world-famous and its High Street is much admired.

Like Cambridge, Oxford is an ancient university city, but also has important pressed steel and motor works. It is famous for its Colleges and gardens and is surrounded by beautiful countryside. As an intellectual centre, Oxford, again like Cambridge, has attracted students of all kinds and from all parts of the world so that today those following local authority, private and other courses (about 6,000) almost equal those who attend the University.

EDUCATION

University of Oxford. In existence since the twelfth century, 32 colleges, 5 of which are for women. Colleges are self-governing, within the University, they have their own buildings and facilities. Lectures, etc., are not open to students outside the University.

Faculties: Theology, Law, Medicine, *Literae Humaniores* (Classics and Philosophy), Modern History, English Language and Literature, Medieval and Modern European Languages and Literature, Oriental Studies, Physical Sciences, Biological Sciences, Social Studies, Anthropology and Geography, Music, Psychological Studies and Mathematics.

Technical Colleges, etc.
Oxford College of Technology, Headington, Oxford.
College of Further Education, Cowley Road, Oxford.

Private
Oxford Academy of English, 18 Bardwell Road, Oxford.
Eckersley School of English, 45 St. Giles, Oxford.
St. Clare's Hall, 141 Banbury Road, Oxford.
Oxford and County Secretarial College, 34 St. Giles, Oxford.
Oxford School of English, Godmer House, 90 Banbury Road, Oxford.

ACCOMMODATION

Boarding-houses
Names and addresses may be obtained from:
✣ The Oxford Information Centre, 140 High Street, Oxford.
or:
The Oxford Association of Hotels and Guest Houses, 75 Iffley Road, Oxford.

Hostels and Residential Clubs
Y.M.C.A., 262 Iffley Road, Oxford.
Y.H.A., 32 Jack Straw's Lane, Headington Hill, Oxford.
Commonwealth Lodge (Warden), Commonwealth Services Club, 3 South Parks Road, Oxford.

HOSPITALITY, SOCIAL CLUBS AND SOCIETIES: apply to:
British Council, 1 Wellington Square, Oxford.
Oxford Council of Social Service, Greyfriars, Paradise Street, Oxford.
Commonwealth Services Club, 3 South Parks Road, Oxford.
English-Speaking Union, 19 Beaumont Street, Oxford.

POLICE STATION AND ALIENS REGISTRATION OFFICE, ALSO
LOST PROPERTY

Police Station (Headquarters), St. Aldate's, Oxford.

EMPLOYMENT: Ministry of Labour, Floyd's Row, St. Aldate's.

PUBLIC LIBRARIES

Central Library, St. Aldate's, Oxford.
Summertown, South Parade, Oxford.
Temple Cowley, Temple Road, Cowley, Oxford.
Bury Knowle, North Place, Headington, Oxford.

MUSEUMS AND MONUMENTS

Pitt-Rivers Museum, Parks Road, Oxford.
Museum of the History of Science, Broad Street, Oxford.
University Museum, Parks Road, Oxford.
Ashmolean Museum and Taylor Institution, Beaumont Street,
Oxford.
Martyrs' Memorial, St. Giles Street, Oxford.
For information on sport, theatres, concerts and cultural
activities, and for publications, apply to The Oxford Information
Centre, address as given above.

Reading, Berkshire

The County Town of Berkshire (population exceeding 123,000).
It lies on the Great West Road and is a railway junction. It has
an important agricultural market and a flourishing shopping
centre. An expanding town with a University now being rebuilt
and a new Technical College, its industries have increased from
mainly biscuits, seeds and beer to a number of engineering firms
and to scientific research. It stands on the River Thames within
easy reach of Thames Valley holiday resorts such as Henley,
Marlow and Goring.

EDUCATION

University of Reading, London Road, Reading. Number of
Students: (1965) 2,600 (4 per cent overseas).
Faculties: Agriculture, Letters, Science.

Technical Colleges, etc.
Technical College, King's Road, Reading.
For all information concerning local authority courses, apply to the:
Education Offices, Blagrave Street, Reading.

Private
Wilson's Secretarial College, 220–2 King's Road, Reading; and others.

ACCOMMODATION

Boarding-houses
Names and addresses may be obtained from:
Foley Hall, Citizens' Advice Bureau, *or* Y.M.C.A.

Hostels and Residential Clubs
Foley Hall of Overseas Students, 60 London Road, Reading.
G.F.S. Hostel, 62 London Street, Reading.
Y.M.C.A., Parkside Road, Reading.

HOSPITALITY, SOCIAL CLUBS AND SOCIETIES: apply to:

International Friendship League, 129 Headley Road, Reading.
Reading and Berkshire International Society, 31 Castle Street, Reading.
United Nations Association, 31 Castle Street, Reading.
Reading International Social Club, c/o Watlington House, Reading.
Victoria League, c/o Barclays Bank, St. Mary's Butts, Reading.
Rotary Clubs (see Foley Hall).
Citizens' Advice Bureau, Watlington Street, Reading; and others (see Local Directory).

POLICE STATION AND ALIENS REGISTRATION OFFICE, ALSO LOST PROPERTY

Borough Police Station, Valpy Street, Reading.

EMPLOYMENT

Ministry of Labour (Men), 21 South Street, Reading.
Ministry of Labour (Women), Abbey Square, Reading.

Youth Employment Service, Northern Rock House, Cheapside, Reading.

See also Employment, Section I, pages 46–52.

PUBLIC LIBRARIES

Central Public Library, Blagrave Street, Reading and branches. (Also Town Hall.)

Apply to Reference Library, address as for Central Library, for general information about town and neighbourhood.

MUSEUMS AND MONUMENTS

Reading Abbey, Museum of English Rural Life.
Municipal Museum and Art Gallery.
See Town Guide for surrounding area.

For information on sport, concerts and entertainment, and for publications, apply to the Reference Library, address as given above.

Sheffield, Yorkshire

Sheffield (population 490,930), near the Derbyshire moors, is the centre for the production of special and alloy steels, cutlery, silverware, tools and engineering, both heavy and light.

EDUCATION

University of Sheffield. Founded 1905; approximately 4,500 students, 6 per cent from abroad. Institute of Education.

Faculties: Arts, Architectural Studies, Economic and Social Studies, Engineering, Law, Medicine, Metallurgy, Pure Science.

Technical Colleges, etc.
College of Commerce and Technology, Pond Street, Sheffield 1.
Central Technical School, Gleadless Road, Sheffield 12.
College of Art, Psalter Lane, Sheffield 11.

ACCOMMODATION

Boarding-houses
   Names and addresses from the City Librarian and Information
Officer, *or* Y.M.C.A., *or* Y.W.C.A.

Hostel and Residential Clubs
   Y.M.C.A. (hostel), 11 Broomhall Road, Sheffield 10.
   Y.W.C.A., 10 Endcliffe Crescent and Division Street, Sheffield 1.
   Salvation Army Hostel, Charter Row, Sheffield 1.
   Christian Alliance of Women and Girls' Club, 50 Kenwood
Park Road, Sheffield 11.

HOSPITALITY, SOCIAL CLUBS AND SOCIETIES
   Details from:
   British Council, 25 Broomhall Road, Sheffield 10.
✤ Civic Information Service, Surrey Street, Sheffield 1.
   The Sorby Natural History Society, City Museum, Weston
Park, Sheffield 10.
   Council of Social Service, 69 Division Street, Sheffield 1.
   United Nations Association, 30 Rockingham Lane, Sheffield 1.
   International Centre, 25 Broomhall Road, Sheffield 10.

POLICE STATION AND ALIENS REGISTRATION OFFICE, ALSO
LOST PROPERTY
   Police Headquarters, Castle Green, Sheffield 3.
   Lost Property: Police; Water Lane, Sheffield; *and* Transport:
33 Division Street, Sheffield 1.

EMPLOYMENT
   Ministry of Labour, Employment Exchange, West Street,
Sheffield.
   See also Employment, Section I, pages 46–52.

PUBLIC LIBRARY
   Central Library, Surrey Street, Sheffield 1.

MUSEUMS AND MONUMENTS
   The Graves Art Gallery, Surrey Street, Sheffield 1.
   The Mappin Art Gallery, Weston Park, Sheffield 10.

The City Museum, Weston Park, Sheffield 10.

For information on sport, cultural activities and entertainment, and for publications, apply to The Civic Information Service, address as given overleaf.

Southampton, Hampshire

Southampton (population 208,710) is a great seaport, with interesting ancient remains. One of the best natural harbours in England.

EDUCATION

University of Southampton. Founded 1902. Granted University College status 1952; approximately 2,100 students. Main University precinct 2 miles from town centre, including Nuffield Theatre.

Faculties: Arts, Education, Engineering, Law, Science, Social Sciences.

Institute of Education.

Technical Colleges, etc.

Southampton College of Technology, East Park Terrace, Southampton.

ACCOMMODATION

Boarding-houses

Names and addresses may be obtained from Y.M.C.A., *or* Y.W.C.A., *or* Y.H.A.

Hostel and Residential Clubs

Y.M.C.A., Cranbury Place, Southampton.

Y.W.C.A., Bellevue Road, Southampton; *and* 55 Christchuch Road, Winchester.

Y.H.A. (South Coast Registered Office), 374 Shirley Road, Southampton. (Hostel) 461 Winchester Road, Southampton.

INFORMATION

❖ Entertainments and Publicity Department, Civic Centre, Southampton.

HOSPITALITY, SOCIAL CLUBS AND SOCIETIES: apply to:

British Council, 6 Northlands Road, Southampton.

Guildhall, West Marlands Road, Southampton.

Bitterne Park Social Club, 76 Manor Farm Road, Southampton.

Boy Scouts (Southampton Local Association), 72 Copperfield Road, Southampton.

British Legion Club Ltd., Thornfield, Upper Deacon Road, Bitterne, Southampton.

British Red Cross Society, 14 Northlands Road, Southampton.

Citizens' Advice Bureau, 3 Havelock Road, Southampton.

POLICE STATION AND ALIENS REGISTRATION OFFICE, ALSO LOST PROPERTY

Headquarters at Salisbury.

Police Block, Civic Centre, Southampton.

EMPLOYMENT

Ministry of Labour Employment Exchange, 16 Millbrook Road, Southampton.

Youth Employment Service, 148 Shirley Road, Southampton.

See also Employment, Section I, pages 46–52.

PUBLIC LIBRARIES

Central Library, Civic Centre, Commercial Road, Southampton.

Branch Libraries: Shirley Road; Oak Road; Woolston; Portswood Road; Burgess Road; Swaythling, etc.

MUSEUMS AND MONUMENTS

Art Gallery, Civic Centre, Commercial Road, Southampton.

God's House Tower (Museum of Archaeology), Winkle Street, Southampton.

The Bargate, Above Bar, Southampton.

Tudor House, St. Michael's Square, Southampton.

West Gate and Guardroom, Western Esplanade, Southampton.

War Memorial, London Road, Southampton; etc.

For information on sport, cultural activities and entertainment, and for publications, apply to The Entertainment and Publicity Department, Civic Centre, address as given overleaf.

Note also at PORTSMOUTH (approximately 30 miles from Southampton):

Portsmouth College of Technology, 9 Burnaby Road, Portsmouth. *Students' Union*, Park Road, Portsmouth, Hants.

Portsmouth College of Art, Hyde Park Road, Portsmouth.

INFORMATION

✠ Information Bureau, Castle Buildings, Clarence Esplanade, Southsea.

York, Yorkshire

York (population 105,230) is famous for its medieval Minster (Cathedral), one of the most beautiful in Europe, and its city walls; Headquarters of the northern military district, and a railway centre.

EDUCATION

University of York. Founded 1963; approximately 1,000 students.

Faculties: Education, Economics, English, History, Language, Mathematics, Music, Philosophy, Politics, Sociology.

Graduate and Research Institutes: Borthwick Institute of Historical Research; Institute of Advanced Architectural Studies; Institute of Social and Economic Research.

Technical Colleges, etc.

Central College of Further Education, Tadcaster Road, York.

York School of Art, Exhibition Square, York.

St. John's Training College, Lord Mayor's Walk, York.

ACCOMMODATION

Boarding-houses

Names and addresses may be obtained from:

✠ The City Information Centre, Central Library, Museum Street, York.

Hostel
  Y.H.A., Haverford, Water End, Clifton, York.

HOSPITALITY, SOCIAL CLUBS AND SOCIETIES: apply to:
  English-Speaking Union, 15 Coney Street, York.
  International Club, Y.W.C.A., Cumberland House, Cumberland Street, York.
  York Civic Trust, The Orchards, Upper Poppleton, York.
  British Legion, 61 Micklegate, York.
  A comprehensive list of York societies may be consulted in The City Information Centre.

EMPLOYMENT
  Ministry of Labour, Piccadilly, York. See also Employment, Section I, pages 46–52.

POLICE STATION AND ALIENS REGISTRATION OFFICE
  Clifford Street, York.

LIBRARIES
  The City Public Library, Museum Street, York.
  Minster Library, Dean's Park, York.
  University Library, University of York, Heslington, York.
  For information on historical monuments, sport, cultural activities and entertainment, and for publications, apply to The City Information Centre, address as given above.

Aberystwyth, Cardiganshire

Aberystwyth (population 10,500) one of the leading health resorts in Wales; home of the University College of Wales, College of Librarianship, Wales, the National Library of Wales and the Welsh Plant Breeding Station. Situated on the west coast in the centre of Cardigan Bay, its climate is dry, sunny and mildly bracing. It is a touring centre for the magnificent scenery of Wales.

EDUCATION
  University College of Wales. Founded 1872; approximately 1,750 students.
  Faculties: Art, Science, Rural Science, Law, Music, Social Studies.

  T—K

Technical Colleges, etc.
   College of Further Education, North Road, Aberystwyth.
   Commerce Department, Portland Street.

ACCOMMODATION AND SOCIAL CLUBS
   Apply to:
✠   The Entertainments and Publicity Department, The Town
   Hall.
   Y.M.C.A., Chalybeate Street.
   Y.W.C.A., North Parade; and others.

POLICE STATION AND ALIENS REGISTRATION OFFICE, LOST
PROPERTY
   Marine Terrace.

EMPLOYMENT
   Ministry of Labour, Employment Exchange, 16 Terrace Road,
Aberystwyth.
   See also Employment, Section I, pages 46–52.

PUBLIC LIBRARY
   Cardiganshire Joint Library, Corporation Street.

MUSEUMS
   National Library and University College.
   For information on sport, theatres and concerts, and for pub-
lications, apply to: The Entertainments and Publicity Office, The
Town Hall.

Bangor, Caernarvonshire

Bangor (population 14,200) is important for its Cathedral and its
University College, and is also a convenient tourist centre. Industrial and business centre on South Bank; residential on North-
west, overlooking Menai Straits. Mountain scenery, climbing
and walking, sea-bathing.

EDUCATION
   University College of North Wales, Bangor. Founded 1884;
approximately 2,000 students.
   Faculties: Arts, Education, Theology, Science.

Technical College
Caernarvonshire Technical College, Ffriddoedd Road.

Theological Colleges
St. Mary's College; Normal College; Teacher-Training Colleges.

ACCOMMODATION

Boarding-houses
Names and addresses may be found from:
The Information Bureau, City Library, Bangor.

Hostels and Residential Clubs
Y.H.A., Tan-y-Bryn.

HOSPITALITY, SOCIAL CLUBS AND SOCIETIES: apply to:

Rotary Club at Gwynedd Hotel, High Street, Bangor.
Citizens' Advice Bureau, Town Hall.
Boy Scouts Association, 96 Caernarvon Road, Bangor.
Girl Guides Association, Caerhun Farm, Caerhun, nr Bangor.

POLICE STATION AND ALIENS REGISTRATION OFFICE, ALSO LOST PROPERTY

Bangor. Tel. Bangor 3333.

EMPLOYMENT

Youth Employment Service, City Library.
Ministry of Labour, Glyn House, High Street, Bangor.
See also Employment, Section I, pages 46–52.

PUBLIC LIBRARY

Ffordd Gwynedd, Bangor.

MUSEUMS AND MONUMENTS

Penrhyn Castle.
University College of North Wales, Museum of Welsh Antiquities.

For publications apply to:
The Information Bureau, City Library.

Cardiff, Glamorgan

Cardiff is the Capital of Wales, its largest city with a population of 260,340. The old Castle and public buildings combine to make the City Centre most attractive. Port traffic comprises iron ore, timber, oil, etc., and all types of general cargo. Nine dry-docks are situated here. Llandaff Cathedral is situated to the West of the City Centre.

EDUCATION

University College of South Wales and Monmouthshire. Founded 1893; approximately 2,500 students, 7 per cent from abroad.

Faculties: Arts, Science, Architecture, Education, Law, Music, Rural Sciences, Technology, Theology, etc.

Technical Colleges, etc.

Welsh College of Advanced Technology, Cathays Park, Cardiff.

College of Food Technology and College of Commerce, Crwys Road, Cardiff. (Colchester Avenue, Cardiff after 1966).

Llandaff Technical College, Western Avenue, Cardiff.

City of Cardiff Training College, Cyncoed, Cardiff.

The Reardon Smith Nautical College, Fairwater, Cardiff.

The City of Cardiff College of Art, The Friary, Cardiff.

South Wales and Monmouthshire College of Domestic Science, Llantrisant Road, Cardiff.

City of Cardiff College of Music and Drama, Cardiff Castle.

ACCOMMODATION

Hotel, etc., accommodation. Details from:—

The Information Officer, Municipal Offices, Greyfriars Road, Cardiff.

Hostels

Y.M.C.A., Station Terrace, Cardiff.

Y.W.C.A., 126 Newport Road, Cardiff.

Young Women's Residence, Glenhurst, 38 Cathedral Road, Cardiff.

International House of South Wales, Plymouth Road, Penarth, Glamorgan.

HOSPITALITY, SOCIAL CLUBS AND SOCIETIES

There are a large number of Youth Clubs in the City. Details can be obtained from:

British Council, Caroline Street, Cardiff.

The Youth Organizer, Jackson Hall, Westgate Street, Cardiff.

POLICE STATION AND ALIENS REGISTRATION OFFICE, ALSO LOST PROPERTY

Central Police Station, Law Courts, Cardiff.

INFORMATION AND CITIZEN'S ADVICE BUREAUX

Cardiff Municipal Offices, Greyfriars Road, Cardiff.

✠ Wales Tourist and Holidays Association, 7 Park Place, Cardiff.

EMPLOYMENT

Ministry of Labour (Regional Office), Dominions House, Queen Street, Cardiff.

Employment Exchanges, Westgate Street; *and* Bute Docks.

See also Employment, Section I, pages 46–52.

PUBLIC LIBRARY

Central Public Library, Trinity Street, The Hayes, Cardiff.

MUSEUMS, MONUMENTS AND ART GALLERIES

Cardiff Castle, City Centre.

National Museum of Wales, Cathays Park, Cardiff.

Howard Roberts Gallery, 69 St. Mary Street, Cardiff.

Arts Council, Holst House, Museum Place, Cardiff.

Welsh National War Memorial, Alexandra Gardens, Cathays Park, Cardiff.

Welsh Folk Museum, St. Fagan's Castle, nr Cardiff.

Turner House Art Gallery, Penarth, nr Cardiff.

For information on sport, cultural activities, lectures and theatres, apply to The Information Officer, Municipal Offices.

Swansea, Glamorgan

Swansea (population 170,160), is an important metal-working town. Area 40 square miles. On the north-west shore of Swansea Bay; a large seaport and industrial town, especially steel and tinplate working.

EDUCATION

University College of Swansea. Founded 1920; approximately 2,370 students.

Faculties: Arts, Science (Zoology), Applied Science (Metallurgy), Economics, Social Studies.

Technical Colleges, etc.

Swansea College of Technology, Mount Pleasant, Swansea.

Swansea College of Art, Alexandra Road, Swansea.

Swansea College of Further Education, Old Guildhall, Somerset Place, Swansea.

Private

Details from:

❖ Information Office, Guildhall, Swansea.

ACCOMMODATION, HOSPITALITY, SOCIAL CLUBS AND SOCIETIES

A list may be obtained from The Central Library's Bureau, *or* Y.M.C.A., *or* Information Office, Guildhall.

Y.M.C.A., St. Helen's Road, Swansea.

POLICE STATION AND ALIENS REGISTRATION OFFICE, ALSO LOST PROPERTY

Central Police Station, Alexandra Road, Swansea.

EMPLOYMENT

Youth Employment Bureau, Somerset Place, Swansea.
Employment Exchange, Northampton Lane, Swansea.
See also Employment, Section I, pages 46–52.

PUBLIC LIBRARIES

Central Library, Alexandra Road, Swansea.
Reference Library, Alexandra Road, Swansea.
Branch Libraries in most Wards.

MUSEUMS AND MONUMENTS

Royal Institution of South Wales, Victoria Road, Swansea.
The Glynn Vivian Art Gallery, Alexandra Road, Swansea.
The New Guildhall and Law Court, Victoria Park, Swansea.
For information on sport, cultural activities and entertainment, and for publications, apply to The Information Office, address as given overleaf.

Aberdeen, Aberdeenshire

Aberdeen (population estimated 187,000), the 'Granite City'; a good harbour at the mouth of the River Dee. Chief exports are granite, fish and cattle, engineering products. University city with a cathedral. Scotland's leading seaside holiday resort and third largest city.

EDUCATION

University of Aberdeen. Founded 1494. University precinct is scattered in different parts of the City. Approximately 3,000 students, 10 per cent from abroad (will be 4,000 by 1967).
Faculties: Arts, Divinity, Law, Medicine, Science, Engineering, Forestry.

Technical Colleges, etc.

Aberdeen Technical College, Gallowgate, Aberdeen.
North of Scotland College of Agriculture, 41 Union Street, Aberdeen.

Robert Gordon's Technical College, Schoolhill, Aberdeen.

Aberdeen College of Commerce, Holburn Street, Aberdeen; and others.

ACCOMMODATION

Boarding-houses

Names and addresses may be obtained from:

✤ Corporation of the City of Aberdeen Information Bureau, 20 Union Street, Aberdeen.

Hostels and Residential Clubs

Y.M.C.A. Residential Club, 5 Golden Square, Aberdeen.

Y.W.C.A., The Residence, 24 Spital, Aberdeen.

Y.W.C.A. (Hostel), 55 Dee Street, Aberdeen.

Y.M.C.A., Forces and Civilians' Hostel, 78 College Street, Aberdeen.

Church of Scotland Young Women's Hostel, 78 Dee Street, Aberdeen.

HOSPITALITY, SOCIAL CLUBS AND SOCIETIES: apply to:

British Council, Provost Ross's House, Shiprow, Aberdeen.

The Information Bureau, 20 Union Street, Aberdeen.

Aberdeen Association of Social Services, 38 Castle Street, Aberdeen.

Society of Friends, 98 Crown Street, Aberdeen.

South Aberdeen Constituency Labour Party, 70 Kildrummy Road, Aberdeen.

South Aberdeen Unionist Association, 23 Crown Terrace, Aberdeen.

Rotary Club (Secretary), 2 Bon Accord Square, Aberdeen.

POLICE STATION

Lodge Walk, Aberdeen.

ALIENS REGISTRATION OFFICE (Passport Office)

49 Market Street, Aberdeen.

LOST PROPERTY

City Police Office, Lodge Walk, Aberdeen.

If anything left on buses: Corporation Transport Department, Lost Property Office, 54 Castle Street, Aberdeen.

EMPLOYMENT

Ministry of Labour (Men), 49 Market Street, Aberdeen.

Ministry of Labour (Women and Juveniles), Greyfriars House, Gallowgate, Aberdeen.

City Youth Employment Committee, Flourmill Brae, Aberdeen.

See also Employment, Section I, pages 46–52.

PUBLIC LIBRARIES

The Central Library, Rosemount Viaduct, Aberdeen; and numerous branches throughout the City.

MUSEUMS AND MONUMENTS

Art Gallery, Provost Skene's House (opposite Marischal College). Temporarily closed.

Marischal College.

For information on all kinds of sport, theatres and entertainment, and for publications, apply to The Information Bureau, address as given above.

Dundee, Angus

Dundee (population 185,679) is the second largest industrial city in Scotland and is a thriving seaport situated on the north shore of the Tay Estuary.

Its industries now produce a very wide range of goods including accounting machines, refrigerators, dentures, carpets, chemicals, electrical goods, shipbuilding, structural and marine engineering, light engineering, and confectionery and preserves, in addition to jute and flax products.

A number of internationally known industrial firms have opened plants in Dundee during the last twenty years.

EDUCATION

University: Queen's College. (Meantime part of St. Andrews University, but soon to obtain independent status.)

Technical Colleges, etc.

  Institute of Art and Technology (Advanced Technology).
Technical College; College of Art; School of Architecture.
College of Education (Teacher-Training).
Commercial College (Business Training).
Kingsway Technical College (Trades and Crafts).

CITY INFORMATION CENTRE

  City Chambers, Dundee.

HOSPITALITY, SOCIAL CLUBS AND SOCIETIES: apply to:

  British Council, 29 Bank Street, Dundee.

  For information on employment, all kinds of sport, theatres
and entertainment, and for publications, apply to The City
Information Centre, address as given above.

Edinburgh, capital of Scotland

The capital of Scotland (population 476,600), seat of chief Scottish Law Courts, ancient University and many well-known schools. One of the most beautiful cities in Britain, with many eighteenth-century buildings, it is a tourist centre, famous for its romantic history and fine situation. Home of the Edinburgh International Festival of Music and Drama, held in August–September. With printing, brewing and other industries, it is also a manufacturing town.

EDUCATION

  University of Edinburgh. Founded 1583, main University offices near the centre of City. Other departments are scattered. Considerable new building is in progress. Approximately 8,000 students, including 1,000 part-time; 15 per cent from abroad.

  Faculties: Arts, Divinity, Law, Medicine, Music, Science, Social Sciences, Veterinary Medicine, Schools of Scottish Studies.

  Laboratories, Library, etc., and Theatre.

Technical Colleges, etc.

  Heriot-Watt University, Chambers Street, Edinburgh 1; Engineering and other technical subjects.

  Napier Technical College, Colinton Road, Edinburgh 10.

Edinburgh College of Art, Lauriston Place, Edinburgh 3.

Edinburgh College of Domestic Science, 5 Atholl Crescent, Edinburgh 3; *and* Castlehill School of Baking and Catering, Castle Hill, Edinburgh 1.

Lorne Street Technical Institute, Inchview Terrace, Edinburgh 7.

W. M. Ramsay Technical Institute, Inchview Terrace, Edinburgh 7.

The Edinburgh and East of Scotland College of Agriculture, West Mains Road, Edinburgh 9.

Leith Nautical College, 59 Commercial Street, Leith, Edinburgh 6.

Private

Basil Paterson (Tutors), 23 Abercromby Place, Edinburgh; and others.

ACCOMMODATION

A Register of Accommodation may be obtained from the Edinburgh Accommodation Bureau, 11 Cambridge Street, and from the City of Edinburgh Publicity Department, 343 High Street, Edinburgh 1.

Hostels and Residential Clubs

Y.M.C.A., 14 South St. Andrew Street, Edinburgh.

Y.W.C.A., 116 George Street, Edinburgh.

S.Y.H.A., 7 Bruntsfield Crescent, Edinburgh.

The Overseas League, 100 Princes Street, Edinburgh.

HOSPITALITY, SOCIAL CLUBS AND SOCIETIES: apply to:

The British Council, 3 Bruntsfield Crescent, Edinburgh.

English-Speaking Union, 22 Atholl Crescent, Edinburgh.

Edinburgh Christian Council for Overseas Students, 22 Buccleuch Place, Edinburgh 8.

Saltire Society, 483 Lawnmarket, Edinburgh.

Citizens' Advice Bureau, 4 Pitt Street, Edinburgh 3.

Elcho House Social Centre for Women, 35 Drummond Street, Edinburgh 8.

INFORMATION BUREAUX

✤ City of Edinburgh Publicity Department and Tourist Information Service, 343 High Street, Edinburgh 1.

City of Edinburgh Tourist and Transport Information Centre, Waverley Bridge, Edinburgh 1.

Scottish Tourist Board, Rutland Place, Edinburgh 3.

Festival Offices, Cambridge Street, Edinburgh. (Festival only.)

POLICE STATION AND ALIENS REGISTRATION OFFICE

Police Chambers (Headquarters), Parliament Square, High Street, Edinburgh.

LOST PROPERTY

Police Lost Property Office: Police Chambers, Parliament Square, Edinburgh.

Railway Lost Property: Station of arrival.

City Transport Lost Property: 14 Queen Street, Edinburgh.

Scottish Omnibuses Lost Property: Bus Station, St. Andrew Square, Edinburgh.

EMPLOYMENT

Ministry of Labour Exchange (Men), 174 Lauriston Place, Edinburgh.

Ministry of Labour Exchange (Women), 19 Rose Street, Edinburgh.

See also Employment, Section I, pages 46–52.

PUBLIC LIBRARIES

Central Public Library, George IV Bridge, Edinburgh 1.

National Library of Scotland, George IV Bridge, Edinburgh 1.

MUSEUMS AND MONUMENTS

Royal Scottish Museum; Huntly House; Museum of Childhood; National Museum of Antiquities; Royal Scottish Academy; National Gallery of Scotland; National Gallery of Modern Art; Edinburgh Castle; Palace of Holyrood House; St. Giles Cathedral; Scott Monument; Parliament House with Law Courts; John Knox's House; Royal Botanic Garden and Herbarium; Scottish Crafts Centre; Tolbooth.

For information on sport of all kinds, on entertainment, cultural activities and concerts, and for publications, apply to The City of Edinburgh Publicity Department, address as given overleaf.

Glasgow, Lanarkshire

Glasgow is the most important seaport of Scotland and the third largest city in the U.K. (population 1,089,700). A commercial community and the centre of a large industrial district. Shipbuilding yards and large docks on the River Clyde, engineering, iron and steel works, textile factories.

EDUCATION

University of Glasgow. Founded 1451. Approximately 6,000 students, 7 per cent from abroad. University is scattered, principal offices at Gilmorehill.
Faculties: Arts, Divinity, Engineering, Law, Medicine, Science.
University of Strathclyde (formerly Royal College of Science and Technology and Scottish College of Commerce).

Technical Colleges, etc.
The David Dale College.
Glasgow and West of Scotland College of Domestic Science.
The West of Scotland Agricultural College.
The Scottish College of Commerce (in University of Strathclyde).
The Scottish Hotel School.
Glasgow College of Building.
Stow College of Engineering.
Glasgow College of Printing.

Private
Skerry's College, 13 Bath Street, Glasgow C.2 and others.

ACCOMMODATION

Boarding-houses
Names and addresses may be found from the:
✤ Municipal Information Bureau, George Square, Glasgow.

Hostels and Residential Clubs
Scottish Youth Hostels Association (Hostel), 13 Woodlands Terrace, Glasgow.
Young Scots' Society, 22 Burgh Hall Street, Glasgow, W.1.
Y.M.C.A., 7–9 Beaconsfield Road, Glasgow, W.2.
Y.M.C.A., 100 Bothwell Street, Bath Street, Glasgow, C.2.

HOSPITALITY, SOCIAL CLUBS AND SOCIETIES: apply to:

British Council, 6 Belmont Crescent, Glasgow, W.2.
Boys' Brigade (headquarters), 168 Bath Street, Glasgow, C.2.
Girl Guides (headquarters), 1 Scott Street, Glasgow, C.2.
Women's Voluntary Service, 38 Bath Street, Glasgow, C.2.
English-Speaking Union, 74 Berkeley Street, Glasgow, C.2.
Student International Club, 11 University Gardens, Glasgow, W.2.
Royal Overseas League, 3–4 Claremont Terrace, Glasgow, C.3.
Rotary Club, 34 West George Street, Glasgow, C.2.
Scottish Youth Hostels Association (Office), 108 Renfield Street, Glasgow, C.2.
Holiday Fellowship, 45 Drumbeg Drive, Glasgow, S.W.3.
Y.W.C.A. of Great Britain, 80 Bath Street, Glasgow, C.2.
Y.W.C.A. of Scotland (Office), 12 Newton Terrace, Glasgow, C.3.

POLICE STATION AND ALIENS REGISTRATION OFFICE

Police Headquarters, 21 St. Andrew's Street, Glasgow, C.1.

LOST PROPERTY

Municipal Transport: 46 Bath Street, Glasgow, C.2.
Buses: Office of Bus Company.
Trains: Station of arrival.
Elsewhere in City: Central Police, Lost Property Department, 21 St. Andrew's Street, Glasgow, C.1.

EMPLOYMENT

Ministry of Labour, 103 Waterloo Street, Glasgow, C.2.
See also Employment, Section 1, pages 46–52.

PUBLIC LIBRARIES

The Mitchell Library, North Street, Glasgow, C.3; and branches.

MUSEUMS AND MONUMENTS

Art Gallery and Museum in Kelvingrove Park; The Old Glasgow Museum; Tollcross Museum; Camphill Museum; Museum of Transport.

For information on sport of all kinds, on cultural activities and concerts, on all entertainment, and for publications, apply to The Municipal Information Bureau, address as given overleaf.

Perth, Perthshire

Perth (population 41,199), cattle-markets, dye works, distilleries, glass works, insurance.
A railway centre and gateway to the Highlands of Scotland.

EDUCATION

Airwork Service Training, Perth Aerodrome.
Lawers School of Agriculture, Comrie, Perthshire.

CITY HALL

King Edward Street.

CITY INFORMATION CENTRE

Information Kiosk, St. John's Square, Perth.
For information on accommodation etc., employment, sport, cultural activities, and all entertainment, and for publications, apply to The Information Kiosk, address as given above.

St. Andrews, Fife

St. Andrews (population 10,000) is a small town, but an important city in Scottish history. The University, the first in Scotland, was founded in the fifteenth century. Situated on a rocky headland with the sea and hills in the background. Famous golf-course.

EDUCATION

University of St. Andrews – St. Salvator's College. Founded 1410. Approximately 3,000 students.
Faculties: Applied Science, Arts, Divinity, Law, Medicine, Science, Social Sciences.

ACCOMMODATION

Boarding-houses
Names and addresses may be obtained from The Information
Bureau.

Hostels and Residential Clubs
Several University Hostels.

HOSPITALITY, SOCIAL CLUBS AND SOCIETIES
Apply to:
St. Andrews Publicity and Information Association.
✠   Information Bureau, Town Hall, South Street, St. Andrews.
St. Andrews Citizens Office, 107 South Street, St. Andrews.

POLICE STATION AND ALIENS REGISTRATION OFFICE,
ALSO LOST PROPERTY
North Street, St. Andrews.

PUBLIC LIBRARY
University Library.

MUSEUMS AND MONUMENTS
St. Andrews Castle: Cathedral.
For information on employment, sport, cultural activities and
entertainment, and for publications, apply to The Information
Bureau, address as given above.

Belfast, capital of Northern Ireland

Belfast is the capital of Northern Ireland and the latter is an
integral part of the United Kingdom. It is the centre of the Irish
linen trade, also renowned for shipbuilding. The Government,
through its grant schemes, has attracted a wide variety of industries, especially in the field of synthetic fibres and light engineering.

EDUCATION
The Queen's University of Belfast. Founded 1908, originated
1845. Approximately 4,300 students.

Faculties: Arts, Science, Applied Science and Technology, Law, Economics, Medicine, Agriculture, Theology. The faculty of Arts includes Education.

Technical Colleges, etc.

College of Technology, Belfast (including a College of Art and a College of Domestic Science).

Jordanstown Physical Education College, Jordanstown, Belfast.

There are three Teacher-Training colleges:

Stranmillis College, Stranmillis Road, Belfast 9.

St. Mary's (for Girls), 191 Falls Road, Belfast 12.

St. Joseph's (for Men), Trench House, Stewartstown Road, Belfast 11.

Private

Orange's Academy, Institution Place, Belfast 1.

Shaftesbury House Tutorial College, 75 University Street, Belfast 7.

ACCOMMODATION

Boarding-houses

Names and addresses may be obtained from the:

✠ Tourist Information Centre, 6 Royal Avenue, Belfast 1; *or* Bryson House, 28 Bedford Street, Belfast 2; *or* Y.M.C.A., *or* Y.H.A.

Hostels and Residential Clubs

Y.M.C.A., 12 Wellington Place, Belfast 1.

Y.W.C.A., 3–5 Malone Road, Belfast 9.

Y.H.A., 28 Bedford Street, Belfast 2.

The Presbyterian Hostel, Howard Street, Belfast 1.

HOSPITALITY, SOCIAL CLUBS AND SOCIETIES: apply to:

British Council, 1 Chlorine Gardens, Belfast 9.

Belfast Council of Social Welfare, Bryson House, 28 Bedford Street, Belfast 2.

Royal Overseas League, 31 Wellington Place, Belfast 1.

Rotary Club of Belfast, Grand Central Hotel, Royal Avenue, Belfast 1.

King George VI Youth Centre, May Street, Belfast 1.

Y.M.C.A. National Office, 22 Howard Street, Belfast 1.

Belfast Corporation, City Hall, Donegall Square, Belfast 1.

Belfast Welfare Department, 16 College Street, Belfast 1.

Belfast Corporation Transport Social Club, 112 Ann Street, Belfast 1.

Belfast Girls' Help Society, 21 Hartington Street, Belfast 7.

Youth Hostel Association, 28 Bedford Street, Belfast 2.

POLICE STATION AND ALIENS REGISTRATION OFFICE, ALSO LOST PROPERTY

General Headquarters, Brooklyn Knock Road, Belfast 5.

Police Office (Lost Property and Charge Office), Chichester Street, Belfast 1.

EMPLOYMENT

Ministry of Labour, Dundonald House, Upper Newtownards Road, Belfast 4.

Employment for Young Persons, 38 Alfred Street, Belfast 2.

See also Employment, Section I, pages 46–52.

PUBLIC LIBRARIES

Linen Hall Library (membership of this Library is by subscription), Donegall Square North, Belfast 1.

Central Library, Royal Avenue, Belfast 1; and branches.

MUSEUMS AND MONUMENTS

St. Anne's Cathedral, Donegall Street, Belfast 1.

St. Peter's Pro-Cathedral, Derby Street, Belfast 12.

Ulster Museum and Art Gallery and Botanical Gardens, Stranmillis Road, Belfast 9.

Belfast Transport Museum, Witham Street, Belfast 4.

Belfast Castle, Antrim Road, Belfast 15.

Albert Memorial Clock, High Street, Belfast 1.

The City Hall, Donegall Square, Belfast 1.

Parliament Buildings, Stormont, Belfast 4.

N.B. – Also the City of LONDONDERRY, with University College, and an interesting historical past. (See map.) A new university is to be built at Coleraine, County Antrim.

For information on sport of all kinds, theatres and cultural activities, and for publications, apply to The Tourist Information Centre, address as given overleaf.

Audio-Visual Education
and Additional Bibliography

Audio-Visual Education

The organization responsible for the development and policy of Audio-Visual Aids in Education in Britain – covering all aspects of these methods from blackboard work and wall-charts to closed-circuit television and overhead projection – is:

The National Committee for Audio-Visual Aids in Education, 33 Queen Anne Street, London, W.1.

Other organizations with particular functions in this field are:

Overseas Visual Aids Centre, 31 Tavistock Square, London, W.C.1; gives advice and help on audio-visual aids to teachers, community development workers and others from overseas countries; permanent displays, library, etc.; training courses, organized.

Audio-Visual Language Association, 53 Kensington Gardens, Cranbrook, Ilford, Essex; informs members about developments in equipment, course material and teaching techniques.

British Association for Commercial and Industrial Education, 26A Buckingham Palace Road, London, S.W.1; specializes in giving advice on the education and training of employees. Corporate membership only.

British Film Institute, 81 Dean Street, London, W.1; administers the National Film Archive and National Film Theatre. The Institute's Education Service provides courses and single lectures on film and television as well as publishing pamphlets; concerned to help teachers and lecturers.

British Universities Film Council, College of Technology, Loughborough, Leicestershire; co-ordinate and develop the use of the film and related material in British universities and institutions of university standard, for purposes of teaching and research.

Central Film Library, Government Building, Bromyard Avenue, Acton, London, W.3; distributes for non-theatrical showing

16 mm. and 35 mm. versions of films produced or acquired by
the Central Office of Information.

Central Gramophone Library, 38 Russell Square, London, W.C.1;
collections of gramophone records available on loan to adult
education lecturers, music and gramophone societies, hospitals, prisons and other organizations.

Educational Films of Scotland, 16–17 Woodside Terrace, Charing
Cross, Glasgow, C.3; advise on visual material for Scottish
schools.

Educational Foundation for Visual Aids, 33 Queen Anne Street,
London, W.1; concerned with the production and distribution of audio-visual material for schools, and with all aspects
of audio-visual aids equipment.

Foundation Film Library, Brooklands House, Weybridge, Surrey;
National Library of educational films set up by the Educational
Foundation for Visual Aids.

Scientific Film Association, 55A Welbeck Street, London, W.1;
promotion of national and international use of scientific and
industrial films; specialized film catalogues.

Scottish Central Film Library, 16–17 Woodside Terrace, Glasgow,
C.3; to promote the use of the educational film and all other
visual aids in Scottish schools.

Scottish Film Council, 16–17 Woodside Terrace, Glasgow, C.3;
to encourage the use of the film as an educational, instructional
and cultural medium; performs the same function for Scotland
as the British Film Institute performs for England and Wales.

Society for Education in Film and Television, 34 Second Avenue,
London, E.17; an independent organization for those interested in teaching film and television appreciation, membership
being open to all who are engaged in education.

Museums Association, 87 Charlotte Street; to collect and dissemin-
ate information about museums and subjects they deal with.

National Audio-Visual Aids Centre, Paxton Place, Gipsy Road,
London, S.E.27 (operated jointly by E.F.V.A. and the
N.C.A.V.A.E.); facilities are provided for the demonstration
of equipment and materials, the organization of courses,
collation of information, etc.

World Council of Christian Education, Annandale, North End
Road, London, N.W.11; Audio-Visual Aids Department which
arranges lectures, conferences and demonstrations of the use
of audio-visual aids in Christian education.

Publications

For books: apply to The Visual Education Book Service, 33 Queen Anne Street, London, W.1.

For periodicals:

Visual Education, monthly; from the N.C.A.V.A.E.; *also*

O.V.A.C. Bulletin, twice yearly; O.V.A.C.

Contrast, quarterly; the British Film Institute.

Film User, monthly; Current Affairs Ltd.

Scientific Film, bi-monthly; Scientific Film Association.

Sight and Sound, British Film Institute.

Screen Education, 5 issues per year; Society for Education in Film or Television.

Additional Bibliography

(A) *Current Affairs*

1. CENTRAL OFFICE OF INFORMATION. Reference pamphlets. Available from H.M. Stationery Office. Various prices.
2. KING-HALL, STEPHEN. *Our Times 1900–1960.* Faber, 1961. 28s.
3. THOMSON, DAVID. *England in the Twentieth Century.* Penguin, 1965. 5s.

(B) *Government*

4. DU SAUTOY, PETER. *The Civil Service.* O.U.P., 1957. 10s. 6d.
5. GORDON STRATHEARN. *Our Parliament.* Revised edn. Cassell, for Hansard Society, 1964. 30s.
6. JACKSON, R. M. *Machinery of Justice in England.* 4th edn., C.U.P., 1964. 45s.
7. JACKSON, W. ERIC. *Local Government in England and Wales.* Penguin, 1959. 3s. 6d.
8. JENNINGS, IVOR. *The British Constitution.* 4th edn. C.U.P., 1961. 21s. (paperback, 10s. 6d.).
9. MACKENZIE, KENNETH. *English Parliament.* Revised edn., Penguin, 1959. 5s.
10. WALKER, PATRICK GORDON. *The Commonwealth.* Secker and Warburg, 1962. 36s.

(C) *History*

11. CLAPHAM, J. H., and COURT, W. H. B. *Concise Economic History of Great Britain*. C.U.P., 2 vols., 1949–54. 62s. 6d. (paperback, 2 vols., 30s.).
12. SIMMONS, JACK, ed. *A Visual History of Modern Britain*. Vista Books, published 1962. 5 vols 1–6, 35s. each, vol. 7, 63s.
13. STEINBERG, S. H. *Historical Tables 58 B.C. – A.D. 1958*. 6th edn., Macmillan, 1961. 30s.
14. STEINBERG, S. H., ed. *A New Dictionary of British History*. E. Arnold, 1963. 30s.
15. TREVELYAN, G. M. *History of England*. 3rd edn., Longmans, 1945. 40s. (abridged version: Penguin, 1959, 8s. 6d.).

(D) *The Arts*

16. PEVSNER, N. *The Englishness of English Art*. New edn. Penguin, 1964. 10s. 6d.
17. GAUNT, WILLIAM. *A Concise History of English Painting*. Thames and Hudson, 1964. 35s.
18. ROTHENSTEIN, SIR J. *Modern English Painters*. New edn., Arrow, 1962. 2 vols., 7s. 6d. each.
19. LAMBERT, SAM, ed. *New Architecture of London*. British Travel and Holidays Association, 1963. 7s.
20. PEVSNER, N., ed. *Buildings of England Series*. Penguin. These are issued county by county. Prices vary.
21. TUBBS, RALPH. *The Englishman Builds*. Penguin, 1945. 3s. 6d.
22. NICOLL, ALLARDYCE. *British Drama: An Historical Survey from the Beginnings to the Present Time*. 5th edn., Harrap, 1962. 25s.
24. MASON, COLIN. *Music in Britain*. Longmans, 1963. 3s. 6d.
25. WALKER, ERNEST. *A History of Music in England*. 3rd edn., O.U.P., 1952. 45s.

(E) *Literature*

26. ALLEN, WALTER. *The English Novel*. New edn. Penguin, 1958. 6s.
27. BURGESS, ANTHONY. *The Novel Today*. Longmans, 1963. 2s. 6d.
28. ENTWISTLE, W. J., and GILLETT, E. *The Literature of England A.D. 500–1960*. 4th edn., Longmans, 1962. 18s.

29. FRASER, G. S. *The Modern Writer and his World.* 2nd edn., Penguin, 1964. 6s.
30. JENNINGS, ELIZABETH. *Poetry Today.* Longmans, 1961. 3s. 6d.
31. SAMPSON, GEORGE. *The Concise Cambridge History of English Literature.* 2nd edn., C.U.P., 1961. 32s. 6d.

(F) *Finance, Trade and Industry*

32. ALLEN, G. C. *British Industries and Their Organization.* 4th edn., Longmans, 1959. 30s.
33. FERRIS, PAUL. *The City.* Penguin, 1962. 4s. 6d.
34. HOBSON, OSCAR. *How the City Works.* 7th edn., Dickens Press, 1963. 8s. 6d.
35. PAYNE, PETER F. *British Commercial Institutions.* 2nd edn., Harrap, 1964. 15s.

(G) *Broadcasting*

36. CENTRAL OFFICE OF INFORMATION. *Sound and Television Broadcasting Services in Britain.* H.M.S.O., 1964. 3s.
37. CROZIER, MARY. *Broadcasting — Sound and Television.* O.U.P., 1958. 10s. 6d.
38. *B.B.C Handbook.* B.B.C.; Annual. 6s.

(H) *The Press*

39. TAYLOR, H. A. *The British Press: A Critical Survey.* Barker, 1961. 21s.
40. WILLIAMS, FRANCIS. *Dangerous Estate: The Anatomy of Newspapers.* New edn. Arrow, 1959. 3s. 6d.

(I) *Sport and Country Life*

41. CENTRAL OFFICE OF INFORMATION. *Agriculture in Britain.* H.M.S.O., 1964. 3s. 6d.
42. ERNLE, LORD. *English Farming Past and Present.* 6th edn., Heinemann, 1961. 50s.
43. *Lonsdale Library,* edited by Lord Lonsdale and Eric Parker. Seeley Service, 22 volumes on various sports. 21s. to 35s. each.

(J) *Science*

44. CARDWELL, D. S. L. *The Organization of Science in England.* Heinemann, 1957. 18s.
45. CENTRAL OFFICE OF INFORMATION. *British Inventions: Story of Discovery and Development.* H.M.S.O., 1963. 2s. 6d.
46. CENTRAL OFFICE OF INFORMATION. *Nuclear Energy in Britain.* H.M.S.O., 1962. 7s.
47. CLEMENT, A. G., and ROBERTSON, R. H. S. *Scotland's Scientific Heritage.* Oliver and Boyd, 1961. 18s.
48. *Scientific and Learned Societies of Great Britain.* 61st edn., Allen and Unwin, 1964. 45s.
49. *Trend Report.* Committee of Enquiry into the Organization of Civil Science. (Cmnd. 2171) H.M.S.O., 1963. 4s.

(K) *Education*

50. ALEXANDER, SIR WILLIAM. *Education in England: the National System, How it Works.* 2nd edn., Newnes Educational Publishing Co., 1964. 25s.
51. BARNARD, H. C., and LAUWERYS, J. A. *A Handbook of British Educational Terms, including an Outline of the British Educational System.* Harrap, 1963. 15s.
52. BRITISH COUNCIL AND ASSOCIATION OF COMMONWEALTH UNIVERSITIES. *Higher Education in the United Kingdom: A Handbook for Students from Overseas and their Advisers.* Revised edn., Longmans, 1964. 7s. 6d.
53. CENTRAL OFFICE OF INFORMATION. *Technical Education in Britain.* H.M.S.O., 1962. 3s.
54. *Commonwealth Universities Yearbook*: A Directory to the Universities of the Commonwealth. Association of Commonwealth Universities; Annually. 105s.
55. DENT, H. C. *British Education.* Longmans, 1962. 2s. 6d.
56. HASTINGS, MERLE. *Grants for Higher Education.* Cresset Press, 1964. 10s. 6d.
57. MADDOX, HARRY. *How to Study.* Pan, 1963. 3s. 6d.
58. UNESCO. *Study Abroad.* H.M.S.O.; Annually. 20s.

(L) *General*

59. BRITISH COUNCIL. *How to Live in Britain: A Handbook for Students from Overseas.* Revised edn., Longmans, 1965. 1s.

60. BROMHEAD, PETER. *Life in Modern Britain*. Longmans, 1962. 13s. 6d.

61. CENTRAL OFFICE OF INFORMATION. *Social Services in Britain*. H.M.S.O., 1964. 7s.

62. HALL, WENDY. *This is Britain: Everyday Life*. Methuen, 1962. 6s. 6d.

63. OSBORNE, J. F. *Britain* (*Sunday Times* World Library). Heron Books, 1961. 21s.

64. SCOTT, J. D. *Life in Britain*, Eyre and Spottiswoode, 1956. 25s.

65. TREGIDGO, P. S. *A Background to English: A book about Britain for African and Asian Students*. Longmans, 1962. 10s.

(M) *General Reference Books*

66. CENTRAL OFFICE OF INFORMATION. *Britain: An Official Handbook*. H.M.S.O.; Annually. 27s. 6d.

67. *Titles and Forms of Address: A Guide to their Correct Usage*. 12th edn. Black, 1964. 12s. 6d.

68. *Whitaker's Almanack*. Whitaker; Annually. 25s.

69. *Who's Who*. Black; Annually. £7 7s.

(N) *Dictionaries*

70. *The English Duden*: A Pictorial Dictionary with English and German indexes. 2nd edn. Harrap, 1960. 30s.

71. HORNBY, A. S., and others. *The Advanced Learner's Dictionary of Current English*. 2nd edn., O.U.P., 1963. 21s.

72. *Oxford Illustrated Dictionary*. O.U.P., 1962. 50s.

(O) *Encyclopaedias*

73. *Chamber's Encyclopaedia*. Centenary edn., Newnes, 1959, 15 vols. £75.

74. *Hutchinson's New 20th Century Encyclopaedia*. 4th edn., Hutchinson, 1964. 40s. (1 vol.)

75. *Pears Cyclopaedia*. Pelham Books; Annually. 21s. (1 vol.).

(P) *Maps, Atlases and Guides*

76. BICKMORE, D. P., ed. *Atlas of Britain and Northern Ireland*. O.U.P., 1963. £26 5s.

77. MUIRHEAD, L. R., ed. *The Blue Guides to England, Scotland, Wales, Ireland, London, Oxford and Cambridge.* Benn, 6 vols. 50s., 40s., 30s., 40s., 22s. 6d., 4s. 6d.
78. NAGEL. *Great Britain and Ireland.* Muller, 1953. 40s.
79. PIEHLER, H. A. *England for Everyman.* Revised edn., Dent, 1960. 10s. 6d.
80. ROYAL AUTOMOBILE CLUB. *Guide and Handbook.* R.A.C.; Annually. 15s.
81. *A to Z Atlas of London and Suburbs.* Geographer's Map Co. 3s. 6d.
82. *Bartholomew's Reference Atlas of Greater London.* 12th edn., Bartholomew, 1963. 50s.
83. *Benn London Pocket Guide.* Benn, 1962. 3s. 6d. (in English, French, German, and Italian).
84. NATIONAL UNION OF STUDENTS. *The Student Guide to London.* N.U.S.; Annually. 3s.

November, 1965

Main centres of study and counties.

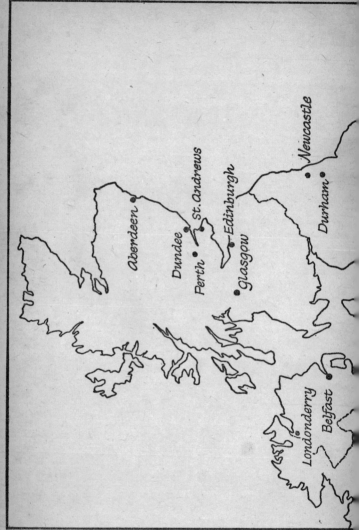

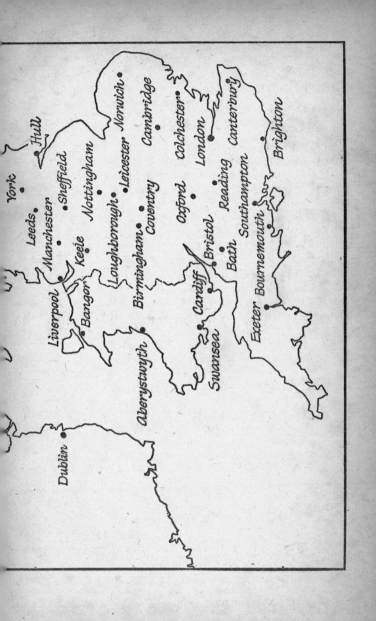

These are PAN PIPER Books

Gavin Brown

CAREERS FOR BOYS
CAREERS FOR GIRLS

PAN ORIGINALS. Two up-to-date handbooks of immense value to school-leavers, graduates, parents, and teachers. Each covers a wide range of opportunities and jobs with full information about examinations, prospects, etc. (each 5/–)

Gilbert Phelps

A SURVEY OF ENGLISH LITERATURE

Main themes and developments in English Literature from Beowulf to 1939. Not just another History of English Literature, but a fresh, fascinating approach to the great classic authors, their books, poems and plays. (7/6)

Books for the taste of today